Research and Education

Educational researchers take a number of decisions that define the credibility and scope of their enquiry – the approaches they adopt, the strategies they employ, the methods they use and the ways they present their findings. This core text provides an easy-to-read, comprehensive introduction to educational research that will develop your understanding of research strategies, theories and methods.

Specifically written for undergraduate education studies students, the book guides you through the process of planning a research project, the different research methods available and how to carry out your research and write it up successfully. Highlighting the theoretical and methodological debates and discussing important ethical and practical considerations, the book is structured to help you tackle all the different aspects of your project from writing your literature review, designing a questionnaire and analysing your data to the final writing up. The book will give you the confidence and enthusiasm to discuss and write about your research effectively.

Features include:

- extension tasks – to introduce new material and encourage you to think critically
- case studies – with information on important studies and examples of research that have utilised specific approaches
- practical advice and tips – to help you relate the topics discussed to your own on-going project work
- annotated further reading lists – providing you with an opportunity to access more detailed and specific resources.

Part of the *Foundations in Education Studies* series, this timely textbook is essential reading for students undertaking a research methods course or a piece of educational research.

Will Curtis is Director of part-time and 2+2 degrees in the Centre for Lifelong Learning at the University of Warwick, UK.

Mark Murphy is Reader in Education and Public Policy at the University of Glasgow, UK.

Sam Shields is Lecturer in Education at the University of Hull, UK.

Foundations of Education Studies Series

This is a series of books written specifically to support undergraduate education studies students. Each book provides a broad overview to a fundamental area of study exploring the key themes and ideas to show how these relate to education. Accessibly written with chapter objectives, individual and group tasks, case studies and suggestions for further reading, the books will give students an essential understanding of the key disciplines in education studies, forming the foundations for future study.

Research and Education, Will Curtis, Mark Murphy and Sam Shields

Policy and Education, Paul Adams

Forthcoming titles

Philosophy and Education, Joanna Haynes, Ken Gale and Mel Parker

Sociology and Education, Richard Waller and Chrissie Rogers

Research and Education

Will Curtis, Mark Murphy and
Sam Shields

Routledge
Taylor & Francis Group

LONDON AND NEW YORK

First published 2014
by Routledge
2 Park Square, Milton Park, Abingdon, Oxon OX14 4RN

and by Routledge
711 Third Avenue, New York, NY 10017

Routledge is an imprint of the Taylor & Francis Group, an informa business

© 2014 W. Curtis, M. Murphy and S. Shields

British Library Cataloguing in Publication Data
A catalogue record for this book is available from the British Library

Library of Congress Cataloging in Publication Data
Curtis, Will, Dr.
Research and education / Will Curtis, Mark Murphy, Sam Shields.
pages cm. -- (Foundations of education studies)
1. Education--Research. I. Murphy, Mark.
II. Shields, Sam. III. Title.
LB1028.C87 2013
370.72--dc23
2013021837

ISBN: 978-0-415-80958-0 (hbk)
ISBN: 978-0-415-80959-7 (pbk)
ISBN: 978-1-315-85832-6 (ebk)

Typeset in Bembo Std and Helvetica Neue LT Pro
by Saxon Graphics Ltd, Derby

Contents

Introduction

Aims of the book

Research and Education is designed to provide an easy-to-read, comprehensive introduction to educational research for Education Studies undergraduate students. The book aims to develop your understanding of research strategies and methods within the study of education. It highlights theoretical and methodological debates and discusses important ethical and practical considerations. Educational researchers take a number of decisions that define the credibility and scope of their enquiry, in terms of strategies employed, methods used, sampling, positionality, analysis and presentation.

The book is designed to support you in undertaking your own piece of independent educational research. It covers all the popular approaches to educational research, providing contemporary examples of research, critical discussion and practical advice. Many students find their research project one of the most daunting pieces of work they undertake (often because it is one of the longest and it requires a high degree of independent working). At the same time, it can be your most exciting piece of work, in which you have freedom in choosing your topic and your approach to data collection. While we were writing this book we reflected on the different research project topics we have supervised, so that many of the examples in the book relate to examples of research you may find interesting and relevant. The book has been written in an accessible style, and we hope that reading this book will give you confidence and enthusiasm in discussing and writing about your own research. The book is structured to help you tackle all the different aspects of your project, from writing your literature review, designing a questionnaire and analysing your data to the final writing up process.

Structure of the book

The book is divided into four sections:

- Part 1: Planning an education research project
- Part 2: Research strategies
- Part 3: Methods of data collection
- Part 4: Theorising research

Part 1 outlines the kinds of issues that need to be considered when planning a research project. These include choosing a topic and writing a proposal, reviewing the literature, choice of methodology and sampling technique, analysing the data and writing up the results. This first section is full of practical ideas and advice, and is designed to help you complete your research project. The ideas and information provided in subsequent chapters should provide a strong basis from which to build on this section, and will help you to complete the last stage of writing up your research.

Part 2 on research strategies aims to introduce you to the various approaches that can be taken within the field of education research, and includes chapters on surveys, experiments, case studies, ethnography and action research. Each of these chapters includes a description of the nature and purpose of the different approaches, while also highlighting their potential benefits and drawbacks. It should be emphasised that in the real world of education research there can be considerable overlap between these different approaches – for example, some case studies can also be classed as ethnographies. Therefore it is important to remember that these are not mutually exclusive categories – much can be gained from cross-pollination.

Part 3 on methods of data collection details the various tools that can be used to gather evidence for research projects. Chapters cover questionnaires, interviews, focus groups, observations and documents. There is also a chapter on how to use the internet for research purposes. The chapter includes examples of existing research that has utilised these different methods, using examples from across the education sector. It should be noted that there are education research studies in existence that have used *all* of these methods in their research. Therefore it is important that you do not view the methods in isolation, but rather as potential contributions to your research, depending on its purpose and scope.

Part 4 focuses on the relationship between theory and education research, not just in the sense of how we apply theory in research settings, but also in terms of how we theorise *about* research and education. This section includes chapters on using theories and concepts in research, evaluating methods, the position of the researcher, ethical issues in educational research and also a chapter on the involvement of children and young people in research. It is important that researchers have a strong understanding of the kind of concepts and ideas that are being utilised (either implicitly or explicitly) in their research, as this can provide a strong basis from which to develop high quality research outcomes. Also, taking a reflective and critical stance on educational research, both as a practitioner and as a member of the academic community, is an important professional and ethical requirement.

How to use the book

The book contains a number of features to help you understand and apply important research concepts and theories, as well as encouraging you to think about your own educational research project. Features include:

- **Activities** – these extension tasks introduce new material and encourage you to think critically. We suggest you engage in these activities with a peer, interrogating one another's perspectives.
- **Case studies** – throughout the book you will encounter boxes that contain further detail about important studies or examples of research that have utilised specific approaches. Use these to identify material that may provide helpful examples for your own project.
- **Practical advice** – while many of the topics covered during the book are abstract and theoretical, we have aimed throughout to relate the discussion back to your own ongoing project work. You will find practical advice and tips in each chapter.
- **Further reading** – each chapter concludes with some recommended texts, providing you with an opportunity to access more detailed and specific resources.

We do not expect you to read this book from front to back cover in one sitting, but rather to use it as the sort of resource you can 'dip' in and out of. You will find the first section very useful as you plan and undertake your own research project, providing an overview of what you are aiming for. As your research gathers momentum and you start to write up different sections, this section will prove invaluable as a detailed guide to what to include and how to present information. You should familiarise yourself with the issues covered in Section 4 before you begin your project, because these theoretical concerns should frame your thinking and the choices you make. For instance, you are likely to have to consider ethical issues before you are allowed to carry out your data collection. Data analysis will also be a lot easier if you know how you are going to do this before you gather your research.

Sections 2 and 3 will help you to make the most appropriate choices in terms of the methods and strategies you employ. As your project progresses, these chapters will provide you with a reference point, enabling you to draw from existing literature to view the choices other researchers have taken and to consider the advantages and limitations of your chosen approaches.

We wish you all the best with your research project. Follow the guidance in this book and your project should prove to be the most rewarding experience of your degree.

1

Approaches to educational research

Introduction

This chapter introduces students to the nature of research, considering in particular the meaning of 'research' and its purposes and uses within the specific context of education. It will look briefly at how research in education has developed historically and will highlight recent trends, emphasising the growing importance of educational research. The chapter also looks at key research paradigms, presenting the critical differences between scientific (i.e. positivist) and interpretivist perspectives. It will consider how these different theoretical perspectives relate to different research strategies and methods of data collection, looking in particular at quantitative and qualitative approaches to educational research.

What do we mean by educational research?

Booth *et al.* (1995) provide a good definition of what research is: 'gathering the information you need to answer a question and thereby help you solve a problem' (Booth *et al.*, 1995: 6). Swap the word 'question' for the term 'education question' and you arrive at a fairly concise statement of the focus of this book. Gathering information in order to answer an education question is the raison d'être of educational research, and if the amount of educational research in existence is any indication, the field of education is awash with questions to be answered. This makes sense, because what happens in the field of education is hugely significant for a host of reasons – political, personal, social and cultural. Developments in education, along with the health sector, arguably receive the most coverage in the media, with newspapers and the wider media understanding the implications of educational findings not just for parents and pupils but also for policy makers (see the coverage in the Education Guardian, for example – www.educationguardian.co.uk).

Much more so than in other academic research areas such as anthropology or history, most research in education has practical as well as theoretical implications, with the results of studies often finding their way into policy and thereby shaping pedagogical practice. Given the kinds of questions that are often asked in education research, this is entirely to be expected:

- How do children learn?
- What are the most effective approaches to teaching in the classroom?
- Does social class matter in the classroom?
- What curriculum works best for primary children?
- What subjects should pupils study in secondary school?
- How may we best understand the nature of teacher professionalism?
- How do students experience study in higher education?

These are just some of the common kinds of question asked in education research, but the list is endless, with more and more specialised questions engaging researchers. This vast field of research is also reflected in the ever-increasing number of academic journals devoted to the topic area, including journals devoted to specific subjects such as music education, maths education and physical education, as well as journals that focus on specific thematic areas such as special educational needs, teaching and learning in higher education, quality assurance in education and so on.

Approaches to educational research

Alongside this diversity of context, there is also a clear diversity of research *design* to be seen in the field of theoretical application. Research is conducted for a variety of reasons in parallel with the core reason stated above, which will have a clear impact on the analysis of the findings and also the implications that are drawn from the research. The forms of application can be roughly divided into the following categories (Murphy, 2013a):

- Research as *exploration*
- Research as *interrogation*
- Research as *reconstruction*
- Research as *testing*
- Research as *critique*

Education research as *exploration*   A large percentage of education research papers set out to explore specific educational phenomena, which can range from policies, curriculums or aspects of teaching practice to forms of social reproduction. A common approach to research generally, this form of educational research aims to flesh out and broaden our understanding of specific issues.

Research as *interrogation*   A second common strand of education research takes theoretical concepts and uses them to 'expose' or reveal that which is hidden from view – to make explicit that which is implicit. This research tends to have a more political edge, much of it aiming to unmask the power relations behind seemingly neutral policies and practices. Therefore it should come as no surprise that various understandings of power have been applied across this sector, since a fascination with 'what lies beneath' state imperatives is a common professional response to the whirlwind of policy change in education.

Research as *reconstruction* Another strand of education research uses research to propose possible alternatives to the subject matter at hand – whether this is a policy, a practice or an idea. Sometimes this takes the form of action research, which has the production of new models as its aim, or sometimes it comes in the form of theoretical arguments that make the case for such models.

Research as *testing* Some researchers aim to 'test' a particular idea or hypothesis that has become central to a specific understanding of educational practice, policy or theory. Although this approach may be considered to align itself with a strictly scientific understanding of research, this is not always necessarily the case (see Chapter 18 for examples of this kind of approach that are more geared towards theoretical constructs).

Research as *critique* A welcome addition to the literature comes in the form of publications that question the relationships between education research and theoretical approaches drawn from other disciplines. These publications are welcome since they offer some balance with other forms of research that can sometimes be guilty of viewing research as an applied field only, thereby providing a kind of self-criticality that the field needs. The applications of this kind of research fall into three categories. The first is characterised by research that is critical of the relevance of the specific theory under scrutiny. The second category of critical research applications is exemplified by research that problematises the ways in which theory is applied. The third category is illustrated by researchers who use their own research to critique an original theory – a form of theory generation in its own right.

Key research paradigms in educational research

Often research in the social sciences is thought of in terms of two opposing paradigms. These have been given a range of names, but a useful way of understanding the key distinction is to think of research from either a *positivist* or an *interpretivist* point of view: The 'traditional' positivistic stance on research (sometimes known as the scientific, objectivist or normative approach), has some key basic tenets that for many decades were assumed to be the only way of conducting research:

- The assumed neutrality and objectivity of a detached researcher, who should attempt to minimise his or her impact on the object of research and who is believed to be free from any bias related to social, political or cultural context.
- Data which can be quantified, that is, turned into a number, in order that statistical relationships between variables can be discerned.

■ Research which is oriented towards establishing overarching patterns and
   trends and building theory from generalisable results (Curtis and Pettigrew,
   2010: 58).

As Curtis and Pettigrew point out, the positivistic approach, which held sway for so
long across the social sciences in the first half of the twentieth century, became the
focus of sustained criticism once the sheen of 'science' had worn off the study of the
social world. An alternative framework was offered 'by those who saw research as
an interpretive rather than scientific act' (2010: 58). However, it was always bound
to be thus since ideas, concepts and intellectual frameworks borrowed from another
sector, in this case the natural sciences, can never be copied and transplanted
wholesale into another sector (the social sciences) without a certain amount of
disjuncture and dissonance. Thus a movement that Cohen *et al.* (2007: 19) labelled
'anti-positivism' developed in the latter half of the twentieth century, staking a
claim for a more appropriate framework for social science research. Cohen *et al.*
provide a useful summary of this position below.

> In rejecting the viewpoint of the detached, objective researcher – a
> mandatory feature of traditional research – anti-positivists would argue that
> individuals' behaviour can only be understood by the researcher sharing
> their frame of reference: understanding of individuals' interpretations of the
> world around them has to come from the inside, not the outside. Social
> science is thus seen as a subjective rather than an objective undertaking, as a
> means of dealing with the direct experience of people in specific contexts,
> and where social scientists understand, explain and demystify social reality
> through the eyes of different participants; the participants themselves define
> the social reality.
>
> (Cohen *et al.*, 2007: 19)

These 'paradigm wars' have seen numerous battles over the years which have
been well documented elsewhere.[1] There is also a range of other approaches to
research, including critical theory, that have further contributed to the discussion
about correct and appropriate methods in the social sciences.[2] However, suffice to
say that these two broadly opposed positions result in different sets of assumptions
regarding the nature and purpose of educational research, revolving around a
value-free (positivist) versus a value-laden (interpretivist) notion of the researcher
and their relationship to their research subjects. Furthermore, this distinction
sometimes gets translated into the *quantitative* vs. *qualitative* debate, but while there
are certainly parallels in that positivist research tends to favour quantitative
approaches, these two dichotomies are not the same. The decision to use a
quantitative approach (i.e. an approach that places emphasis on the analysis of
numbers) as opposed to a qualitative approach (i.e. one that places emphasis on
meaning) should be centred on whether or not the respective methodologies are
fit for purpose. After all, any form of research has both a qualitative and a
quantitative element; at some stage all research must unavoidably involve some
form of observation and some kind of measurement, regardless of the phenomenon
under investigation.

Types of education question – core thematic areas

Although there is considerable overlap, research questions in education can be broadly grouped into the following key thematic areas (Murphy, 2013b):

- Inequality, inclusion and education
- Identities: Notions of educational selves and subjectivities
- Teaching and learning: Curricular and pedagogical practice
- Governance and management.

Inequality, inclusion and education   The ways in which schooling and learning generally are mediated by, and impact on, issues of class, race and gender have concerned education researchers for decades, with the ideas generated by research providing a valuable foundation for discussion and policy making. Questions of power and privilege and their relationship with educational processes, systems and outcomes are also reflected in the extensive field of special educational needs research, which takes issues of inclusion as its starting point.[3]

Identities: Notions of educational selves and subjectivities   Questions of identity have come to the fore in social science research. In particular, questions of professional identity have received much attention, with the field of education providing a rich source of information. This is because educational identities are open to multiple interpretations and cover a wide range of professional formations and issues – becoming a teacher, transformations in teacher professionalism, sources of academic identity and the challenges of teacher education, to name but a few.[4] Another area of identity studies in education concerns student identity. There is a growing body of research literature that examines the relationship between educational processes and forms of selfhood, with questions such as the formation of learner identities receiving a great deal of attention.[5]

Teaching and learning: Curricular and pedagogical practice   The field of teaching and learning has understandably become a mainstay of educational research, encompassing an extensive range of studies on issues such as assessment, curricula, student support and teacher efficacy. The specialist fields of subject education are also well catered for, with published research available on every curriculum subject.[6]

Governance and management   Educational governance provides a political and economic context for the previous three thematic areas, but it is also an important focus of research in its own right. In education, much of the governance research centres on policies to do with regulation, marketisation and accountability, and the impact of these on educational values, professionalism, provision and delivery.[7]

Chapter summary

In this chapter we have explained what is meant by educational research, and outlined its links to educational policy and professional practice. The chapter details the various approaches that can be adopted in educational research – exploratory, interrogative, reconstructive, testing and critical. We have also provided an overview of the two core research paradigms – positivist and interpretivist – that are used in education research, concluding with an outline of the field's four core thematic areas – inclusion, identities, teaching and learning, and governance.

Further reading

Punch, K. (2005) *Introduction to social research: Quantitative and qualitative approaches*. London: Sage.

■   Keith Punch's *Introduction to social research* (2005) provides a strong overview of both quantitative and qualitative research methods in a coherent and accessible manner, using many relevant examples throughout.

Creswell, J. (2013) *Research design: Qualitative, quantitative, and mixed methods approaches* (4th edition). London: Sage.

■   In the fourth edition of John Creswell's *Qualitative, quantitative, and mixed methods approaches* (2013), the individual chapters provide useful advice on how to implement mixed methods designs as well as how to tackle quantitative and qualitative approaches in research. Each chapter also concludes with writing exercises so that readers can practice the principles learned in the chapter.

Notes

1   Numerous books document these battles and the differences between the two broad approaches. For useful sources on this, see Crotty (1998), Pring (2004) and Punch (2005).

2   Cohen *et al.* (2007) deliver a succinct overview of some of these approaches in the second half of Chapter 1 in their textbook (pp. 22–48), including discussion of complexity and feminist theory. See also the likes of Biel (2007) and Popkewitz (2012) for further analysis of alternative paradigms in social research.

3   Useful resources on current research in SEN include the likes of Cigman (2006), Cline and Frederickson (2009) and Hodkinson and Vickerman (2009).

4   See the likes of Alsup (2005) and Kanes (2012) for strong studies of identities and teacher professionalism.

5   There are some excellent book sources for research in the field of learner identities – for example, see Carr and Lee (2012), Francis *et al.* (2012), and Chappel *et al.* (2013)

6   There are plenty of resources on teaching and learning research available, but Moore (2012) provides a strong overview of the field, while Swann (2011) looks at the literature on teaching and learning from the perspective of teachers.

7   Two excellent sources of research on the governance of education are Huisman (2010) and Ozga *et al.* (2011).

Planning an education research project

2

Choosing a topic and writing a proposal

Introduction

Planning a research project begins with choosing a topic to research, and then writing a research proposal that describes the aims, objectives and rationale of the research (including its key research questions), the theoretical framework, the literature in the field, and the methodology and data collection methods that will be adopted in order to carry out the research. This chapter will look at how to choose a worthwhile topic to research in the field of education, and will consider the importance of choosing a topic that is interesting (to the researcher as well as to others), relevant, and feasible. It will then move on to consider how to formulate a project title and key research questions from the general topic that was selected, and how to formulate the rationale of the project. The next section will discuss the purpose and importance of the research proposal and provide a suggested format for writing the different sections of the proposal.

Choosing a topic

As outlined in the introductory chapter, there are four broad areas of research in the field of education. While there is considerable overlap between them, they centre around the following key thematic areas:

- Inequality, inclusion and education
- Identities: notions of educational selves and subjectivities
- Teaching and learning: curricular and pedagogical practice
- Governance and management.

So, broadly speaking, there is a selection of areas that you can focus on in your research. These are not mutually exclusive, but you will find that you are predominantly drawn to one or another – it's wise to consider the broad category carefully, because it can have an impact on your focus throughout your research project. Ask yourself whether you are more or less interested in one of these topics:

- How do schooling and education foster or hinder people's attempts to better their lives, or help to promote democratic values in society? Education is a political battleground – for good reason, since it is firmly connected to political and economic imperatives while offering one of the few legitimate routes to social mobility. As a result, it is seen to occupy one of the key sites of struggle over social inclusion and equality. Unsurprisingly, this attracts a considerable number of researchers, so consider whether you are a like-minded traveller.

- What kind of self and social understandings do teachers and students have of themselves and their roles/identities? Consider their perceptions, their attitudes towards their position, their functions and so on. If this is the kind of question that draws you to the field of education, then exploring issues of educational identities would be the best 'fit' for you in your research career. For example, you might want to pursue questions around the kind of expectations that students bring to their own learning.

- How people learn and how teachers teach/assess/design the curriculum. Are you especially interested in the 'mechanics' of this aspect of educational practice? If so, you should focus your research topic on some aspect of teaching and learning.

- How are educational institutions and professions governed and managed? Are you fascinated by how education policy is manufactured and how it impacts on professional practice and learning outcomes? If so, you should think seriously about looking into the area of governance and management.

It is important to consider some additional basic principles before you choose your topic:

- Is your area something you are *passionate* about? Is your research topic something you *feel* strongly about? While it is beneficial to exercise dispassion when conducting the research itself, it is rare to find an educational researcher who does not have some form of emotional attachment and interest in their chosen field of study – after all, most people have inevitably been 'schooled' in some form or another, or at the very least have engaged with learning processes of various types.

- Is the research *feasible*? Is the topic of your choosing researchable? That is to say, is it something that you can gather evidence about, from which you can draw some reasonable conclusions? It is vital that you engage with this question in a concrete fashion, rather than situating yourself purely within the world of abstractions (education as a regime of control, for example). If you can't imagine how you might gather your evidence, this is probably a sign that the research itself is impractical and not worth pursuing. However, it's not just abstractions that can make a research project unfeasible. For example, you may want to examine how different forms of assessment impact on learning, but given that the connection between these two variables is contested and open to discussion, you may be unable to carry out research that links the two together adequately in the manner that you would like.

- Is the research *manageable*? Do you have access to the data that you need? Is there enough time for you to carry out your research? Will you be given permission to carry out the research? Is it likely that you will be able to gather enough data in the time allowed? Are there sufficient resources at your disposal? These are all significant questions to ask at this early stage, so be truthful and realistic in how you respond to them.

Examples of research topics

Below are some examples of the kind of topics that researchers have investigated previously (with citations for researchers in these areas). Of course, this is far from a comprehensive list; rather, it is a set of indicative research questions to give an idea of the scope of the existing research.

Inequality, inclusion and education

- Exploring pupil segregation between specialist and non-specialist schools (Exley, 2009).
- The relationship between forms of special educational needs and educational attainment (Mykelburst, 2007).
- The rationale behind students' choice of university (Ball *et al.*, 2002).
- The relationship between social class, culture and educational attainment (Barone, 2006).
- The role of parents in their children's education (MacFarlane, 2008).

Notions of educational selves and subjectivities

- Self-perceptions of teachers and learners in higher education (Booth *et al.*, 2009).
- The presentation of education in the media (Haahr, 2003).
- Women's learning experiences in the workplace (Gouthro, 2009).
- The impact of policy on teachers' professional identity (Bushnell, 2003).

Curricular and pedagogical practice

- Lecturers' interest in forms of leadership (Garcia, 2010).
- Teacher effects on social and behavioural skills in early elementary school (Jennings and DiPrete, 2010).
- The relationship between forms of assessment and subject-based knowledge (Sanders, 2008).
- The role of faith and philosophy in Muslim teacher education (Scott-Baumann, 2003).
- Exploring the rationale behind changes in the English national curriculum (Winter, 2006).

Governance and management

- School surveillance as a form of social control (Hope, 2009).
- How power relations within the British special educational needs system affect parental choice (Morgan, 2005).
- The role of accountability in the governance of higher education institutions (Murphy, 2009).
- The impact of marketisation on professional identities and work practices in FE colleges (Smith, 2007).
- School-sponsored health programmes and neo-liberal education policy (Vander Schee, 2008).

What should go in a proposal?

If there is one guiding principle when putting together a research proposal, it should be clarity. How clear is your research topic? How well-defined is your research design? How explicit is the rationale, and how convincing is the stated significance of your proposed research? Clarity of thought is a must at any stage of the research process, but it is particularly essential at the proposal stage because this document forms an intellectual and practical plan for the rest of your study. As a result, any lack of clarity will have consequences for the quality of your research outcomes.

A secondary principle would be to 'keep it real' – be realistic about what you can achieve, and don't set yourself impossible targets that you have no hope of meeting. Of course, this is common sense, but all too often new researchers may feel they have to aim high, making bold claims and setting out to achieve startling originality. However, a good start to a successful research career would be more about making a useful and relevant contribution to the educational research community via a well-managed and thought-through project.

A proposal will usually have the following parts (with minor variations):

Background to the research question   This section of your proposal should aim to both introduce the research area and provide the context within which it is situated. You are explaining to the reader why your topic might be timely and appropriate, and pointing out where the research question 'fits' within the overall education community and its set of interests. This section effectively functions as a narrative 'frame' within which the importance of your own research topic is highlighted – you are making a claim for the usefulness of your proposed research.

For example, take the debate over the relationship between diet and learning in primary school classrooms. Some argue that there is a strong link between the two: do pupils learn more effectively if they have had a proper breakfast, or does it matter what kind of breakfast they have? It might be the case that not many researchers have focused on the importance of *lunch*, and what kinds of foods are eaten at lunchtime. This gap in the established knowledge base could be used as background context for your own research.

This section should include some references to the existing research on the topic, so you should include some of the relevant literature while also making reference to the policy context. This is a vital aspect of your proposal – while it is not expected that you will have read the literature in great detail, it is useful to indicate that you know what it includes and what kinds of general research results have been gathered.

Statement of research question   Based on the narrative you provided in Section 1, you should then go on to provide a statement of your own research question – for example, what impact do different types of lunch have on afternoon learning outcomes? How are notions of teacher professionalism shaped by different forms of management? What is the role of parental expectations in educational achievement? Whatever your focus, the statement of your research question must be as precise as possible.

Aims and objectives   The aims and objectives should follow logically from the statement of your research question. The aim refers to the general rationale for the project, while the objectives detail the steps by which you will achieve the aim. This part of the proposal can cause as much anxiety as the statement of the research problem, but any anxiety is usually worth it because the clarity of these aims and objectives is a significant indicator of whether or not the research project will be a success – i.e. whether it will achieve its aims. Any ambiguity at this stage is a clear indicator of an ambiguous design, which will result in ambiguous findings. Therefore it is recommended that conceptual and definitional vagueness should be avoided at this early stage.

The aims and objectives section should look something like this:

Aim: The aim of the study is to (e.g.) examine the relationship between parental expectations and pupils' educational outcomes in secondary schools.

The *objectives*:
- To examine the existing research base on the relationship between expectations and outcomes.
- To collect data on parental expectations and student outcomes from the case study sample.
- To analyse the findings from the data collection phase.
- To draw some conclusions about the expectations/outcomes relationship.

Research design   This is where you outline the methods you are going to use to gather your data, i.e. the evidence that will help you answer the question that you have posed. This section should also provide justification for why you have chosen particular methods – for example, why you will use a case study as opposed to a more broad-based approach, why you will employ questionnaires when interviews might be more feasible, and so on. This section needs to be convincing, and it must also indicate the clarity of what you are trying to achieve.

Timeline   Depending on the length of your project, you should give some indication of the duration of each part of the study, estimating the length of time you will devote to reading the literature, gathering the evidence, analysing the results and writing up. Try and be realistic in this timeline, and try not to put too much pressure on yourself to achieve unrealistic targets.

Significance of the study   It is important to include a section in your proposal that makes the case for the significance of the research, because it allows you to reiterate the rationale for carrying out the research in the first place. Why is this research necessary? Why do we need it? What kind of contribution does it make to the existing knowledge base? Here you are effectively making an assertion about the future worth of your work. This might seem artificial on paper, but in practice it 'sets the scene' while clarifying the kind of potential contribution that you can make.

The limitations of the study   It might seem counter-intuitive to include a section which details the shortcomings of the research (especially when you have devoted a lot of effort to 'bigging it up' earlier in the proposal), but it does your research no disservice to outline the limits of its reach and scope. No study can avoid such limits, and a built-in statement of intellectual and professional modesty does the proposal no harm.

Examples of research limitations might include the lack of time for a more in-depth approach to the research question, or the fact that your study is questionnaire-based and therefore lacking a qualitative dimension (or vice-versa). Whatever these limits might be, a demonstration of your knowledge and awareness of their existence allows you to make reasonable claims on behalf of the evidence that you have gathered.

A note on the challenges of (inter)disciplinarity

Designing a research project based on a vague research question is an occupational hazard in any research discipline, but it has particular implications for fields such as education. Because it is a field of study and practice as much as it is a 'discipline', education tends to be grounded in the ideas and theories of other disciplines such as history, politics, psychology and sociology as much as its own. So while the education researcher must be answerable to the ongoing paradigmatic debates in education (e.g. continuous vs. final assessment, play vs. structured learning and so on) and must situate their research within these paradigms and debates, often they also need to be at least on nodding terms with the paradigms and debates of other disciplines as well. This can cause confusion among education researchers, in a way that might not happen in disciplines such as sociology, for example. After all, any research findings are geared towards making contributions to existing debates, although this purpose is often forgotten for some reason – no research operates in a vacuum or has no precedent. Research should add to the stock of knowledge in a specific way, by confirming or rebutting existing theories of behaviour or at least adding to the complexity of understanding on the topic at hand. This tends to be more straightforward in other disciplines, but given the often dual body of knowledge underpinning a good deal of education research, it's often the case that researchers will effectively attempt to deliver *two* research questions in one. It is vital to avoid this, and to ensure that you have focused on *one* research question, and also that there is a definable field of study to research and an academic debate within which to situate your findings and analysis.

Chapter summary

This chapter began by identifying four broad research themes in the education sector and describing some of the issues that should be considered when choosing a specific research topic (personal interest, feasibility, manageability). It also provided some examples of research topics within the four themes. It went on to suggest what should be included in a research proposal, including some information on the background to the research question, a statement of the research question itself, the aims and objectives of the research, the research design, a timeline and an indication of the significance and limitations of the study. The chapter concluded by discussing the challenge of interdisciplinarity in terms of conducting educational research in the context of ideas generated within other disciplines.

Further reading

Booth, W.C., Colomb, G.G. and Williams, J.M. (1995) *The craft of research*. Chicago: University of Chicago Press.

■ See in particular Chapter 3, 'From Topics to Questions', which emphasises the movement from the general to the specific when it comes to identifying a topic for your research.

Punch, K. (2006) *Developing effective research proposals* (2nd edition). London: Sage.

■ In the updated second edition of *Developing effective research proposals* (2006), Keith Punch offers an excellent guide to the issues involved in proposal writing and presenting a well-considered plan for the execution of research. It is organised around three central themes: what is a research proposal, who reads proposals and why? How can we go about developing a proposal? Finally, what might a finished proposal look like?

Krathwohl, D. and Smith, N. (2005) *How to prepare a dissertation proposal: Suggestions for students in education and the social and behavioral sciences*. Syracuse, NY: Syracuse University Press.

■ David Krathwohl and Nick Smith's (2005) book *How to prepare a dissertation proposal: suggestions for students in education and the social and behavioral sciences* includes three annotated proposals from former students which provide examples of the guidance offered. They also include a range of chapters devoted to a mixture of qualitative, quantitative and mixed methods studies.

3

Reviewing the literature

Introduction

This chapter offers guidance on the selection, use and presentation of the existing literature in a research project. It outlines different strategies for accessing material and identifies some of the most important journals in the study of education. Electronic literature searches are increasingly important, and the chapter identifies a number of useful databases and approaches for managing the process of electronic searching effectively. The chapter suggests strategies for managing and engaging critically with your selected literature. In the final section, it outlines effective approaches for writing up a literature review.

What is a literature review and what is it for?

A literature review is an essential component in any research project. Your project does not stand alone. It needs to be situated within the existing literature in your chosen field of study, allowing you to justify and contextualise your project and create a space for your work.

The literature review surveys the body of existing scholarly articles in your chosen area of study. It is written from 'a particular standpoint to fulfil certain aims or express certain views on the nature of the topic and how it is to be investigated' (Hart, 1998: 13). In other words, your literature review will use scholarly articles to develop an argument about the research, concepts and theories that relate to your study. In doing so you are not simply listing relevant literature. Rather, you are critically engaging with it – analysing, organising, evaluating and synthesising.

By reviewing existing work you can increase your understanding of your topic and demonstrate this knowledge to your reader. You can also show your skills at selecting and interpreting relevant material. You can identify common themes, competing perspectives and approaches to gathering information, and different uses and meanings of the concepts you intend to use. Engagement with the literature can also help you to develop, consolidate and question your own developing perspectives. Most importantly, the evidence you gather here will prove invaluable when you analyse your own research findings.

Steps in a literature review

A literature review is not linear; it will evolve constantly as you identify new research and develop new concepts and arguments. Nevertheless, there are a number of useful steps in the process (and it should be noted that most of them take place before you start writing up!).

- *Research focus* – identify your topic and develop clear aims and objectives.
- *Gather relevant material* – from a range of scholarly writing. Keep detailed reference notes or use a software package like *Refworks* (http://www.refworks.com/) or *Endnote* (http://endnote.com/) to save a considerable amount of time later on.
- *Read, take notes and develop ideas* – begin by reading broadly on your topic. Then as you become more familiar with the literature, start to focus on your specific research aim.
- *Organise, analyse and evaluate* – group your literature around concepts and approaches, identifying relationships, similarities and differences, strengths and weaknesses.
- *Synthesise* – develop a table or concept map that organises the literature to form your own independent and coherent argument.
- Write it up!

ACTIVITY

Take a journal article or chapter from a book that is relevant to your chosen topic of study. Skim it to identify important ideas. Now read key sections carefully, using different colours to highlight useful quotes, key points, ideas that support and challenge your own thoughts, and strengths and weaknesses. Write a brief summary of these points and make an accurate note of the reference details.

Accessing a range of literature

The literature review is generally the most substantial and time-consuming part of your project. There is simply so much information you could access. There is some good news, though – whereas twenty years ago you would have had to spend hours hunting through and photocopying books and paper copies of journals, today you can access tremendous amounts of material from your computer. Search engines and databases provide mechanisms by which you can narrow and refine your search, sifting out inappropriate material and giving you control over the search parameters.

Because you are engaging in an academic enquiry, journal articles should be your main source for your literature review. Not only are journal publications often among the most contemporary of sources, but published articles also have the advantage of having undergone a peer review process. Authors submit their work for review by other academics, and only work that has passed through this process successfully will be published. Of course, there are thousands of journals in education today, with wide variation in the rigour of this review process. However, as a general rule, the more prestigious the journal, the more thorough the review process will be. Among the most important British education journals are:

- *British Journal of Educational Studies*
- *British Educational Research Journal*
- *British Journal of Sociology of Education*
- *Gender and Education*
- *Journal of Philosophy of Education.*

Alongside journal articles, other sources of scholarly writing include books, conference proceedings, reports, government publications, newspaper articles and other students' dissertations and theses. With access to so much academic writing, the search process can feel very daunting and it can be difficult to know where to start. One effective strategy is to begin with a landmark essay or piece of research – you might obtain this from notes from study modules, in a relevant textbook, or by asking your supervisor. After reading the seminal article you can use the reference list at the end of the paper to identify other relevant literature. You can also search the article and author names, identifying more recent scholarly work that has responded to or expanded the original ideas. These strategies mean your literature base 'snowballs' as you access more and more sources.

Before long, the difficulty becomes knowing when to stop. You cannot access all the literature in your topic. The relevant literature is not static, clearly defined or readily identifiable. You need to make choices about what is significant, and you must reach a point where you feel you have enough evidence to develop your argument. The literature is a continuously evolving network of scholarly writing, which interacts with itself to develop, challenge, expand and contradict an ever-growing body of knowledge. Your literature review needs to position your own work within this network.

Different sources

While journal articles should be your starting point in identifying scholarly writing, you should also try to use a range of other sources. Each source has strengths and limitations. For instance, academic books contain a lot of information and have the space to develop detailed arguments. However, books can be difficult and/or expensive to access, and due to publishers' lead-in times they are seldom up-to-the-minute or current. Newspaper articles are accessible and come in bitesized chunks, but journalistic writing is quite different from academic writing and newspapers are likely to present information in a partial, biased and sensationalised manner.

One of the most common ways of accessing relevant literature is via the internet. It is quick and easy to use a search engine to locate publications on your topic, and there is an enormous amount of freely accessible information. Most important is the emergence and rapid expansion of 'creative commons' licensing and open educational resources. Of course, you have to be especially careful when using scholarly writing from the web, since this material is less likely to have gone through an editorial or peer review process. Having said that, online 'web 2.0' communities increasingly self-regulate content – in some ways, Wikipedia has the most rigorous peer review system of all. The democratic nature of the web is both its strength and its weakness – multiple perspectives are readily available and anyone can publish anything.

Most importantly, whichever source you use, you need to develop what Postman and Weingartner famously termed 'crap-detecting skills' (1971). As you read, question the credibility and accuracy of the source, distinguishing 'good' from 'bad' information. You can find excellent YouTube videos by Howard Rheingold exploring internet literacies and crap detection.

Using databases

A database is an organised collection of material. It is like an electronic filing system, helping you to access the resources you require. In general, you can define and narrow your search according to criteria such as keywords, titles, authors, dates, names and types of publication. Each database has distinct mechanisms for managing data, so it is crucial that you familiarise yourself with the processes.

Some databases provide access to a limited range of resources, for example peer-reviewed journal articles. Others list a wide range of materials, including books, policy documents, newspaper articles, blogs and so on. Some databases provide title and abstract information while others provide links to full articles, although many very recent articles will be embargoed for between six and eighteen months. While a growing number of databases are free to access, some require a personal or institutional subscription – check to see if you can access the latter via your university network or using your library login details.

There is a large number of databases which all provide excellent access to literature in education. Among these are:

- **Education Research Complete (ERC)** – indexing and abstracts for more than 2,400 journals, and full text access to more than 1,400.
- **British Education Index (BEI)** – the main education index covering the UK, including titles and abstracts from more than 300 education journals.
- **Education Resources Information Centre (ERIC)** – free, international database with more than 1.4 million bibliographic records of education material.
- **Current Educational and Children's Services Research (CERUK+)** – a free database of education and children's services research in the UK.

Some databases are specific to particular areas of educational enquiry. For instance:

- **Higher Education Empirical Research Database (HEER)** – summaries of the latest published research in higher education.

- **International Education Research Database** – free database of more than 5,000 articles in the field of international education.
- **Directory of UK ELT Research** – research in English language teaching since 2005.

Many more generic databases will also prove useful, including:

- JSTOR
- Academic Search Premier (EBSCO)
- JORUM
- Springerlink
- Swetswise
- ZETOC
- Google Scholar
- Directory of Open Access Journals (DORJ)
- Social Sciences Citation Index
- Applied Social Sciences Index and Abstracts (ASSIA)
- Scopus
- Lexis.

ACTIVITY

Try using a database to find scholarly writing in your chosen field of study. Access one of the online databases listed above. Start with a general keyword search. Now try to narrow your search – your database might allow you to refine your search parameters by:

- date
- type and title of publication
- keywords in title or abstract only
- peer reviewed only.

Now try the same process with a different database. Do you get similar or different results?

Critically engaging with the literature

A literature review is certainly more than a list of books and studies that relate to your topic; it is not merely a series of annotated articles. The most important characteristic of a successful literature review is critical engagement. To help you to analyse and evaluate the literature, you might ask the following questions:

- How recently was the research undertaken?
- Do the local, social, historical, cultural, political and economic contexts match with your own study?

- Who is the intended audience?
- What evidence is used to justify the author's claims?
- Has the literature been scrutinised by peer review?
- How trustworthy is the source or the publication?
- If the paper is based on primary research, is the methodological approach sound? Consider, for example:
  - How large is the sample?
  - Is there any evidence of bias?
  - Are the findings based on small-scale qualitative research, large-scale survey, mixed methods…?
  - Can you challenge the research on grounds of reliability, validity, representativeness, generalisability, reflexivity…?

Your literature needs to identify scholarly work that is relevant to your project, outline what you consider to be the important ideas in the literature, and analyse and evaluate this literature using questions like the ones listed above. However, your review also needs to *synthesise* this literature, combining it to say something new. This is the most important characteristic of critical engagement – *using* the literature to help you develop your own argument. To do this, as you read you need to consider a number of further questions:

- How does it correspond with other scholarly writing I have read?
- How does it match and contradict my own thinking?
- What have I learnt?
- How can I use it?
- How does it fit into my developing arguments?

ACTIVITY

The following extract is taken from the literature review in a recent article on mobile learning (m-learning). Read the extract and consider the following:

- Identify where the authors are:
  - Describing existing literature
  - Evaluating literature
  - Using literature to define concepts
  - Using ideas from literature to develop their own arguments
  - Identifying relationships between different literatures.
- Can you set out their argument as a list of short bullet points?
- How does this review of literature support the research?

From: Kearney, M., Schuck, S., Burden, K. and Aubusson, P. (2012) 'Viewing mobile learning from a pedagogical perspective', in Research in Learning Technology. Vol. 20, 2012

M-learning is described in numerous ways, but these descriptions all consider the nexus between working with mobile devices and the occurrence of learning: the process of learning mediated by a mobile device. Numerous characteristics of m-learning have been identified in the literature. Koole's (2009) FRAME model sits well with socio-cultural views of learning, taking into consideration both technical characteristics of mobile devices as well as social and personal learning processes. She refers especially to enhanced collaboration, access to information and deeper contextualisation of learning. Our paper extends Koole's model, to include understandings of "mobile pedagogy" which draw on socio-cultural understandings presented in her model.

Danaher, Gururajan, and Hafeez-Baig (2009) propose a framework based on three key principles: engagement, presence and flexibility. "Presence" refers to the "simultaneous awareness and locatedness of self and others ... encompassing the emotional element of being human" (26). They further break down "presence" into three sub-group "interaction types": cognitive (student-content), social (peer) and teaching (student-teacher). Inherent in this model is implicit discussion of pedagogy; the aim of our paper is to make this discussion central and explicit.

Other researchers have provided insights into different social aspects of m-learning. Traxler (2009: 30) described m-learning as "noisy" and problematic, featuring three essential elements: the personal, contextual and situated; while Klopfer, Squire, and Jenkins (2002) identified five features: portability, social interactivity, context sensitivity, connectivity and individuality. Pachler, Cook, and Bachmair (2010) analysed the interrelationship of learners with the structures, agency and cultural practices of what the authors call the "mobile complex" (1). The identification of these sets of characteristics and relationships established core features that we had to ensure were addressed in the development of our framework.

Larger-scale, more complex conceptual frameworks for m-learning design and evaluation have been proposed. Parsons, Ryu, and Cranshaw (2007) proposed a complex conceptual framework for m-learning with four perspectives: generic mobile environment issues, learning contexts, learning experiences and learning objectives. Vavoula and Sharples (2009) proposed a three-level framework for evaluating m-learning, comprising a micro-level concerned with usability, a meso level focusing on the learning experience (especially on communication in context) and a macro level dealing with integration within existing organisational contexts. Our framework aims to further interrogate this "meso level" of learners' experience.

Hence numerous frameworks have been proposed in the literature, ranging from complex multi-level models (e.g. Parsons, Ryu, and Cranshaw 2007) to smaller frameworks that often omit important socio-cultural characteristics of learning or of pedagogy. Common themes include portability of m-learning devices and mobility of learners; interactivity; control and communication. These descriptions acknowledge the prime importance of context, including spatial and temporal considerations, for analysing m-learning experiences. However, they typically attempt to merge affordances of mobile devices or characteristics of applications with features of the learners' experience. While acknowledging that the features identified in other frameworks are important in characterising technology-mediated learning by mobile users, we propose a succinct framework highlighting a unique combination of distinctive characteristics of current mobile pedagogy to bring socio-cultural insights to the literature on m-learning.

Writing up your literature review

Your literature review is your own piece of original work and there are numerous ways in which you could write it. Nevertheless, there are some strategies that might help you write a good one:

- **Link clearly to your overall project aims and objectives** – start by explaining how the selected literature relates explicitly to your project. You might choose to summarise the argument of your literature review here.

- **Contested concepts** – define the key concepts at the heart of your study. During your reading you are likely to recognise that different authors use concepts in different ways. An excellent start is to consider different interpretations and uses of your key concepts before outlining the definition you intend to use.

- **Building from landmark literature or classic studies** – another excellent way to begin is to outline one or two seminal pieces of work in your field. From this, you can discuss work that followed, considering how the original ideas have been challenged and refined over time.

- **Inverted pyramid argument** – you might follow a structure that starts with a broad exploration of the literature, before increasingly focusing on localised examples and narrowing definitions and uses.

- **Structured around key themes or topics** – grouping your argument around key themes helps you to maintain clarity and structure in an extended piece of writing. These themes will also prove useful when analysing your own data.

- **Maintain your voice** – because you are discussing other people's work, you can easily lose your own voice. Remember you are analysing their work rather than summarising it. By offering your interpretations of their arguments, you minimise the risk of plagiarism.

- **Using evaluative language** – make sure you are not simply describing or listing existing scholarly work by using phrases like '....overstate the case', 'a problem with…', 'this is limited because…', 'others have argued…', 'while this is persuasive…', 'a convincing argument…'.

- **Developing a coherent, integrated and sustained argument** – the literature review is an essay, and it should have a clear structure with an introduction and conclusion.

- **Signpost** – tell the reader why you have selected specific literature and what you are using it for. Clearly indicate how your argument is developing.

■ **Finish** – oddly, it is much harder to finish than to start a literature review. New research is always being published and the enormous amount of scholarly work means you can never fully complete a review. Although you will need to revise and extend your literature review throughout the period of your study, you need to reach a point where you are happy with it.

Chapter summary

This chapter has outlined the main sources of literature, providing details of useful databases and key journals. It has encouraged you to reflect on the relative merits of different sources, most notably the increasing use of the internet as a gateway to a wide range of materials. It has helped you to develop strategies for critically engaging with literature and for writing your literature review as a discursive and coherent argument. To maximise your chances of producing an excellent literature review, remember the following 'top tips'.

Ten top tips for writing a successful literature review

1 Your best source of literature is the online database.
2 Read literature reviews that already exist in your topic of study.
3 Use a wide range of types of literature – theoretical, conceptual, empirical, contemporary, historical, statistical, landmark....
4 Ensure that you review some literature from the last two years.
5 Be prepared to modify and redefine your research topic as you identify new relevant literature.
6 Identify themes in the literature and group your discussion around these themes.
7 Keep a track of your references – you might use software like *Endnote* or *Refworks*.
8 Don't list – always critically engage with the literature.
9 Use the language and 'signposts' you would normally use when writing a critical essay.
10 USE your literature to help you develop your own conceptual framework and argument.

Further reading

Ridley, D. (2012) *The literature review: A step-by-step guide for students* (2nd edition). London: Sage Study Skills Series.

■ This updated edition is filled with useful examples and guidance to help you develop your own literature review. Chapters 4 and 5 provide especially good advice on gathering material, reading and referencing.

Hart, C. (1998) *Doing a literature review: releasing the social science research imagination*. London: Sage.

■ This more advanced book provides a framework for using literature to think creatively in developing your own arguments.

4

Sampling

Introduction

Sampling is the term used when picking participants to take part in a study derived from the population of interest. Population refers to the larger group from which individuals are selected to participate in a study. The description below of the sample used in Read's research tells us a great deal about the participants in her study. It also allows us to evaluate the findings about the two populations of teachers and pupils in these regions.

> The research was conducted in 51 different Year 3 primary school classes (involving 7–8-year-old children) in London (25 classes) and North-East England (26 classes). Twenty-five classes were taught by a male teacher and 26 by a female teacher (with an even split between London and the North-East). Interviews were conducted with three girls and three boys in each of the classes (307 pupils in total; 153 boys and 154 girls). Of these pupils, 207 are White, 52 are Black, 25 are South Asian, five are dual heritage, one is Chinese, and the ethnicity of 17 was not classified. Only 10 of the minority ethnic pupils were located in North-East England.
>
> (Read, 2011: 4)

Sampling techniques fall into two main categories – probability and non-probability sampling. Sampling is a way of 'picking' individuals from a population you want to find out more about. The way you choose your sample will depend on your research approach. This chapter will help you to choose your research sample, and it will be organised under three sections: why you should use a sample, different types of sampling, and sampling bias.

Why use a sample?

In most cases it is unrealistic to expect to be able to work with a whole population. For example, it is not realistic to ask every teacher in England about their views on the implementation of the new National Curriculum in 2014. However, it would be possible to pick a sample of teachers whose views are likely to be representative of all the teachers in England.

The use of a sample saves time and money! This statement may sound like an advertising gimmick, but there are important methodological reasons for using a sample. One of the key reasons is to be able to generalise your findings to a wider population. The key methodological reasons for using a sample are:

- It is not always feasible to survey every person in the population you wish to study.
- There is little evidence that asking every member of a population will increase the validity and reliability of your findings.
- A representative sample enables you to make generalisations to the wider population you are studying.
- A representative sample increases the confidence you can have in generalising to the wider population you are studying.

As well as these advantages, there are also a number of obvious practical reasons for using a sample:

- It would take a long time to include every person in the population you wish to study.
- It is very expensive (e.g. in terms of the cost of researchers and travel) to ask every person in the population you wish to study.

However, you will need to explain the decisions you have made in regards to how you selected your sample of the population, because the participants you choose will influence the findings of your research.

ACTIVITY

You want to find out about Year 6 pupils in transition to secondary school. Logistically you cannot ask every Year 6 pupil in the country, and they (or their parents and teachers) might not all agree to take part in your research anyway. This is where sampling comes in. You have already identified the population you wish to research – Year 6 pupils. Now you will select a smaller number from this population – this is your sample. You decide to select Year 6 pupils from schools in a small coastal town. Now there are a range of strategies you can use to choose the Year 6 pupils who will take part in your study.

- How would you pick the Year 6 pupils to be involved in the research?
- Why do you need to explain to the reader why you chose this sample?
- Could you generalise your findings to every Year 6 pupil in the country? Why? Why not?
- Discuss your responses with a partner.

Many of the factors which influence how you select your sample will be dependent on the type of research you are carrying out. In the next section we will discuss different sampling strategies based on conducting quantitative and qualitative research.

Different types of sampling

Probability sampling

The next part of this chapter explains how to pick a 'probability' sample for studies which are using large numbers of participants, or researchers who believe that participants are likely to represent a cross-section of the population being researched. Probability sampling is based on the assumption that the people or events chosen as part of the sample are selected because it is likely that they have characteristics which represent the wider population that the research is trying to find out about. The most popular types of probability sampling are random, systematic, stratified, quota and cluster sampling.

- **Random sampling** – gives all the members of a population an equal chance of being selected. For example, if a number is given to each name on a list of Year 7 pupils, these numbers can then be picked at random to achieve a sample. Assume you have one hundred Year 7 pupils and they are all given a number from one to one hundred. You need to pick twenty out of your one hundred pupils. As in a tombola for a charity raffle, you could simply pick twenty numbers out of a hat to give you your sample. Alternatively the same principle can be applied using a computer random number generator, which will generate the twenty numbers you require.

- **Systematic sampling** – is an alternative type of random sampling. For example, you may decide to pick every seventh name on a list. This is fine, but make sure that the list itself will not inadvertently influence the sample. A boy/girl/boy/girl list may mean that if you pick an even number, such as every fourth name, you will always get a girl. If you require a balance of male and female pupils you need to ensure that your systematic sampling pattern will provide representativeness.

- **Stratified sampling** – this means that each member of a population has an equal chance of being selected based on the degree to which they represent part of the whole population. Stratified samples are more complicated than random samples since cases are selected in proportion to one or more characteristics in the population. For example, if socio-economic class is considered relevant to the study and this is determined by entitlement to free school meals, you need to select the appropriate proportion of participants who are entitled to free school meals. If the proportion entitled to free school meals is 20 per cent of the overall population, then 20 per cent of your sample needs to be selected on this basis. This becomes problematic because some schools may have a significantly higher proportion of children with entitlement to free school meals, while other schools may have a significantly lower proportion. Also, bear in mind that the assumptions you are making about a population will ultimately affect the results of your research. This is also problematic because you may want to select your sample based on sensitive issues such as age or sexual orientation, or very complex categories such as ethnicity or occupation.

- **Quota sampling** – this means that the members of the population who are targeted for inclusion in your sample are focused on because they meet the criteria of the predefined quota. For instance, the research may decide to interview ten newly qualified male teachers and ten newly qualified female teachers. This type of sampling is sometimes conducted on the high street by market researchers.

- **Cluster sampling** – sometimes the population you are interested in naturally occurs in clusters, such as schools. In this way, rather than focusing on individuals, the population can be selected based on the cluster in which it occurs. An advantage of this technique is that if many of the individuals we wish to include in our study belong to a cluster, we can save travelling time because the individuals are often in the same location.

ACTIVITY

Read the following extract:

> The purpose of the study was to gain a greater understanding of the sense of empowerment achieved by women in Pakistan through participation in higher education. The target population were female faculty members and female students drawn from 10 public universities in Pakistan. Data were collected in two parts.
> For the initial part, a survey instrument was used to obtain feedback from female faculty and students, using a five-point Likert scale with possible responses of 'strongly disagree', 'disagree', 'neutral', 'agree', and 'strongly agree' for the majority of questions. The full survey contained 98 questions, out of which 14 were selected as a basis for this paper. The questions selected relate thematically to issues of gender parity and include two open-ended questions. The survey was presented to faculty members and students on paper. Out of 102 public universities in Pakistan, 10 were selected, two from each of the four provinces of Pakistan and two from the Federal capital of Pakistan, Islamabad. Across all 10 universities, the sample comprised 1500 female postgraduate students from a cross-section of departments (5% of female students from each university) and 320 female faculty members (50% of female faculty members from each university). Participants were selected randomly.
> The researcher visited five out of these universities to administer the questionnaire in person, while postal questionnaires were sent to the remaining universities.
> Out of 1500 questionnaires distributed to students, 1290 (86%) were returned, and out of 320 faculty members approached, 290 (92%) responded.
>
> (Malik and Courtney, 2011: 33)

- How would you define the type of sampling used? Why?
- How representative do you think the sample is of women in higher education in Pakistan? Why?

Non-probability sampling

This section explains how to choose a 'non-probability' sample for studies which are using smaller numbers of participants, or where the researcher does not have enough information about the 'sample' to know if they are 'representative'. Non-probability sampling is more likely to be used in qualitative studies. Common types of non-probability sampling, such as purposive, snowball, convenience and theoretical sampling, are outlined. In qualitative research this type of sampling is generally not seen to be problematic as small-scale research does not often attempt to generalise to a wider population; it is much more interested in providing an in-depth portrait of the experiences of those participants who are taking part in the research.

- **Purposive** – the sample is chosen specifically for the research because the researcher knows that these participants will be able to provide the best account of the phenomena that they wish to study. Purposive sampling is an approach which indicates that you know who the best participants for your research are, because they are the population who are most likely to know the most about your area of research. For example, if you are interested in NQTs' experiences of teaching in their first few months, the NQTs themselves are much more likely to give an informative account of this experience than their mentor or the other teachers they work with. Interpretivist research approaches are not concerned with bias in the same way that positivist research is. The random selection used by positivists is undertaken to ensure that the researcher does not bias the research. However, the interpretivist stance is different because it acknowledges that researcher bias is inevitable – we are all shaped by the environment we live in, our life experiences and the views of those around us. Therefore, interpretivists argue that it is impossible not to bias the sample. After all, the very topic which is being researched will be based on the researcher's predisposition to an interest in this area. With purposive sampling the researcher acknowledges their bias and how it may affect the research process, and the choosing of research participants will be part of this. Crucially, a researcher using purposive sampling will not try to make broad generalisations to the wider population based on their findings. They may suggest that their findings are potentially indicative – for example, of the experiences of all NQTs within their first few months of teaching – and they may indicate that their findings correspond with other research in this area. However, they would not suggest that the findings are completely representative because there will be many other factors which have shaped the findings based on other factors related to the research process, the participants and the researcher. Consequently it is important to remember the limitations of generalisability with purposive sampling, and to keep in mind the fact it is much more closely aligned with research within the interpretivist paradigm.

- **Snowballing** – this involves asking participants if they are aware of other individuals who would also be interested in participating in the research, and recruiting participants via other participants who act as gatekeepers. Perhaps the best example of the appropriate use of a non-probability sample is where a snowball technique is necessary. In some studies of truancy, for example, it may be difficult to find people belonging to this population. In such a case we may start with a convenience sample of one or two pupils who agree to take part in the study. Then we can ask these participants to introduce us to or put us in contact with other pupils who also play truant. This approach should not be confused with convenience sampling.

- **Convenience** – this involves using the most easily available participants. By its very nature, this sampling technique can skew the findings of the research. Convenience sampling is not an approach that is generally considered within educational research because of its lack of methodological rigour. It is normally used by market researchers who have a quota to fill – for example, interviewing ten women and ten men. Generally within educational research you will wish to be more specific about who your research participants are based on what you wish to find out – for example, teachers who have qualified in the last three years, or Year 6 teachers. However, to achieve a level of validity and reliability in your findings you may still have in mind the number of participants that you need to include in your research to have confidence in your findings (more information on evaluating research can be found in Chapter 19). Engaging enough participants in your research to reach a saturation of themes – which suggests that if you interviewed any more participants you would not find any new themes – is not the same principle as convenience sampling.

ACTIVITY

- Which types of sampling could you use to find out about primary teachers' views on the Special Educational Needs and Disability Green Paper 2012?
- How would the sampling approach influence the type of data collected?

Sampling bias

There will always be a chance that the particular sample selected will give inaccurate results, although it is possible to minimise the probability of this happening. Piaget's well-known research on children's developmental stages was derived from carrying out experiments with his own three children and his friends' children (Gallard and Garden, 2011). Like his own children, the children of his friends were from an advantaged socio-economic background and therefore his sample was not representative of the population, indicating a sampling bias. Advances in statistical techniques give us greater confidence in making generalisations from a sample to a whole population, but in truth, when using a sample we cannot be completely sure about how representative it is of the population. There are several factors that influence sampling bias:

- The size of the sample influences both the representativeness of the sample and the statistical analysis of the data.
- Larger samples are more likely to detect a difference between groups.
- Smaller samples are less likely to be representative.

- Non-probability sampling increases the likelihood of sampling bias.
- Probability sampling is free of bias that might stem from choices made by the researcher.
- A problem in sampling arises due to bias from the use of 'volunteers'. Whether or not you provide an incentive for participants to take part in your research, the participants who choose to be involved in your study are likely to be different from those who do not.

ACTIVITY

Read the extract below:

> The sampling strategy underlying the initial questionnaire survey was informed by two main concerns. Firstly, we sought to generate a representative sample of student teachers (in England) for each of the ITT routes being studied – namely university-administered PGCE, Flexible PGCE, BEd, BA/BSc with QTS, SCITT, and GRTP. Secondly, it was hoped to ensure that a sufficient number of trainees were recruited from among the routes with the least training places, in order to enable viable statistical analysis by route up to the end of the project in 2009 (allowing for attrition over a 5 year period). ITT providers were thus stratified by route and a random sample of providers within each route was selected, with a small number of providers being purposively selected to boost the numbers of trainees from the smaller ITT routes.
> A total of 110 providers were approached to participate in the survey, of which 74 took part. Where possible the self-completion questionnaire was administered face-to-face by a project fieldworker, though in some cases (notably in very small ITT providers) it was necessary for the survey to be administered postally. The Wave 1 questionnaire was completed by 4,790 student teachers; 3,162 trainees took part in the follow-up Wave 2 telephone interview; and, of these, 2,446 (then) NQTs took part at Wave 3.
>
> (Hobson *et al.*, 2007: 5–6)

- What steps did the researchers take to minimise sampling bias?
- Are there any ways in which sampling bias may have crept into the research? Why? How?
- Drawing on your knowledge of sampling, is there anything you would have done differently to minimise sampling bias?
- Discuss your thoughts with a partner.

Chapter summary

This chapter has highlighted the significance of sampling when carrying out research on a population of interest. A range of sampling techniques derived from non-probability and probability approaches have been discussed. Decisions about your method of choosing a sample need to be explained in your research, and any issues regarding sampling bias also need to be highlighted.

Further reading

Gorard, S. (2001) *Quantitative methods in educational research: The role of numbers made easy*. London: Continuum.

■   Chapter 2, 'Sampling: The basis of all research', is an informative and accessible read highlighting the advantages and pitfalls of different types of sampling.

5

Data analysis

Introduction

Analysis in educational research involves discovering the layers of meaning in your data, which means finding the patterns in 'what' and 'how' participants describe or explain educational experiences. However, the *type* of data analysis will depend on the kind of data you have collected. For the purposes of this chapter we will broadly describe data as either *qualitative* or *quantitative*. Qualitative data is in word form – for example, interview transcripts or field notes from classroom observations. Qualitative data analysis can be daunting because there is no set way to interpret the data. The qualitative data analysis section will be split into four sections: beginning qualitative data analysis, analysis techniques derived from grounded theory, language devices for analysis, and absences in the data. The section on quantitative data analysis will also be divided into four sections: frequency, descriptive statistics, measures of central tendency and chi-square tests.

Beginning qualitative data analysis

First, read through all your data and become familiar with its content. This is often easier if you have transcribed your own interview data because you will already (consciously or subconsciously) have started to think about what is being said. As you read through the data, jot down any points that seem significant and stand out to you – for example, particular words or phrases. As you can see from this initial process, qualitative data lends itself to the interpretive paradigm since you are the one interpreting the data. A key way to analyse your data is through coding. The process of coding means putting labels on your data.

There are various ways you can start to identify your codes. For many people a range of coloured highlighters and a large empty space where pieces of paper can be spread out and shuffled is one way of starting to think about the codes for a qualitative data analysis. For the more technically-minded, qualitative data analysis software such as NVIVO can be used.

The principle of qualitative data analysis software is that as you develop codes you can attach appropriate examples to each code. This will enable you to see if some codes have significantly more data attached to them than others. Software also allows you to create models so that you can explain the relationships or patterns in your data visually. A word of caution, – qualitative data analysis software does not do the thinking for you. You still have to identify the themes and codes yourself.

Alternatively you can use a simple Word document and put the appropriate interview quotes under the codes you have created with judicious use of bold text and highlighting. The key to qualitative data analysis is recognising that you are required to do the thinking about what codes and themes are in your data and how these fit together. Miles and Huberman (1994: 9) recommend that your focus should be to identify 'patterns and processes, commonalities and differences'. This can take time and you need to think deeply to identify the layers in your data. You may also find it helpful to talk to other people about your interpretation of the data, or let others look at your data and see if their interpretations are similar to your own.

Analysis techniques derived from grounded theory

There are specific strategies and devices that the qualitative researcher can use for data analysis. Grounded theory is perhaps the best known process for systematically analysing qualitative data. This chapter is not the appropriate place to discuss the history of grounded theory or why some researchers find it methodologically problematic (a good starting point for this debate is the chapter by Charmaz in Denzin and Lincoln, 2011). This chapter will restrict itself to explaining some of the techniques from grounded theory which may aid your analysis.

Strauss and Corbin (1998) are two well-known authors of grounded theory research, and they give useful examples to show how they analysed their data. Examples of the data analysis process are replicated here from interviews with students about their assignment feedback. First Strauss and Corbin (1998) suggest highlighting the words and phrases – *conceptual names* – that are used repeatedly by participants, see Table 5.1.

TABLE 5.1 Conceptual names to analyse data

Interview quote excerpt	Conceptual name
If it says this is absolute rubbish again it is not very constructive because in my mind you think you have done what is necessary but it hasn't worked. (Henry, interview)	Rubbish
Nobody likes being told that they're wrong but I think you've got to do it you know. (Helen, interview)	Being wrong

Second, Strauss (1987) suggests coding for *conditions, interactions among actors, strategies and tactics* and *consequences,* see Table 5.2.

TABLE 5.2 Types of code

Interview excerpt	Type of code	Code
It's the same with the other one – "however try and keep this a little bit more focused." "Good start on a critical analysis" – how could I go a bit more further in that? I mean you can probably see from that you can't get much from feedback like this. (Arvind, interview)	Conditions	Vague feedback
*Subject is a problem, you're just given your assignment and then don't get any help. It's like they are too important and won't touch us. They think they are better than us. (Debbie, interview)	Interactions among actors	Unapproachable staff
Yeah like the last one there was like I really just didn't understand the feedback and I went and had a word with the demonstrators and I didn't find that useful either hence that is why I said to yourself I was just going to pay the money and have private tuition, which as I have said worked. It was a bit of a shock because my grades just went from E to B. (Arvind, interview)	Strategies and tactics	Personalised support
Yeah definitely when I first had mine I was you know I was like am I on the right track, do I want to do this? Am I going to get anywhere? So you know from that point it's left me with I will not approach that demonstrator I just will not go anywhere near her I go to talk to the other person. (Arvind, interview)	Consequences	Damage to self-esteem

ACTIVITY

Using an interview transcript, try to code the data looking for conditions, interactions among actors, strategies and tactics and consequences as suggested by Strauss (1987).

- What patterns do you notice?
- Are there any other significant themes emerging?
- Share your analysis with a partner – have they spotted the same themes?

Qualitative data analysis is aided when you can reflect on your data, mark it up and write memos (Miles and Huberman, 1994). Memos are notes about any thoughts, ideas or questions that you feel are emerging from the concepts in the data. The value of memos is that they are a way of recording new thoughts and enable you to consider different ideas within the data analysis. The content of memos is not limited and could include a wide range of comments, such as hunches and insights. In Table 5.3 there are examples of memos made on interview excerpts.

TABLE 5.3 Memos

Interview excerpt	Memos
Because you know I don't know because like I haven't had the most lavish lifestyle as a kid and I think you know I want to do well so you know just for yourself kind of thing and to prove people wrong.	I think there is a link to the graduate job market here and the idea of a better life. Leathwood and O'Connell's (2003) students felt that the opportunity for graduate employment was a key reason to study and also came from backgrounds associated with poverty, low-paid jobs and unemployment.
I think definitely because last year I was quite annoyed at the people I didn't get feedback from and now I've got loads and I'm like yes.	Students are dissatisfied when they don't receive feedback – does this tell me that students value feedback?

At the beginning of this chapter analysis was described as understanding the 'what' and 'how' participants explain their educational experiences. The 'how' can often be identified through considering different language devices. Three language devices which it may be useful to consider are metaphors, contrastive rhetoric and extremist talk.

Metaphors

Although codes can take the form of a straightforward category label, the use of metaphor is a more complex way of interpreting the data (Miles and Huberman, 1994). A metaphor is a figure of speech which presents strong imagery or symbolism.

Contrastive rhetoric

Making contrasts is a widespread feature of interactional and conversational practice (Hargreaves and Woods, 1984). Contrasts are either explicitly or implicitly involved in all descriptions, since all our conceptions of what things are must also be constructed according to what they are not. The use of such contrastive rhetoric may be identified in many social settings, where participants create accounts based on distinctions between 'us and them', 'past and present' and 'here and there'. The use of 'past and present' is a way to compare previous and current experiences of education, whereas the use of 'us and them' can be employed as a way of differentiating between groups.

Extremist talk

Extremist talk does not involve a comparison; rather, it tends to focus on one end of a spectrum only, and it may be used by individuals who find themselves in subordinate positions, see Table 5.4.

TABLE 5.4 Language devices

Language device	Interview excerpt
Metaphor	*Students only seek help when they hit the buffers.* (Henry, interview) *You feel it is a hostile environment because lecturers just want you to get on with it... you need the tutor to actually pull you out, you need to know where the life-jacket is but I haven't used it because the life-jacket wasn't actually thrown to me.* (Henry, interview)
Contrastive rhetoric – 'past and present'	*Oh I did terrible. I just like messed around you know I wasn't really interested, but as I got older you know you want to do well you are more motivated because you know the outcome in the end. Yeah I was like in the bottom class when I was a little kid about five, then I worked myself up and then in my last year at school I was in the top set which was a good achievement for me. I thought I'd come to uni to be good at Psychology.* (Helen, interview)
Contrastive rhetoric – 'us and them'	*More than I did now yeah. Because you were allowed to take the work to teachers and ask them what's going on kind of thing, but like here they are not allowed to look at it because then they are classed as being biased towards your work or they know you better. Do you know what I mean? So it's kind of harder.* (Shireen, interview)
Extremist talk	*So they can't go to them and say I'm hacked off or I don't understand what you are on about because he thinks he's going to bawl his head off because you know some teachers and tutors like to bawl.* (Henry, interview)

ACTIVITY

- Using an interview transcript from your own data collection – can you identify any language devices being used?
- What do they tell you?

Absences in the data

So far this chapter has concentrated on identifying what is being said, but what about information that is not mentioned explicitly? Absences in the data – topics or themes that you might have anticipated but which are not there – can tell their own story. It is important to consider whether anything is 'missing' and why that might be. Additionally you may have anomalies in your data – that is, information from one or two participants that does not 'fit' with your overall findings. Again, you should consider why this is the case, and it is also important to consider whether these findings are important in themselves and therefore whether they should be included when reporting your findings.

Quantitative data analysis

Quantitative data is numerical, such as numbers of pupils or exam results. In quantitative data analysis, the focus is on variables. A variable is an attribute that describes a person, place, thing or idea. Qualitative variables take on values that are names or labels, such as school subjects or hobbies. Quantitative variables are numeric, which means they can be measured – for example, the number of children in a school, see Table 5.5.

TABLE 5.5 Types of variable

Type of variable	Examples	Statistical application
Nominal data	Male/female Socio-economic status Ethnicity Religion	Counting and descriptive statistics, e.g.: 1 out of 4 respondents was female. 35% of the sample identified themselves as Black and Minority Ethnic (BME).
Ordinal data	Ordinal data often describe perceptions and try to gauge views. The use of the Likert scale is a good example of the use of ordinal data. For example: I think children in my class are good at sharing: 1 Strongly agree 2 Agree 3 Neutral 4 Disagree 5 Strongly disagree	Literally meaning 'in order'. Counting and descriptive statistics again, e.g. 50% of respondents strongly agreed. 30 of the respondents disagreed that the provision of after school activities was good.
Interval data	Interval data can be ranked on a scale because the 'gap' between each category is known, such as months or years. This means the analysis can assess how much more or how much less, rather than just more or less.	E.g. the number of 'A' grade GCSE English results: 2010 – 20% 2011 – 24% 2012 – 23% In this example we could compare the school's results year on year.
Ratio data	Income Distance Weight Ratio data has a true zero. Comparisons can be made using multiplication and division. Ratio data is the most sophisticated type of data in terms of the types of statistical tests that can be done.	For example, you may want to compare the salary of a newly qualified teacher with that of another graduate entry profession, or you may want to identify the distance travelled by pupils to school.
Discrete data	This is about naturally-forming whole units.	For example, children or teachers. It does not make sense to talk about 1.4 children; we can only say 2 out of 3 children.

Frequency

A questionnaire involved data collection from three Year 7 Science classes (100 pupils in total). Question 3 asked pupils their gender – boy or girl. Question 7 asked for pupils Year 6 Science SAT level result.

To make sense of the data it first needs to be counted. This can be done by entering the answers from each participant into a spreadsheet or table. At this stage all you are doing is counting the data. The frequency table shows the number of students who achieved a particular level in their Science test, see Table 5.6.

TABLE 5.6 Frequency table of Science SAT levels

Gender	Level 3	Level 4	Level 5
Boy (51)	12	30	10
Girl (49)	8	25	15
Total: (out of 100 pupils)	20	55	25

If you include a frequency table it is important to highlight to the reader the key patterns you have identified.

Descriptive statistics

Descriptive statistics do just that – they describe. They are generally employed for univariate data which has one variable, such as the pupils' test scores. For instance, looking at the frequency table above we can describe this data by saying that 25 out of 100 pupils achieved a Level 5 in their Year 6 Science SAT. We could also describe this as a percentage and say that 25 per cent of the pupils achieved a Level 5, or report it as a fraction and say a quarter of the students achieved a Level 5.

However, you may also wish to interrogate the data further to identify other patterns. For example, of the 49 girls in the survey, 15 achieved a Level 5 in Science. Therefore you may wish to say that 31 per cent of the girls achieved a Level 5 in Science. A graph can also represent this data. There are a range of different types of graph that may be useful for visual representations, such as bar charts, pie charts, scatter graphs and line graphs. Again, it will be important to highlight to the reader the key patterns you have identified.

Measures of central tendency

The mean, mode and median are called measures of central tendency because they identify a single score as typical or representative of all the scores in a frequency distribution, see Table 5.7.

TABLE 5.7 Measures of central tendency

Measure of central tendency	Method	Example
Mean	The mean is also known as the average. To work out the average, add all the numbers up and then divide them by the total number of measurements.	$\dfrac{4+5+6+4+7}{5} = 5.2$ The mean is **5.2**
Mode	The mode means the most common – that is, the most commonly-occurring number in the data set.	4, 4, 5, 6, 7 The mode is **4**, since it is the most commonly occurring number.
Median	The median refers to the middle value. This means the numbers have to be placed in ascending order.	4, 4, 5, 6, 7 **5** is the median number here, since it falls in the middle.

If more than one number occurs most frequently when you are trying to work out the mode, – for example, as with the data set 4,4,5,6,6,7 – there are two modes, in this case the numbers 4 and 6. This is because both of these numbers occur most frequently (twice). In this instance you may need to consider whether a different measure of central tendency would be more appropriate.

When a dataset has an even number of measurements there is no 'middle' number to give you the median. Instead you need to take the two middle numbers and work out the average. For example, in the dataset 4,4,5,6,6,7 the middle numbers are 5 and 6. Working out the average of these two numbers gives you a median of 5.5.

As measures of central tendency, the mean and median each have advantages and disadvantages. The median may be a better indicator of the most typical value if a set of scores has an outlier. An outlier is an extreme value that differs greatly from the other values in the data set. However, when the sample size is large and does not include outliers, the mean usually provides a better measure of central tendency.

Standard deviation and variance

Standard deviation measures how spread out a set of numbers is. The formula for the standard variation is the square root of the variance. The variance is the average of the squared differences from the mean, see the following example:

To work out the *variance* of a set of reading test scores (scored out of 100):

1 Work out the average reading test score:

$$\frac{80+40+55+75+67}{5} = 63.4$$

2 Subtract the average from each measurement:

$80 - 63.4 = 16.6$
$40 - 63.4 = -23.4$
$55 - 63.4 = -8.4$
$75 - 63.4 = 11.6$
$67 - 63.4 = 3.6$

3 Square the results and sum them:

$$16.6^2 + (-23.4)^2 + (-8.4)^2 + 11.6^2 + 3.6^2 = 1041.2$$

4 Work out the average of the squared differences:

$$\frac{1041.2}{5} = 208.24$$

5 **The variance is 208.24**

The standard deviation is the square root of the variance:

$$\sqrt{208.24} = 14.43$$

The standard deviation is 14

(Decimal answers can be rounded to the nearest whole number – round up whenever the last digit is 5 or greater.)

Chi-square test

This section will outline a chi-square test since this is perhaps the most useful statistical test within educational research. The chi-square test is used to discover the relationship between two categorical variables. Your variables must be ordinal or nominal, and you need two or more groups in each variable. A quantitative data software package such as SPSS will use the correct formulae to complete the statistical test. However, it is important to know when and why you would use this test. An example of when a chi-square test may be applied and advice on interpreting the results are given below.

A science teacher wants to know if boys or girls prefer an online game-based learning simulation or a practical experiment when learning how to create electrical circuits. Our variables are: gender – boy or girl; and preferred learning activity – online or practical. Our statistical test involves bivariate data, meaning that we have two variables.

Once the teacher has collected the data it can be entered into SPSS. SPSS will produce a cross-tabulation table which will look similar to Table 5.8.

TABLE 5.8 Chi-Square test results

	Online	Practical	Total
Boys			
% within gender	20	30	50
% preferred learning activity	40	60	100
% total	20	30	50
Girls			
% within gender	13	27	50
% preferred learning activity	26	54	100
% total	13	27	50
Total			
% within gender	33	57	100
% preferred learning activity	33	57	100
Total	33	57	100

The chi-square test involves taking the sum of the difference between the observed (o) data and the expected (e) data, and dividing it by the expected data in all categories. The formula below shows the chi-square test calculation:

$$X^2 = \sum \frac{(o-e)^2}{e}$$

o = the frequencies observed
e = the frequencies expected
$\sum$ = the 'sum of'

As with most statistics, the results of chi-square calculations have a significance level attached to them. If the significance level is lower than p=0.05 (or one in twenty) this means that the observed effect is highly unlikely to be the result of chance. Therefore, a result of p≤0.05 is generally considered statistically significant. Using the data from the cross-tabulation table above, we can work out the results of the chi-square test, which are that both boys and girls preferred the practical activity for learning about electrical circuits.

Chapter summary

Data analysis is a huge part of a research project. The way in which data analysis is carried out will depend on whether you have qualitative or quantitative data. There are a variety of ways in which qualitative data can be analysed, but they all rely on the researcher to interpret the data. Similarly, there are set ways of analysing numerical data and statistical tests can be used to show the patterns in this type of data.

Further reading

Connolly, P. (2007) *Quantitative data analysis in education: A critical introduction using SPSS.* London: Routledge.

- This book is written in a friendly and accessible manner and it does not assume any prior knowledge of quantitative data analysis. It includes chapters on data sets, variables and how to analyse the relationships between variables. It also explains different ways of presenting your findings and how to conduct statistical tests.

Gibbs, G. (2007) *Analysing qualitative data.* London: Sage.

- This book discusses the nature of qualitative data and the processes by which this kind of data can be analysed. It includes chapters on thematic coding, analysing narrative data and using computer software for qualitative data analysis.

6

Writing up

Introduction

This chapter provides practical guidance for managing the writing up phase of a piece of extended research in Education Studies. This may be the first time you have taken on a large piece of writing like this, so this chapter is full of useful support and advice. It provides examples of possible chapter structures and layout, advice for managing time and material, and hints and tips for writing effectively.

If you choose your topic and your methodology carefully, your extended research project should be the best part of your degree. It is an opportunity for you to investigate an educational topic in greater depth than in other parts of the course. You will be able to use the knowledge and skills you have developed during your degree to produce an independent and original piece of work. It should be the most rewarding piece of work that you complete, but it is also the most demanding. It is therefore very important that you:

- Choose an area of study that is of real interest to you.
- Ensure that you have access to sufficient and appropriate material to support your topic.
- Make sure your project is realistic within your resource and time limitations.
- Develop an appropriate and feasible methodological approach.
- Start writing early – do not leave writing up until the last few weeks!

Getting started

Often the hardest part of writing up is getting started. Somehow your room always seems in need of a good tidy, and TV programmes seem to become much more interesting. Even the most experienced writer procrastinates – especially in the early stages of writing up. Your research project is likely to be the longest piece of writing you will have done, and it can feel very daunting – especially at the beginning.

Luckily, if you have followed the guidance from earlier in this book you will not be starting with a blank sheet of paper. You should have clear aims and objectives, research questions or a hypothesis, which you will have agreed with your supervisor quite early on. You will have lots of reference material, and you may have a draft literature review. You may have kept a 'research log' or 'diary' and undertaken substantial 'thinking on paper' (Wolcott, 1990: 31), keeping notes on your reflections about what worked well and what proved difficult throughout your research, comments on articles you have read, documenting your developing data analysis and so on. To help you make a start, consider:

- Producing a detailed chapter plan and a schedule identifying key deadline dates to complete chapters/drafts.

- Taking each of your aims and objectives in turn and writing a brief description of what each means, which method you used to address it and what you discovered.

- Begin writing with a chapter you already have lots of material for – this is likely to be your literature review or your findings chapter.

- Making the task seem less daunting by thinking of the final project as a series of connected short essays. It is easier to start a 1500-word essay than a 10,000-word thesis!

Structuring your research project

A conventional structure for a research project based on empirical research consists of the following chapters:

1   Introduction
This chapter usually articulates and explains the project's aims and objectives, research questions and/or hypothesis. These aspects of your study are absolutely key in helping you write up – they should frame everything that follows. The introduction often includes a rationale and a justification for the study. Ask yourself why the topic is important and why you are a good person to undertake it. The chapter generally ends with an outline of the overall structure of the report and a summary of each chapter.

2   Context
Here you outline the political, economic, social, cultural, historical, local and personal contexts of the study. Discuss important developments in your field of educational enquiry, and outline key policy developments. Think about important current factors that impact on your topic – changes in technology, the wider economy, funding, participation rates, media stories and so on. In this chapter you are providing a background to your study. If you undertook primary research in a particular school or college, provide some detail about student and staff numbers, specific institutional factors and policies (remembering to adhere to conventions on anonymity).

3   Literature review

Use existing literature to frame your topic, to help you clarify important concepts and develop your own argument. Use a range of sources and types of literature (empirical, theoretical, conceptual, journalistic, academic, statistical, interpretive, seminal, contemporary…). Remember, you are not simply identifying important literature. You are organising and critically analysing it to help you to develop your project. Ideally, try to identify a gap in the literature that your project fills (see Chapter 3 for further guidance).

4   Methodology

This is a really important chapter and it has a number of functions. Firstly, you need to position your research within wider methodological debates – for instance, within the interpretivist and positivist paradigms discussed earlier. Then you need to outline and justify the choices you made – your approach to sampling, the methods you utilised, your data analysis strategies, the ethical issues you identified and the solutions you came up with. Evaluate your own research in relation to concepts like validity, reliability, representativeness, generalisability and reflexivity (see Chapter 4 for further guidance).

5   Results/Findings

Here you outline your main findings. Quantitative data might be presented in tables, graphs and charts. Qualitative data might be presented as quotes from respondents, extracts from fieldwork diaries, detailed life stories, or descriptions of events or encounters. The way you select and present your data demonstrates your analysis and interpretations; grouping your findings around themes is a very good strategy (see Chapter 5 for further guidance).

6   Discussion

This is where you critically examine your data, setting out the implications of your research. The key thing here is to refer back to the literature you discussed in your third chapter. Think about the similarities and differences between the literature and your own findings. Relate back to your aims and objectives or your research questions (see Chapter 5 for further guidance).

7   Conclusion

This chapter provides a summary of the overall project. It refers directly to aims and objectives/research questions as outlined in the introductory chapter. Conclusions often include a series of recommendations (for practice or for future research) that come out of your study. This chapter might also include a discussion of how your research could be improved upon, and an outline of future related research projects.

Of course, this is only one way that your research project could be set out. Some prefer to embed contexts in their introduction or their literature review. Some incorporate findings and discussion into one chapter, while others prefer to have a series of 'findings' chapters, each examining different themes emerging from the data. Some have two chapters on methodology – one that deals with the theory and principles of educational research, and another that describes and justifies the practicalities of the selected research design.

If you are writing a research project based on secondary research (a library-based project, for example) you are likely to develop a very different chapter structure. You might develop four or five 2000-word essays on issues relevant to your topic, with introduction and conclusion chapters to bind them all together and create a coherent narrative. Alternatively you might want to be original and experimental, developing your own very unique chapter structure. If you choose to do this, ask your supervisor to show you some examples of innovative structures and make sure they are happy with your proposed outline. Whichever way you choose to structure your research project, try to include all the features identified above at some stage.

Other components

Your research project should also include the following:

Title page

Along with your name and the title of your project, you will be expected to include information about the assignment and your university. Check your institution's handbook for details of what should be included here.

Abstract

The abstract should appear immediately after the title page. The abstract provides a brief summary of the research project, outlining key arguments and findings. Abstracts are generally between 150 and 300 words in length. This is a really important section. As you will have discovered when doing your own literature review, the abstract is a key source of information for the reader, helping them to decide if something is relevant and interesting to them. A good abstract outlines key aims and objectives, the methodological approach, the main findings, and concludes with an indication of why the project is important. While the rest of your research project will be presented in one-and-a-half or double line spacing, the abstract is always single-spaced. It is best to write the abstract after you have completed the whole research project.

Contents page

The contents page is a list of all chapter headings, subheadings and maybe sub-subheadings, alongside the page number that each begins on. You should also include any appendices with their page numbers. You might also include a list of tables, figures or charts. If your project contains lots of acronyms and/or subject-specific concepts, you might include a list of abbreviations and/or a glossary after the contents page.

Acknowledgements

You might take this opportunity to thank anyone who has helped you with your research project. It is usually a good idea to thank your supervisor. You might also thank any institution you visited for your fieldwork, or anybody that helped you with data collection or analysis. Finally you might want to thank friends and family for giving you the time and space to complete such a lengthy project.

Reference list

The reference list appears at the end of the report, after the Discussion and Conclusion chapters. It includes all the sources you cited in your research project. These are presented in alphabetical order. If you have used a software package like *Endnote* or *Refworks*, it will automatically populate your reference list. A bibliography, which includes all sources read during production of the project irrespective of whether or not they are directly cited, is used less frequently nowadays. See below for guidance on presenting references.

Appendices

The final thing you might need to include in your research project is a list of appendices. These are supplementary documents that are of relevance to the project. As a general rule, keep them to a minimum or avoid them altogether. It is a good idea to include a copy of a questionnaire, a list of interview prompts or an observation schedule if you have used any of these. You might be asked to include your research ethics approval documentation, your informed consent form or copies of letters to head teachers or parents about your project. You might also include other official documentation – copies of school documents, official statistics tables or publicity documentation. Only include documents that you make reference to in the main body of the research report. You should not include copies of all completed questionnaires or full transcripts from interviews or focus groups, but you could provide one (or extracts from a few) as an example. Appendices do not usually count towards your word count, so there is a tendency to throw lots of things into this section if you are struggling to stay below the upper word limit.

Some useful strategies for writing up

Over time writers develop their own strategies for ensuring they are able to submit their work on time. There are a number of tactics that you might find helpful:

■ Draw up a *writing plan* that sets out important deadlines for completing the draft of each chapter. Aim to have a full draft completed well in advance of the final deadline. Your plan will need to be flexible, but it will provide you with a yardstick to measure your own progress.

■ Identify specific *writing days*, especially in the early stages of writing up. Make sure that nothing will interrupt you on these days, so you can dedicate your time to writing. This will really help to give your writing momentum.

■ Develop a *writing routine*, whether this is a daily or weekly pattern. Some people find it easy to get up early and do two hours' writing before the day begins. Others prefer doing a night shift, writing between midnight and 2.00 a.m. As a general rule, our minds are fresher earlier on in the day.

■ Have regular *writing breaks*. Sitting staring at a computer screen is not the healthiest way of spending time. To avoid a stiff neck and a bleary feeling, do some exercise at regular intervals. Light exercise gets your body moving and raises your heartbeat up – but don't overdo it! Fresh air really helps, and many writers find walking to be a great activity for organising thoughts and developing new ideas.

■ Set yourself *writing targets* – in a particular session, aim to write 400 words, or to complete two sub-headed sections. Make sure these targets are feasible and short-range, so that you are breaking an extended piece of writing into small manageable chunks.

■ Give yourself *writing rewards* – gift yourself a cup of tea or half-an-hour's TV viewing when you have successfully achieved a complete section or made your word target.

■ Find your own ideal *writing environment* – some writers require solitude, while others prefer to write alongside a friend or colleague (to encourage and support each other). Some need silence while others like background music.

■ Identify a *writing buddy* – a 'critical friend' who can read and comment on your drafts. Preferably this would be someone who is also writing up their own research project, so that you can reciprocate – critical reading of another person's writing will really help with your own.

Ten 'top tips' for writing a successful research project

1 Aim to finish the final draft of your research project about two or three weeks before the deadline.

2 Develop research questions/aims and objectives that make the project focused and concise. For instance, do not try to explain educational inequalities; rather, concentrate on a specific issue or explanation (like young people with disabilities and their access to higher education, or social capital and the attainment of private school pupils). You might be able to refine a broad topic after you have gathered data and begun to write up.

3 Develop a detailed plan, and be flexible enough to modify this as your writing develops.

4 Introduce and conclude each chapter, indicating how each section fits with those before and after.

5 Keep sentence construction simple and to the point.

6 Support your argument with references, but do not use extensive quotes or build your research project around them.

7   Present a consistent voice throughout – normally in the third person and the past tense.

8   Use chapters, subheadings and sub-subheadings to structure and signpost your arguments.

9   Do not overstate claims or overgeneralise – be tentative and moderate about the conclusions that you can draw from your findings.

10   Carefully check the criteria that your work will be assessed against, and make sure you cover each clearly.

A brief note on ethics

When you write up your research project you must take account of ethical guidelines. BERA's *Ethical guidelines for educational research* (BERA, 2011) are the standard in the UK. Most importantly you need to respect privacy, confidentiality and anonymity. If you have undertaken research in a school or another educational institution, you need to conceal its identity. Either provide it with a pseudonym, or describe it in general terms – for example, as a 'medium sized primary school in the East Midlands'. Likewise, you must maintain the anonymity of any respondents you interview or observe. You can refer to respondents as 'Interviewee 1', 'Interviewee 2' and so on, but your research project will be a more interesting read if you use pseudonyms. It is good practice to add a footnote after the first use of a pseudonym, explaining that all names appearing in the text are fictitious to preserve the anonymity of the participants. Also, only include comments for which you have received consent!

Another strategy you might choose to employ is to send the final manuscript to your respondents. Not only might their comments help you to validate your analysis and interpretations, but in ethical terms you also enable them to take some ownership of the final account (see the ethics chapter for more information on these issues).

Referencing

Different departments and universities expect you to use different referencing approaches. In education, the Harvard and APA styles are the most commonly used referencing systems. Check your course or module handbook to confirm the preferred style. Most importantly, always be consistent and accurate with your references. When paraphrasing or quoting a source in the main text, you should present the reference as (name, date: page number). For example, to reference this page, you would write (Curtis, Murphy and Shields, 2013: 50).

In a reference list, each type of source requires different information, formatting and presentation. The most commonly used types of sources are:

A book:

Fielding, M. and Moss, P. (2011) *Radical education and the common school: A democratic alternative.* London: Routledge.

A chapter in an edited book:

Wenger, E. (2009) 'A social theory of learning'. In K. Illeris (ed.) *Contemporary theories of learning: Learning theorists in their own words.* London: Routledge (209–218).

A journal article:

Sparks, A. (2008) 'Embodiment, academics, and the audit culture: A story seeking consideration'. *Qualitative Research,* 7 (4), October 2007, 521–550.

An article on a website:

Smith, K. (2001) 'Learning in the community and community learning'. http://www.infed.org/lifelonglearning/b-edcom.htm

A website:

McLaren, P. (2013) http://pages.gseis.ucla.edu/faculty/mclaren/ [Accessed: 31 January 2013]

A report:

UCAS (2012) How have applications for full-time undergraduate higher education in the UK changed in 2012?; *UCAS Analysis and Research,* July 2012. UCAS [full report accessible at: http://www.ucas.ac.uk/documents/ucas_how_have_applications_changed_in_2012.pdf]

A newspaper article:

Higgins, C. (2013) 'Arts council chief accuses Gove of abandoning cultural education'. *The Guardian.* 15/01/2013.

A film:

Happy Go Lucky (2008) [Film] Directed by Mike Leigh. United Kingdom: Momentum Pictures.

A radio or TV broadcast:

The Classroom Experiment (2010) [TV programme] BBC, BBC1, 4 December 2010 03.05.

A blog:

Hyland, L. (2012) 'Have chance, will learn'. *Lars is Learning* [Blog] 3 November. Available at http://larsislearning.blogspot.co.uk/ [Accessed 21 January 2013]

As mobile technologies and social media develop there is an increasing range of platforms from which to access information. It is not always obvious how to present references from these sources. Anglia Ruskin University has developed an excellent and wide-ranging guide to Harvard referencing. It can be accessed via their library pages at http://libweb.anglia.ac.uk/referencing/harvard.htm

Plagiarism

Plagiarism is an attempt to gain an advantage by unfair means, and it is taken very seriously by universities. There are a number of potential sanctions, which will get more severe the further you are through your degree. Plagiarised work will almost certainly get a mark of zero and will have to be rewritten with a capped mark. Students can be thrown off the course if they are found guilty.

Plagiarism includes:

- Copying from a text (book, article, website) without acknowledgement.
- Purchasing work from an assignment-writing website.
- Copying another student's work.
- Paraphrasing – putting arguments you have read into your own words without acknowledging the source.
- Submitting work as your own when it has been produced with someone else or by a group.

Universities generally use a software tool like *Turnitin* to identify any correlations between your work and existing literature. Not only does this check your assignment against published work, it also checks against other students' work already submitted through the system. This is an ever-growing database, and it is certainly not worth taking any chances.

To ensure you do not plagiarise, always:

- Write in your own words.
- Reference accurately.
- Acknowledge all sources for your material.
- Make a note of any reference you use.
- Clearly identify any quote you use.
- Be especially careful when using material from websites. It is easy to cut and paste and then forget to rephrase and reference.
- Submit a full reference list.

Proofreading your work

When you have completed a full draft of your research project, you need to read it through carefully. It is worth reading aloud – this allows you to hear how your writing sounds. Because your report is an extended piece of writing, you need to be especially careful that you have written in a consistent style and in a coherent manner. When you have completed a full draft, proofread your work against the following checklist:

Presentation

1 Consistency and accuracy of referencing
2 Grammar, spelling and punctuation
3 Follow in-house presentational guide (line spacing, font size, margins)
4 Consistent tense and 'voice'
5 Research findings presented clearly and accurately

Coherence

6 Chapters are introduced and concluded
7 Aims and objectives/research questions are stated clearly and related throughout
8 Conclusions refer directly to aims and objectives/research questions
9 Clarity and independence of argument
10 Writing is balanced, evaluative and does not overstate claims

Use of evidence

11 Range of literature (current, historical, academic, theory, empirical)
12 No assertions – claims that are not justified with reference to evidence
13 Evidence used to develop your own argument
14 Define and explain specialist language and jargon
15 Research findings not simply described, but interpreted and analysed.

Chapter summary

This chapter has provided support for the process of writing up your research project. It has discussed strategies to help you get started and then maintain your writing over time. It has provided 'top tips' for producing a successful piece of extended writing, and outlined potential chapter structures and core components. This was followed by guidance on referencing and avoiding plagiarism. The chapter ended by offering a checklist to help you proofread your full draft.

Further reading

Sharp, J. (2012) *Success with your education research project (Study Skills in Education Series)* (2nd edition). Exeter: Learning Matters.

Walliman, N. and Buckler, S. (2008) *Your research project in education (Sage Study Skills Series)*. London: Sage Publications.

Bell, J. (2012) *Doing your research project: A guide for first-time researchers in education, health and social science (Open Up Study Skills)*. Maidenhead: Open University Press.

■ There are many books that provide advice and guidance on completing an education research project. These three books will provide excellent support throughout your project. Extensive practical advice and a highly accessible approach have made Bell's book the 'go to' text. You will also find the practical tasks in Sharp's book really helpful as you progress with your own work.

Research strategies

7

Surveys

Introduction

Surveys enable us to collect a representation of the population of interest by the same information being collected from each participant (more information about population samples can be found in Chapter 4). Surveys may collect information on attitudes, perceptions or behaviour, and they may be able to access information that is not already easily available. By the use of a survey the researcher can make claims about a wider population based on the results from a sample. Surveys lend themselves to quantitative designs, and the large number of respondents required by the survey method means that statistical tests can be used. Therefore, survey results are generally reported in numerical form and are widely used within educational research. For example, headline findings from recent educational surveys include 'Four out of ten headteachers are concerned about crumbling school buildings' (Shepherd, 2012) and '83% of teachers see pupils who are hungry in the morning' (Evans, 2012).

A well-known educational survey is the 'Programme for International Student Assessment' (PISA). This international study is participated in by over seventy countries. It aims to evaluate education systems worldwide by undertaking three-yearly assessments of fifteen-year olds' competencies in reading, mathematics and science. National surveys such as the General Household Survey (GHS), the Labour Force Survey (LFS) and the British Household Panel Study (BHPS) all include sections on education. They cover current educational status, educational attainment and the establishment last attended full-time by participants. These surveys have been particularly useful for looking at patterns within education and other aspects of peoples' lives. This chapter will outline different types of survey, practical issues to consider when conducting a survey, and survey response rates.

Types of survey

There are a range of different types of survey, and some surveys may combine more than one approach – for example, a survey may be longitudinal, but it may also use a panel of participants.

Cross-sectional

This means that responses are collected at one point in time from a sample selected to represent a larger population. The survey about volunteers in schools from the National Foundation for Educational Research (NFER) demonstrates the characteristics of a cross-sectional survey: 'A panel of 1567 practising teachers from 1211 schools in the maintained sector in England completed a survey about volunteering in schools. Teachers completed the survey online between the 20th April and 2nd May 2012 ... the cross sectional survey included teachers from the full range of roles in primary and secondary schools, from headteachers to newly qualified class teachers. Fifty-five per cent (859) of the respondents were teaching in primary schools and 45 per cent (708) were teaching in secondary schools' (Lewis and Brzyska, 2012: 1–5). This means that a range of teachers from a range of state schools completed the survey, representing a cross-section of the different characteristics of the teaching profession, such as type of school they work in, their level of experience and their seniority. Therefore the findings from this cross-sectional survey about volunteering are likely to be representative of the broader perceptions of teachers about patterns of volunteering within state schools.

Longitudinal

Longitudinal studies are carried out over a period of time. This type of survey can be more accurate than cross-sectional surveys, and it helps us to understand changes over a period of time. This type of survey is expensive and it may be many years before results can be compared. Comparability over time can also be problematic, and so the significance of findings need to be considered within the context they are located. For example, the proportion of individuals holding a university degree has changed significantly over the last fifty years due to shifts in the economic needs of society and educational policies, not because people are more intelligent than in the past. Over time a number of respondents are likely to drop out of any longitudinal study, thereby making it more difficult to justify comparisons over time with a diminishing number of participants. The '7up' longitudinal study is a famous documentary which has tracked fourteen children from the age of seven every seven years (Apted, 1999).

Trend

This type of survey uses a new sample population at different points in time. This can overcome the drop-out rate among respondents that may affect a longitudinal survey. However, changes in individuals cannot be identified because different populations are used each time. Comparative statistical tests are problematic if the population changes each time the survey is conducted. A rolling sample, in which a proportion of the sample in the survey is longitudinal, is a potential compromise. An example of a trend survey in education was a study carried out by the Qualifications Assurance Agency for Higher Education. 'In Autumn 2008, the Quality Assurance Agency for Higher Education (QAA) undertook a data trends survey to explore the reasons for a fall in the number of Access to HE students between 2005–06 and 2007–08' (QAA, 2009: 1).

Cohort

This is a study of the same population each time data are collected, but the samples may be different. An example of a cohort survey is the one undertaken by the Education and Youth Transitions in England, Scotland and Wales project. 'The Youth Cohort Study of England and Wales (YCS) is a major programme of longitudinal research designed to monitor the behaviour and decisions of representative samples of young people aged sixteen and upwards as they make the transition from compulsory education to further or higher education, or to the labour market. It tries to identify and explain the factors which influence post-sixteen transitions, for example, educational attainment, training opportunities, experiences at school. To date the YCS covers ten cohorts and over twenty surveys. The first survey was carried out in 1985 and the most recent in 2002' (Croxford, 2002: 2).

Panel

A panel survey involves the collection of data at various time points with the same sample of respondents. The BHPS is a major research resource in which a representative sample of the same 10,000 people have been interviewed annually since 1991. Since 1994 a Young Persons Survey has also been carried out for those between the ages of eleven and fifteen living in the sample households. In a further wave of the panel survey, information was obtained about whether or not they had actually stayed in education post-sixteen, and about the qualifications they had obtained in public examinations taken at the age of sixteen or just after (Papasolomontos and Christie, 1998: 249).

Retrospective

This type of survey asks respondents to recall past events, and it therefore has the advantage of hindsight. However, retrospective surveys can be criticised since the accuracy of respondents in recalling past events may be called into question. In particular, attitudes may shift over time. An example of a retrospective survey is the Chicago Longitudinal Study (CLS). Parents in the CLS were interviewed retrospectively about their involvement with their child's education. Telephone interviews were conducted, and where this was not possible a mailed survey was used (Miedel and Reynolds, 1999). The limitation of this retrospective survey was the accuracy of the accounts given by parents of their child's participation. Often reports on individuals' past actions can be prone to reconstruction according to more socially desirable recollections (Finney, 1981). A study by Finkel and McGue (1993) suggested that parents may answer questions based not on the time period of interest, but rather on their entire experience.

ACTIVITY

Read the extract below:

With citizenship education moving rapidly from a policy proposal to a real school subject there is a need to identify, measure and evaluate the extent to which 'effective practice' in citizenship education develops in schools so that such practice can be promoted more widely. To do this, the research design of the study employs four interrelated methods:

- Four nationally representative cross-sectional surveys of students, school leaders and teachers undertaken in the school years 2001–02, 2003–04, 2005–06 and 2007–08, with the first survey acting as a pre-compulsory baseline.
- A longitudinal tracking survey of a whole year group of students in a representative sample of 100 schools, starting in Year 7 in 2002-03, and following them up in Year 9, Year 11 and Year 13 (or the equivalent when they are aged 18).
- Twenty longitudinal school case studies – 10 schools drawn from schools participating in each of the longitudinal and cross-sectional surveys – that will be revisited once every two years over the duration of the study.

The overarching aim of the study is to assess the short- and long-term effects of citizenship education on the knowledge, skills and attitudes and behaviour of students. In addition it aims to identify the different processes (in terms of school, teacher and student effects) that lead to differential outcomes and to assess changes in levels of joining and participation in voluntary bodies.

This report sets out the findings from the first cross-sectional survey. The survey was carried out in summer term of the academic year 2001–02 and its findings are important in three respects:

- they offer an invaluable baseline of the attitudes of students, teachers and school and college leaders to citizenship and citizenship education prior to the formal introduction of citizenship education into schools in September 2002. The findings provide an indication of how well informed schools are about the new National Curriculum of Citizenship and the strengths and weaknesses of their preparation and planning for its introduction.
- they lay a strong foundation for the future conduct of the study and help to clarify the purpose of the cross-sectional surveys and their interrelationship with the study's three other components.
- they provide continuity with the existing research literature on citizenship education and political socialisation in England. Three questionnaires (a student questionnaire for Year 8, Year 10 or Year 12 students, a teacher or college tutor

questionnaire and a senior manager questionnaire) were sent to each school and college that agreed to take part. A nationally representative sample of schools and colleges was selected using stratified random sampling techniques and was invited to participate in the survey in January 2002. A total of 318 schools and colleges agreed to take part, 297 of which completed questionnaires between March and May 2002.

(Kerr *et al.*, 2003: v–vi)

- Based on your understanding of different types of surveys, identify the different types of survey design used in this study.
- What are the strengths of this survey design?
- Is there any part of the survey design that you would have changed? Why?
- Visit the National Foundation for Educational Research website http://www.nfer.ac.uk/index.cfm and identify the types and characteristics of surveys that have been conducted.

Practical issues to consider when conducting a survey

Be aware that surveys and questionnaires must not be confused. A questionnaire is a *research tool*. A survey is a *research approach* which:

- Asks standardised questions
- Uses a sample of a population
- Focuses on attitudes, perceptions and behaviour.

However, to make matters slightly more complicated, a survey may use a questionnaire as a research tool. Indeed, a questionnaire is perhaps the most common tool used in surveys, but it is not the only possibility – for example, surveys may also use face-to-face interviews, telephone interviews, observations or document analysis. There are also several other ways in which a survey can be conducted. Table 7.1 below highlights the different approaches and their relative advantages and disadvantages.

TABLE 7.1 Different approaches to survey delivery

Survey delivery approach	Advantages	Disadvantages
Face-to face	✓ High response rate ✓ Complex questions can be asked	✗ Costly ✗ Time-consuming ✗ Interview bias ✗ Difficult to target a large population without a lot of interviewers
Telephone	✓ Better response rate than a letter ✓ Quicker than face-to-face	✗ Not all telephone numbers are available ✗ Not all of the target population will respond ✗ Difficult to target a large population without a lot of interviewers

TABLE 7.1 continued

Survey delivery approach	Advantages	Disadvantages
Postal	✓ Cheap (in comparison to using interviewers) ✓ Large numbers of the survey can be posted ✓ Slower response rate than face-to-face or telephone ✓ Can access populations who are difficult to contact face-to-face or via telephone	✗ Low response rate ✗ Complex questions cannot be asked ✗ Reliant on respondents understanding the questions fully ✗ Reliant on respondent to answer questions without interviewer present
Online/weblink	✓ Cheap (if survey software is already available) ✓ Professional-looking survey ✓ No paper, making it environmentally friendly ✓ Calculates the results for you, reducing time and human error in inputting data ✓ Quick access to results	✗ Lower response rate than face-to-face or telephone ✗ Population samples who are less likely to use a computer/internet or who are less confident with technology will not be fully represented ✗ Software compatibility issues

ACTIVITY

Read the extract below:

To study self-directed informal learning using the sample survey techniques normally required for representative readings of human behaviour, we have to strike a resolve to focus on those things that people can identify for themselves as intentional learning projects or deliberate learning activities beyond prescribed curricula and without externally authorized instructors. Documenting informal training requires a similar reliance on respondents' self-reports. More sensitive ethnographic case study research should be encouraged. But 'thin' versions of adults' intentional informal learning and training generated through survey research can at least provide more complete profiles of their actual array of learning practices. Well designed surveys of intentional informal learning may therefore contribute to more nuanced appreciation of the multiple dimensions and relationships of the learning continuum. Such measures can at least provide benchmarks for understanding the extent and changing patterns of informal learning activities.

(Livingstone, 2006: 208)

■ What factors does this extract highlight about the advantages and disadvantages of survey research?

Response rates

Response rates will vary markedly within social research depending on the methods being used, the nature of the respondents and the types of issues being investigated. There is no hard and fast rule about what constitutes an acceptable response rate. With large-scale postal questionnaires it is not uncommon to get a response rate as low as 15%. Interviews arranged by personal contact between the researcher and the interviewee are at the other end of the spectrum, since very high response rates can be expected – much closer to 100%. Rather than look for a figure above which a response rate is acceptable and below which the results become more suspect, it is more productive to evaluate the response rate that is actually achieved in terms of whether it is reasonable and in line with comparable surveys. The researcher can look to similar studies as a way of gauging whether their own response rate is acceptable. The methods, the target group, the topic of the research and the use of prior contact are all important here. Each has a bearing on the level of response.

As you have already seen, the different delivery approaches of your survey are likely to influence the number of responses you receive. The delivery approach you use should reflect your target group – for example, a retrospective survey about educational experiences of pupils in the 1950s may not be best administered via the internet, but may work well using face-to-face interviews. Equally a study of university students may not achieve a good rate of return if the survey is administered by post, but a weblink on a social media site may achieve a high response rate. The topic of your survey is also influential, because if the questions are deemed to be of a personal nature your respondents may be reluctant to complete it. Also if the survey is not of interest or is not relevant to the respondents they will be much less likely to respond. Finally, if you have had contact with your potential respondents before asking them to complete the survey, this may increase the response rate rather than sending the survey 'cold'. In summary, the benchmark for an acceptable response rate needs to be set by reference to the experience of similar surveys.

Validity

The validity of your survey results will be measured in part by your response rate. However, the analysis of your findings also needs to be conducted carefully and should avoid overly-simplistic causal links. For example, a survey which found that specialist schools achieved better GCSE results than non-specialist schools was criticised. The surveys were carried out and reported by Jesson (2004). The surveys used DfES data to compare examination results among specialist and non-specialist schools, and it was claimed that in 2003, 56 per cent of pupils in the 938 specialist schools gained five or more GCSEs at A–C grades, compared to 47 per cent in comprehensive and secondary modern schools. The methodology of these surveys was queried because the surveys did not factor in the additional funding received by specialist schools (Tomlinson, 2005).

Non-response rate

Non-response rate is an interesting aspect to consider when analysing your survey results. In theory, the larger your number of respondents, the less likely it is that you will have missed out a significant part of a population. However, administering and analysing a survey is costly in terms of resources and time, and this has to be balanced against how many respondents you can manage. This section will consider the implications of non-response rates. The last respondents in your survey – those who returned the questionnaires at the last minute – were almost non-respondents. It is useful to identify the characteristics of your final respondents as well as those who did not respond at all.

Questions to consider with late respondents and non-respondents

- Are their characteristics any different to the earlier respondents (apart from being less organised!)?
- Do the characteristics of late respondents reflect those of non-respondents?
- Does the non-response rate and the late response rate bring an element of bias into your sample?
- Is there a significant group of a population that your survey has missed out? How does this change your results?
- Do their responses affect the survey results?

Chapter summary

Survey checklist – have you included...

- An explanation of the survey instrument (e.g. is it one you have developed, or has it been used in other research projects?).
- An explanation of how validity and reliability were measured.
- A copy of your survey tool in an appendix.
- Information about your sample.
- Information about non-respondents.
- Data analysis.

This chapter discussed well-known examples of surveys which ask questions about educational experiences and attainment. The chapter then examined the different types of survey that may be used and evaluated their characteristics, such as longitudinal and cross-sectional surveys. Examples of different types of survey were given. The differences between questionnaires as a research method and surveys as a research approach were explained. The chapter then discussed some of the practical aspects of carrying out a survey, and highlighted issues surrounding response rates. The key characteristics of a survey are:

- Asks standardised questions
- Uses a sample of a population
- Focuses on attitudes, perceptions and behaviour.

Further reading

Fink, A. (2013) *How to conduct surveys: A step-by-step guide* (5th edition). Thousand Oaks: Sage Publications.

- A friendly and accessible text with judicious use of subheadings and examples, many of which are education-related. It begins by providing an answer to the question 'What is a survey?', and moves on to give information about different types of question and response rates. It also tackles more complex issues such as sampling, reliability, validity and analysis.

8

Experiments

Introduction

Experiments involve the researcher intervening in the site of investigation. Traditionally common in the psychology of education, experiments can be conducted in a laboratory, but they are more likely to take place in the 'field' – in everyday environments such as the classroom. This chapter introduces some of the more famous educational experiments, identifies some of the key aspects such as intervention and control groups, variables and causality, and distinguishes between different experimental designs. It considers issues related to internal and external validity, and examines some important ethical concerns associated with the empirical approach.

Characteristics of experiments

Experiments entail the creation of a contrived situation, so that a researcher is able to manipulate, control and measure specified 'variables'. The term variable 'refers to some defined property or characteristic of a person, thing, group or situation that can be measured in some way, and for which these measurements vary, so that they can be compared to one another' (Robson, 2002: 100). Generally, an experimental researcher manipulates an 'independent variable' and measures the resulting effect on a 'dependent variable'. In educational research, independent variables might take the form of additional numeracy classes or a new classroom teaching innovation. Dependent variables might be levels of attainment or motivation.

The experimental method is the foundation of the natural sciences. Therefore, when educational researchers 'borrow' an experimental approach they generally utilise scientific strategies. For instance, an educational experiment is likely to attempt to confirm or refute a hypothesis, exert control over the research setting, make use of randomised and representative samples, consist of a group that is subjected to an intervention and another that is not, and use systematic and rigorous testing to measure patterns and relationships. Consequently, while experiments can be designed to generate quantitative or qualitative data, they are more commonly used to generate the former. As with the natural sciences, experiments might be confirmatory (testing the effect of existing variables) or exploratory (discovering the impact of new variables).

Why adopt an experimental approach?

In a seminal work on experimental design, Campbell and Stanley make a strong case in favour of the empirical method. They argue that experiments are:

> the only means for settling disputes regarding educational practice, as the only way of verifying educational improvements, and as the only way of establishing a cumulative tradition in which improvements can be introduced without the danger of faddish discard of old wisdom in favor of inferior novelties.
>
> (1963: 2)

Educational researchers and policy makers value experimental approaches because they have the capacity to identify *causality* – that is, patterns of cause and effect. The experimental researcher controls and manipulates events, and in doing so is able to isolate specific factors and uncover correlations. Researchers can identify the extent that one factor determines or influences another by:

- Influencing an independent variable
- Controlling or removing alternative variables
- Measuring a dependent variable.

This makes experimentation an especially effective approach to test the efficacy of new educational interventions or initiatives. Experimental research can trial an innovation and then measure its degree of success – either by measuring the difference in a before and after test, or investigating the difference between one group that experienced the innovation and one that did not.

Types of experiment design

There are two broad types of experiment in educational research – true experiments and quasi-experiments – with a wide variety of approaches taken within each.

True experiments

For an experiment to be classed as a true experimental design, it generally possesses all of the following key criteria:

- One or more intervention/experimental group(s)
- At least one control group

- Participants must be randomly assigned to groups
- No contamination between the intervention and control groups
- One (in some cases, more than one) variable is manipulated and tested
- A pre-test, to ensure the intervention and control groups are the same
- A post-test, to measure the impact of the intervention on the dependent variable.

Due to the high degree of control required in a true experiment, they are likely to take place in an artificial setting such as a laboratory. An example of a true experimental design is the randomised controlled trial which is common in clinical trials. Participants are randomly allocated to one of two or more groups. All groups are treated in exactly the same way apart from one group which receives an intervention (or treatment). Hutchinson and Styles claim that randomised controlled trials are the 'gold standard for evidence-based educational practice' (2010: 1) because they allow researchers to isolate and measure the specific variable they are studying.

Quasi-experiments

Unlike true experiments, quasi-experimental designs generally lack the component of randomised allocation. They were developed because it is not always practical, ethical, or even possible to assign people randomly to experimental and control groups. These experiments do not take place in the controlled environment of the laboratory. Rather, they take place in the 'field' – for instance, in a natural setting such as the school or the classroom. This means it is far more difficult for the researcher to control all extraneous or 'confounding' variables – factors other than the independent variable that might impact on the findings. While there is some compromise in the extent to which the researcher can control all variables, quasi-experiments benefit by studying participants in their natural environments.

Frequently, quasi-experiments take the form of a non-equivalent group design, whereby the researcher selects two existing or 'intact' comparable groups, employing the intervention with one group but not the other. 'Intact' groups might include local authorities, schools or classes. Another quasi-experimental approach is the regression-discontinuity design, where participants are given a test and those who score above or below a cut-off point are subjected to the intervention. This is an attractive approach if an intervention is best targeted at a specific group that needs or deserves it most – for example, to trial and measure the efficacy of a new intervention to enhance learning for children with low reading ages.

Some design variations

- **Post-test only design** – measures the impact of an intervention on the dependent variable only after it has taken place.
- **Pre- and post-test design** – takes measurements of the dependent variable before and after the intervention. This enables the researcher to identify the

extent to which the intervention has changed perceptions, behaviour or achievement.

- **Post-test with control group** – two groups are established, generally using a randomised sampling approach to ensure the groups are similar. One group is given the intervention and the other is not. A test is conducted after the intervention to measure its effect.

- **Pre- and post-test with control group** – the same as above, except that a test is also conducted ahead of the intervention.

- *Ex post facto* **(after the fact)** – not strictly an experiment because the intervention and control groups are selected after the independent variable has occurred. For example, a researcher examining the impact of attending state versus public schooling on levels of self-confidence might obtain measures from people who attended Eton and people who attended a local state school. This approach eliminates the threat to validity that participants will react differently because they know they are part of an experiment.

ACTIVITY

Devise an experimental approach to explore the following topics in educational research:

- The impact of changes in Sure Start funding.
- The extent to which the use of interactive whiteboards enhances learning in the primary school classroom.
- How secondary school teachers deal with cyber-bullying.
- The impact of new free schools on other schools in a local community.
- The effect of extra reading support for children from deprived socio-economic backgrounds.

Now consider the following questions in relation to each topic:

1   What kind of experiment have you employed?
2   Are there any ethical concerns with the use of experiments?
3   What issues are likely to impact on the validity of the findings?
4   Is experimentation the most effective strategy?

Famous experiments in the psychology of education

There is a long history of experiments in psychological research in education. As Mayer points out, 'experimental methods – which involve random assignment to treatments and control of extraneous variables – have been the gold standard for educational psychology since the field evolved in the early 1900s' (2005: 74). Jean Piaget used experimental approaches in the 1920s and 1930s to develop his theories of cognitive development. He conducted a number of experiments with children in what he termed the 'preoperational stage' (from approximately two to seven years of age), discovering their lack of understanding of abstract concepts like amounts, weight or speed. For example, to test number concepts Piaget showed children two equally spaced rows of six glasses and six bottles and asked whether there were more glasses or more bottles. Children generally recognised that there were equal numbers. The glasses were then stretched to form a longer row. In this situation, when asked whether there were more glasses or more bottles, children generally answered that there were more glasses (in Voyat, 1982: 86).

Rosenthal and Jacobsen (1968) conducted a highly influential educational experiment in California in the 1960s. Testing the hypothesis that self-fulfilling prophecy impacted on educational attainment, they randomly selected a 20 per cent sample of children and informed the teachers that these children could be expected to exhibit accelerated intellectual development. After one year they gave all children an IQ test, and found that the 20 per cent sample broadly achieved higher levels of success. Although the research has since been criticised on a number of grounds, it has become an enduring example of how teacher and student expectations can impact both positively and negatively on attainment.

Perhaps the most infamous example of experimental research was conducted by Stanley Milgram (1974). In his 'shock experiment', subjects were told they were taking part in an experiment on learning and memory. They took on the role of the 'teacher', and Milgram's researchers assumed the role of 'learner'. Learners were asked a series of questions, and the teachers were told to press a button to administer an electric shock if they got answers incorrect. The teachers were informed that the severity of the shock increased with each wrong answer. Twenty-five out of the forty participants continued to give shocks to the maximum 450 volts, even in the face of notices warning of 'danger – severe shock' (of course, in reality there were no shocks). Milgram used the experiment to demonstrate people's obedience to authority in the shape of a scientific researcher. However, it is more frequently used today to highlight the ethical concerns surrounding some approaches to social research.

Since these famous studies, experiments tended to go out of fashion in educational research. With the growth of interpretivist methodologies and an emphasis on conducting research in natural settings, true experiments were challenged for being deceptive, controlling, artificial and manipulative.

Increasing use of randomised trials in educational research

Experiments have become an increasingly popular approach to educational research in recent years, most evidently in the USA. There is a particular attraction to the scientific reputation of experiments and their capacity to verify the effectiveness of interventions. The scientific empirical approach is viewed as bringing educational research in line with higher status research in other areas – for example, medical research. Controlled research settings mean that differences between experimental and control groups can be ascribed reasonably confidently to a specific intervention.

Experiments are increasingly employed to examine the effects of new policies. For instance, Angrist identifies 'dozens' of randomised trials funded by the US Department of Education to evaluate pre-school educational interventions (2004).

He has utilised the approach in his own work on the introduction of voucher schemes in Columbia and incentives to learn for low-achieving American high-school students. Experiments might be used to evaluate the impact of new educational technologies, changes in class or school size, or new academies or free schools.

Bouguen and Gurgand (2012) highlight a number of recent and ongoing European studies which have adopted the empirical approach. Among these is McGuigan, McNally and Wyness's (2012) research on students' awareness of the benefits of staying on in education in the UK. The experiment involved fifty-four schools in London, in which all the Year 10 students were surveyed before and after the intervention. The schools were randomly allocated to the experimental and control groups. The experimental group was given access to an information campaign providing facts about financial aspects of educational decisions. Findings indicated that the information campaign did impact positively on students' knowledge, attitudes and aspirations.

ACTIVITY

Read McGuigan, McNally and Wyness's paper based on their experiment. Now read another of the randomised controlled experiments in education identified in the Bouguen and Gurgand review (see below). Consider the following:

1   What do the two studies have in common?
2   How do they differ?
3   Why might the studies be attractive to:
    a   Educational researchers
    b   Educational policy makers
    c   Teachers and students.

Criticising experimental approaches

As noted earlier, the main advantage that experiments have over other educational research approaches is their capacity to identify causality. However, in the complex education environment it is not always easy to distinguish a particular causal relationship – i.e. to isolate independent variables from other uncontrolled or extraneous variables. Even when a causal link is strongly indicated, experiments often provide little information on why that link exists. For this reason, experiments are sometimes used alongside other research methods that are better at providing explanations, such as in-depth interviews or naturalistic observations.

There are a number of other difficulties with experimental approaches in educational research, which arise chiefly because they involve manipulation and control to a greater or lesser extent. It is not usually possible to control conditions completely in genuine educational settings. Artificial situations give rise to concerns about validity and ethical practices.

Internal validity

Internal validity refers to the potential for findings to be distorted by extraneous factors not controlled by the researcher. According to Campbell and Stanley (1963), there are eight factors that are likely to impact on the accuracy of experimental measures:

- **History** – events that take place between pre- and post-test might influence findings.
- **Maturation** – subjects grow and develop during the course of an experiment (especially a long-term one) which can cause differences.
- **Testing** – improvements between pre- and post-test might be a result of the 'intervention' group having practiced the test.
- **Instrumentation** – if the researcher uses different pre- and post-tests, measured changes may result from differences between the tests.
- **Statistical regression** – there is a tendency for test scores to regress towards the mean when tested on a second occasion. High scores go down and low scores go up.
- **Differential selection** – if the 'intervention' group is selected differently from the 'control' group, any differences might be caused by differences between groups irrespective of the intervention. For instance, if the intervention group volunteered to take part, observed changes may appear because of differences between volunteers and non-volunteers.
- **Experimental mortality** – attrition rates, as subjects drop out of the research process, can bias the findings. For example, if members of the control group drop out because their scores do not seem to be improving, this is likely to distort the extent that an intervention improves test scores.
- **Selection interaction** – the ways the intervention and control groups are selected might combine with any of the other factors identified above.

External validity

External validity refers to the extent that the findings from a piece of research can be applied or generalised to other settings or people. A number of factors impact on the external validity of experimental approaches:

- **Representativeness** – if the 'intervention' group does not accurately reflect the wider population, results are likely to be biased.
- **Experimental (Hawthorn) effect** – people are likely to behave differently because they are the subjects of an experiment/observation.
- **Ecological validity** – because experiments involve the researcher manipulating specific variables, it can be difficult to verify whether behaviour would be the same in natural settings. This is particularly difficult in the case of laboratory experiments.

- **Pre-test sensitivity** – subjects might respond differently to an intervention because they had previously undertaken a pre-test. It is difficult to claim that people who had not taken the pre-test would react in the same way.

- **Operationalising dependent variables appropriately** – dependent variables must be defined and tested in manners that accurately reflect external settings.

- **Multiple interventions** – if an experiment involves a number of interventions, they might have a cumulative effect on subjects' performances. As a result, it is difficult to claim the beneficial impact of a specific intervention.

Ethical considerations

As Chapter 21 indicates, there are many ethical issues the educational researcher must address – and some are especially significant in relation to experimental designs. The researcher who takes participants outside of their natural environment has a particular duty of care for their safety and wellbeing. As Milgram's infamous study clearly shows, there are threats in terms of deception, lack of informed consent and the danger of psychological harm to participants. In fact, it is extremely unlikely that a piece of experimental research such as Milgram's would be allowed to take place today.

As you have seen, many experiments consist of two groups – an experimental group and a control group. Treating these two groups differently raises ethical issues. Either the control group may be adversely affected by being denied an intervention that has positive effects, or the experimental group may be adversely affected by receiving an unsuccessful (or potentially harmful) intervention. Clinical physicians justify differential conduct by pointing out the lack of alternative strategies and the wider benefits of identifying a causal relationship between treatment and health. However, this is not always clear-cut in educational research.

ACTIVITY

One of the most important educational experiments of recent years was instigated by Dr Sugata Mitra. The 'hole-in-the-wall' experiment has had a tremendous impact on educational provision across the world since the first experiment in 1999.

Read the following extract from the 'hole-in-the-wall' project website http://www.hole-in-the-wall.com/Beginnings.html

> On 26th January [1999], Dr Mitra's team carved a "hole in the wall" that separated the NIIT premises from the adjoining slum in Kalkaji, New Delhi. Through this hole, a freely accessible computer was put up for use. This computer proved to be an instant hit among the slum dwellers, especially the children. With no prior experience, the children learnt to use the computer on their own. This prompted Dr Mitra to propose the following hypothesis:
>
> The acquisition of basic computing skills by any set of children can be achieved through incidental learning provided the learners are given access to a suitable

computing facility, with entertaining and motivating content and some minimal (human) guidance.

Encouraged by the success of the Kalkaji experiment, freely accessible computers were set up in Shivpuri (a town in Madhya Pradesh) and in Madantusi (a village in Uttar Pradesh). These experiments came to be known as Hole-in-the-Wall experiments. The findings from Shivpuri and Madantusi confirmed the results of Kalkaji experiments. It appeared that the children in these two places picked up computer skills on their own. Dr Mitra defined this as a new way of learning – Minimally Invasive Education.

At this point in time, International Finance Corporation joined hands with NIIT to set up Hole-in-the-Wall Education Limited (HiWEL). The idea was to broaden the scope of the experiments and conduct research to prove and streamline Hole-in-the-Wall. As part of this, more than 30 such clusters of computers or, as they have come to be known, Learning Stations, have been set up in India and outside India. The results, which have been uniformly encouraging, show that children learn to operate as well as play with the computer with minimum intervention. They picked up skills and tasks by constructing their own learning environment.

Have a look at the website to see how the project has grown and developed. What does this example tell you about the relationships between educational experimentation and practice? Can you think of similar approaches to enhance learning?

Chapter summary

This chapter has detailed educational research that has employed an experimental approach. It has distinguished between different types of experiment. While the attraction of the experiment as a strategy for educational research lies in its capacity to identify causality, this is not entirely straightforward. It is not necessarily possible to isolate and measure one variable, and even when a causal link is suggested, experiments may not specify why. Other concerns have been raised in relation to the internal and external validity of experimental measurements. Nevertheless, experiments, especially in the form of randomised controlled trials, have become an increasingly common approach for evaluating educational policy and innovation.

Further reading

Bouguen, A. and Gurgand, M. (2012) *Randomized controlled experiments in education.* EENEE Analytical Report No. 11 Prepared for the European Commission. European Expert Network on Economics of Education (EENEE), February, 2012. Available at: http://www.eenee.de/portal/page/portal/EENEEContent/_IMPORT_TELECENTRUM/DOCS/EENEE_AR11.pdf

- This is an especially useful resource for identifying important recent projects that have utilised randomised controlled experiments. Tables on pages 25 to 27 provide project details, enabling you to follow up interesting research.

Willer, D. and Walker, H. (2012) *Building experiments: Testing social theory.* Stanford: Stanford University Press.

- While the book covers research in a range of social sciences, it is very useful for educational projects. It details and evaluates experimental design and makes a convincing case for the value of experimental approaches.

9

Case studies

Introduction

Case studies are a very popular research strategy, often used by researchers in education and other social sciences and by researchers in various legal and health-related professions. They are also commonly used by university students undertaking research projects for dissertations and theses. This chapter will look at the key purposes of case study research, and will examine the different types of case studies (single and multiple) and outline their key characteristics. It will consider when case studies should be used, how they can be designed and conducted, and what types of data collection methods can be used. It will also cover the strengths and limitations of case study research.

What is the purpose of case study research?

The purpose of a case study is to explore a specific example of a phenomenon or situation that can help illuminate whatever research question is under investigation. The important issue to note here is that the term 'case' itself is open to interpretation – for example, Judith Bell (1999: 11) calls it an 'instance', which could be the 'introduction of a new syllabus, the way a school adapts to a new role, or any innovation or stage of development in an institution … the case study researcher aims to identify such features and to show how they affect the implementation of systems and influence the way an organisation functions'. Lorna Hamilton (2011: 2) refers to the case study as a 'bounded unit' that the researcher describes and analyses 'in order to capture key components of the "case"'. Regardless of terminology, the important issue here is that the instance or bounded unit can take a diversity of shapes – 'the case might be, for example, a person, a group of particular professionals, an institution, a local authority etc.' (Hamilton, 2011: 2). However, it has a set of defining criteria that justify its definition as a 'case' in point – i.e. it needs to offer a useful example of a broader context or topic under scrutiny (i.e. national curriculum policy, teacher efficacy, etc.).

Types of case study

Case studies don't just come in singular form – there are numerous examples of multiple case studies being used for the purposes of research, often incorporated into broader quantitative studies. A good example of a multiple case study scenario is provided by Murphy *et al.* (2002), a Scottish Executive-funded study on widening participation in Scottish higher education. The research included quantitative analyses of UCAS figures for participation in Scottish HE institutions, exploring issues such as participation rates by class, gender and race. However, a range of institutions were also chosen as case studies for widening access initiatives, in order to try and provide as accurate a representation of widening participation initiatives. Effectively the qualitative aspects of the research had a dual objective – providing a cross-sectional sample of institutions and institutional practices, while also providing adequate representation of the various types of initiative undertaken.

Two examples of case studies in practice

Case study 1: Curriculum policy in England

Source: Pykett, J. (2007) 'Making citizens governable? The Crick Report as governmental technology'. *Journal of Education Policy*, Vol. 22, No. 3, pp. 301–319.

In her paper, Jessica Pykett (2007) provides an excellent example of a case study approach that uses an analysis of a new curriculum subject in England – citizenship education – as a way to better understand the connections between governance, education and the economy. Using a theoretical analysis adopted from French poststructuralism, she explores:

> how the policy behind Citizenship Education, known as the 'Crick Report' [Qualifications and Curriculum Authority (QCA), 1998] was conceived, deliberated and delivered into the public sphere, within a specific social, cultural, political and economic context [analysing] … citizenship education itself as a technology by which central government exercises the 'conduct of conduct'.
>
> (301–302)

The case study method she used was a combination of documentary analysis alongside a series of interviews she carried out with members of the government advisory group on citizenship. Couched within an understanding of the political and social context of the Crick Report, her case study allowed her to 'show how "politics" is erased from policy-making, in effect, putting the consequent policy document beyond political critique' (Pykett, 2007: 303). Design-wise, what her study illustrates is that 'case' can have a diversity of meanings – this 'case' involved the development of a specific curriculum policy, which Pykett used to make more general comments on the relationship between government, education and forms of control.

Case study 2: Parental voice in schooling

Source: Ranson, S., Martin, J. and Vincent, C. (2004) 'Storming parents, schools and communicative inaction'. *British Journal of Sociology of Education*, Vol. 25, No. 3, pp. 259–274.

In their research, Stewart Ranson, Jane Martin and Carol Vincent wanted to explore the phenomenon known as 'storming parents' – i.e. unruly parents who engage in disruptive behaviour with school staff. They wanted to know why 'some parents are driven to march into schools bent on angry encounters with teachers' (Ranson *et al.*, 2004: 260). They believed that such a study was necessary because it 'would provide an opportunity to clarify strategies for improving public policy'.

Their research focused on one secondary school in the English Midlands, involving interviews with twenty-five parents who were asked about their involvement with the school, how they benefited from this participation, and what issues they had or what actions they had undertaken in relation to these issues. The researchers chose the particular school 'because of its leading practice in involving parents, including establishing a forum to involve parents in discussions about the issues facing the school and its policy making' (Ranson *et al.*, 2004: 262).

The focus in the interviews with parents was on what the researchers called 'happenings' – incidents and occasions that generated parental unease, which were linked to a range of aspects: welfare, behaviour, uniform, academic progress and so on. They used the findings to make some general recommendations about school behaviour and approaches to parental interaction.

ACTIVITY

Consider the two examples of case study research mentioned above. Did the approach to the topics under consideration make sense? Why do you think the authors opted for a case study approach as opposed to another method? Would you have done things differently if you were the researcher? For example, could you have incorporated other aspects into your design when researching the nature of parental voices in schooling? This is a useful exercise as it helps you to engage with the thinking behind the design of already existing research.

How to design and implement case studies

There is no one set way to design a case study. The design that is used in a particular study should reflect the purpose for which it is intended, since the case study is an approach to research as opposed to a set of specific strategies. Therefore, the design of case studies is open to creative interpretation, which means that researchers can be imaginative in how they construct their studies. As always, there are a number of issues to take into consideration when designing a case study:

- *Define the 'case' clearly* – although it is difficult to entirely remove ambiguity from any study, try and be as specific as possible. For example, Ranson *et al.* chose to focus on what they referred to as 'happenings', so these became the cases that were used to flesh out troublesome issues of communication between parents and the school.

- *Ensure that the case is researchable* – instead of trying to interview 'storming parents', which could be challenging (legally and otherwise) and might be difficult to source, Ranson *et al.* chose to focus on 'happenings'. These are much more researchable, especially in a school which had low levels of 'storming' (as it were).

- *Choose your sample and location(s) wisely* – consider whether or not the sample and the site(s) of study will provide enough evidence in appropriate forms for your study. If you focus on the wrong case(s), the success of the research project would be open to serious question. Cases are not all the same; some are strategically more effective than others. For example, if you are studying the impact of curriculum change on teacher morale, choosing a school or schools that is or are currently undergoing curriculum change would make much more sense than targeting sites which can only offer retrospective accounts of their experiences.

- *Ensure access to the site(s)* – if the study involves physical access to spaces such as schools, universities, etc., ensure that appropriate access has been granted. This is especially important in case study design, since you are relying on a smaller number of cases to do the work for you. Being granted access early on will make the job of the researcher much easier. Permission to research at this stage is also important because of the issues surrounding anonymity and the ethics of your research – the smaller the research sample, the more important these issues become.

- *Ensuring anonymity* – if the results are to be anonymous, take special care in case study research – avoid concentrating on aspects or characteristics that may potentially allow readers to identify specific institutions, organisations or individuals.

ACTIVITY

Think of a research topic you are interested in exploring further. Would a case study approach be an appropriate one to take? Consider all the points mentioned above – is the 'case' you have in mind clearly defined, or does it have the potential to be so? Is it a researchable topic? Will it provide sufficient evidence to deliver appropriate findings and support a convincing argument? Will you to able to access the 'case' while also ensuring the anonymity of your participants? Use these points as a checklist against your preferred research topic, and consider whether or not the case study approach is right for you.

Analysing data from case studies

Depending on the kinds of data collection methods utilised in a case study, analysing the data can prove a challenge. While this is true for all forms of research, it can be especially problematic for researchers who have used multiple methods or who have researched a number of sites. In this regard, Lorna Hamilton provides some practical and useful advice:

> A starting point and straightforward approach might involve going back to the research questions and, taking each in turn, exploring the data and the possible answers, problems and conflicts which participants face in trying to respond. This can be a slightly messy process or at least one where it is necessary to go to and fro between research questions and data many times, exploring the commonalities and differences, the themes and exceptions which emerge.
>
> (Hamilton, 2011: 4)

Throughout the analysis stage it is vital that the 'case' remains central at all times, because it provides the rationale for the entire project. In this regard, try to avoid going off on intellectual or evidential tangents that can muddy the waters to such an extent that you lose sight of the original reasons behind the research in the first place.

Advantages and disadvantages of case studies

With case studies, there should be no doubt that what you gain in depth you lose in breadth; this is the unavoidable compromise that needs to be understood from the beginning of the research process. This is neither an advantage nor a disadvantage, since one aspect cancels out the benefits and drawbacks of the other. However, there are other positives and negatives that need attention.

Advantages

- **Their flexibility** – case studies are popular for a number of reasons, one being that they can be conducted at various points in the research process. Researchers are known to favour them as a way to identify and develop themes for more extensive research in the future – pilot studies often take the form of case studies. They are also effective conduits for a broad range of research methods; in this sense they are non-prejudicial against any particular type of research – focus groups are just as welcome in case study research as questionnaires or participant observation.
- **Capturing reality** – one of their key benefits is their ability to capture what Hodkinson and Hodkinson call 'lived reality' (2001: 3). As they put it, case studies have the potential, when applied successfully, to:

> retain more of the "noise" of real life than many other types of research. Indeed, other forms of research, such as the experiment or a carefully

structured questionnaire survey, base their success on the ability to exclude such noise, and focus precisely upon the particular phenomenon or possible causal relationship that is to be investigated. There are good reasons for doing much research in this way, but an unavoidable problem with it is that in some circumstances, the excluded noise may be a highly significant part of the story.

(Hodkinson and Hodkinson, 2001: 3)

The importance of 'noise' and its place in research is especially significant in educational contexts, for example in schools where background noise is unavoidable. Educational contexts are always complex, and as a result it is difficult to exclude other unwanted variables, 'some of which may only have real significance for one of their students' (Hodkinson and Hodkinson, 2001: 4).

Disadvantages

- **The challenge of generality** – at the same time, given their specificity, care needs to be taken when attempting to generalise from the findings. While there's no inherent flaw in case study design that precludes its broader application, it is preferable that researchers choose their case study sites carefully, while also basing their analysis within existing research findings that have been generated via other research designs. No design is infallible, but so often have arguments against case studies been raised that some of the criticism (unwarranted and unfair in many cases) has stuck. As Hodkinson and Hodkinson (2001: 10) put it:

    by definition, case studies can make no claims to be typical ... because the sample is small and idiosyncratic, and because data is predominantly non-numerical, there is no way to establish the probability that data is representative of some larger population. For many researchers and others, this renders any case study findings as of little value.

- **Suspicion of amateurism** – case studies, a long-time favourite method of education researchers, tend to carry with them the unfortunate whiff of a suspicion that they offer the time- and finance-strapped education researcher a convenient and pragmatic source of data, providing findings and recommendations that, given the nature of case studies, can neither be confirmed nor denied in terms of their utility or veracity. Who is to say that case studies offer anything more than a story to tell, and nothing more than that?

    However, alongside this suspicion is another more insidious one – a notion that 'stories' are not what social science research should be about. This can be a concern for those who favour case study research, as the political consequences can be hard to ignore precisely because, as Hodkinson and Hodkinson (2001: 10) put it, case study findings 'are easy to dismiss, by those who do not like the messages that they contain'.

However, there are a range of objections that can and should be made against such a bias. So much research is based either on peoples' lives or on the impact of other issues (poverty, institutional policy) on their lives, so the stories of what actually occurs in their lives or in professional environments tend to be an invaluable and rich source of evidence. The fact is that stories (individual, collective, institutional) have a vital role to play in the world of educational research. To play the specific vs general card against case study design suggests a tendency towards forms of research fundamentalism, as opposed to any kind of rational and objective take on the strengths and limitations of case studies.

- **Preciousness** – having said that, researchers should not fall into the surprisingly common trap of assuming that case study data speaks for itself. Rarely if ever is this the case, and it is an assumption that is as patronising to research subjects as it is false. The job of the researcher is both to describe social phenomena and also to explain them – i.e. to interpret. Without interpretation the research findings lack meaningful presentation; they present themselves as fact when of course the reality of 'facts' is one of the reasons why the research is being carried out in the first place.

- **Conflation of political and research objectives** – another trap that education case study researchers sometimes fall into is presenting research findings as if they were self-evidently true, as if the stories were beyond criticism. This is often accompanied by a vague attachment to the notion that research is a political process, one that is performed as a form of liberation – for example, against policies that seek to ignore the stories of those who 'suffer' at the hands of overbearing political or economic imperatives. Case study design should not be viewed as a mechanism for providing a 'local' bulwark against the 'global', but rather as a mechanism for checking the veracity of universalist claims (at least, this should be one of its objectives). The valorisation of particularism can only get you so far in educational research. In this regard, it is important that the researcher maintains an appropriate distance from the case being studied. Otherwise, as Mark (2004: 214) points out, there is the 'possibility that the observer will lose their perspective and could become blind to the peculiarities that they are supposed to be investigating'. Research validity can be affected as a result.

Chapter summary

This chapter explored the key characteristics of case study design, while also providing some examples of research that have used the case study as their framework. Some of the advantages and disadvantages of case studies were outlined, including a focus on the 'generalisability' of case studies and also the potential of this form of research to capture the lived experience of those who are being researched. The important message to take from this chapter is that the case study is as valid an approach to research as any other, but the merits of such studies can often be taken for granted and in some cases they may be abused. The case study is an excellent approach to educational research, but it is also wise to be aware of its shortcomings.

Further reading

Some other useful examples of case study research in education include:

- Di Adams' work (2002) on deregulation in Australian higher education – this is a good example of a study that uses data from multiple sites to provide a foundation for its claims concerning a 'bounded unit' (in this case the introduction of market-oriented policies in the university sector). The study also used a number of other methods in addition to case studies, including documentary analysis, participant observation and individual interviews.

- Richard Harper (2000) provides an excellent case study of one aspect of the work carried out by the International Monetary Fund – its auditing process via what are called 'fund missions'. Here, Harper focuses on one activity, providing a case study of one fund mission couched within an overall ethnographic approach.

- See also Stephen Ball's book *The micropolitics of the school* (1987), in which he uses a variety of case studies, including his own earlier work on Beachside Comprehensive and Casterbridge High, to develop a broader theory of school organisation.

10

Ethnography

Introduction

Ethnography is a fashionable approach to modern educational research. It involves in-depth study of a particular group or setting over an extended period of time. Ethnography requires the researcher to immerse herself within the site of study and attempt to experience it from the perspective of an inhabitant. This chapter identifies important and recent examples of ethnographic research in education. While acknowledging that the term is used in a variety of ways, the chapter outlines some of the common characteristics of the approach. Strengths and limitations are examined and three distinct branches are considered – practitioner ethnography, critical ethnography and autoethnography.

Ethnography in educational research

Ethnographic research attempts to develop an understanding of the shared cultural meanings of a particular group or setting. This might be the culture of an institution (a school or college, for example) or a distinct subculture within the institution – like a gang, a classroom or a friendship group. A group's 'culture' includes their shared behaviours, values, interpretations, artefacts, symbols, norms, assumptions, expectations and meanings. While some aspects of culture are easily identifiable, others lie below the surface – and it is these that the ethnographer attempts to uncover and understand. The ethnographer:

> ...captures and records the voices of lived experience ... goes beyond mere fact and surface appearances ... presents details, context, emotion, and the webs of social relationships that join persons to one another.
>
> (Denzin, 1994: 84)

To gain an understanding of this shared culture, the ethnographer immerses herself in the day-to-day experiences of those who inhabit or participate within it. She attempts to conceive the *world-view* of these actors, to see the world through their eyes.

Some of the most significant studies in education – generally within the discipline of the sociology of education – have been based on ethnographic research within a particular institution. Among the most influential UK studies are the following:

- David Hargreaves identified a link between streaming, labelling and school subcultures in *Social Relations in Secondary School* (1967).

- Paul Willis explored the school experiences of 'the lads' as preparation for working class employment in *Learning to Labour* (1977).

- Stephen Ball identified the impact of teachers' stereotyping, banding and pupil behaviour at *Beachside Comprehensive* (1981).

- Peter Aggleton examined middle-class underachievement at college in *Rebels Without a Cause* (1987).

- Mairtin Mac an Ghaill uncovered the hegemonic 'macho' school cultures in *The Making of Men* (1994).

- Heidi Mirza explored black girls' positive self-esteem and approaches to study despite teachers unwitting failure to meet their needs in *Young, Female and Black* (1992).

- Beverley Skeggs examined the lives of working class women undertaking 'caring courses' in FE as they negotiated social and cultural power relations in *Formations of Class and Gender: Becoming Respectable* (1997).

ACTIVITY

Have a look at some of these important ethnographic studies in education. Using an educational database, try to identify three or four contemporary ethnographic studies.

Make a list of the kinds of educational research topics most suited to an ethnographic approach.

Characteristics of ethnography

There is much disagreement about what counts as ethnographic research. While ethnographic studies vary considerably, they share a number of features in the main:

- **Exploring the shared culture of a group**
  Ethnography developed out of early twentieth century anthropology. Anthropologists like Malinowski believed the best strategy for understanding newly discovered tribes was to go and live among them, and to experience their cultural interpretations first hand. This enables an understanding of their 'way of life' – the shared interpretations and understandings that are considered 'normal' and meaningful within the group. The role of the ethnographer, then, is to get close enough to the group to uncover this 'way of life' or culture, and it is this focus on groups and their shared culture that differentiates ethnography from the other approaches outlined in Part 1 of this book.

■ **Significance of meaning**

The ethnographer is especially interested in the shared meanings that social actors attach to their behaviour, language, events, contexts and lives. Different groups might attach different cultural meanings to the same object or event. For instance, the ASBO (anti-social behaviour order) was designed to attach a cultural stigma to the holder within mainstream society, but many subcultural groups appropriated its meaning, redefining it as a 'badge of honour'. Therefore, the ethnographer will repeatedly ask social actors why they act in particular ways, what their environment means to them, how they understand events and so on.

■ **Insider approach**

To uncover shared culture, the ethnographer attempts to live as a member of the group – to experience the world from the perspective of its participants. This is an 'insider' approach. Rather than standing back as an expert, impartial, social scientist, the ethnographer tries to immerse themselves within the cultures they study, viewing participants as the true experts concerning their own lives.

■ **'Thick descriptions'**

Ethnographers develop detailed descriptions of activities, events and inter-pretations. Distinguishing between ethnographic and everyday descriptions, Hammersley argues:

> ...the "theoretical descriptions" that ethnographers produce are little different from the descriptions and explanations employed by us all in everyday life. What distinctiveness they ought to have concerns not their *theoretical* character but the explicitness and coherence of the models employed, and the rigour of the data collection and analysis on which they are based.
>
> (Hammersley, 1992: 22)

Geertz used the term 'thick description' (1973) to identify the specific features of ethnographic description. He argued that understanding culture involves studying specific events in their contexts and uncovering the meanings of these events to the social actors involved.

■ **Making the familiar strange**

While the ethnographer takes on the role of an 'insider' within the research site, she also needs to view the site as 'anthropologically strange'. She must 'maintain a more or less marginal position' in order to be 'intellectually poised between familiarity and strangeness' (Hammersley and Atkinson, 1995: 112), balancing what Hammersley terms 'involvement and estrangement' (1992: 145). It is the capacity to maintain a distance that enables the ethnographer to uncover and make explicit the common sense knowledge of the group.

■ **Naturalistic settings**

Ethnographers are interested in experiencing the world as it actually is. To do so, they employ methods that enable them to view real people in authentic situations and settings. Most commonly, they use participant observation and in-depth interviews.

- **Longitudinal**
  To uncover 'lived experience' ethnographic studies usually take place over an extended period of time, sometimes over a number of years. It takes a long time to uncover levels of reality beyond the surface, so ethnographic research is usually prolonged and repetitive.

- **Range of data collection techniques**
  While participant observation and in-depth interviews are the most common data collection techniques employed by the ethnographer, other methods are frequently utilised. For instance, ethnographers might use surveys to examine issues they have identified during observations. They are highly likely to employ multiple methods to add context and depth to their study, such as diaries, films, photographs, analysis of institutional documentation and so on.

- **Evolving study**
  The ethnographer does not enter the site of study with pre-existing research structures. As the study develops, aspects of culture will be identified and appropriate data collection techniques will be employed to study these aspects in further depth.

- **Theory deriving from data**
  Likewise, theories to emerge from ethnography derive from the data that is collected. The ethnographer does not enter the research site with a hypothesis to 'test'. Rather, she develops theories from her experiences within the site and from the conversations she has with participants. Like other qualitative approaches, ethnographers generally employ what Glaser and Strauss term 'grounded theory' (1967), whereby early observations give rise to theory that is explored further by additional data collection. Frequently, ethnographers will take their descriptive accounts back to social actors to check that they are recognisable as accurate reflections of their culture.

- **Reflexivity**
  Because of the kinds of methods commonly employed, ethnographers are very likely to consider issues of reflexivity. Their research is inevitably shaped by existing assumptions, relations, prejudices, values and experiences, as well as by the data collection processes. 'Personality' will impact on choice of topic, who takes part in the research, which events are considered important, and how events are analysed, interpreted and reported. Many ethnographers today would accept that the account they produce is one of numerous possibilities. Therefore, ethnographers are generally reflexive – taking themselves, and their role in the field of study, as a serious object of research. This involves being thoughtful and open about their own position and the impact of their methodological choices and processes on the final account they produce (see Chapter 20 for a more detailed discussion of reflexivity).

ACTIVITY

Ethnographers frequently adopt a role of 'acceptable incompetence' in the site of study –
cultivating and conveying an identity of friendly ineptitude. Given the characteristics
identified above, why might a role like this be of benefit to the educational ethnographer?
What other qualities might an effective educational ethnographer require?

Evaluating ethnography in educational research

Because the ethnographer immerses herself in the cultures she studies, she is able to elicit rich, detailed insights. She can understand complex and fluid meanings and interpretations within settings such as the classroom, a friendship group or the playground. Developing relationships with inhabitants of these settings (such as pupils and teachers) gives a human face to the research. By utilising a range of methods over an extended period of time, she is able to uncover meanings and understandings under the surface of everyday life. The combination of commonly-used methods like participant observation and informal interviews means that patterns and discrepancies between what people do and say become apparent. For ethnographers, educational theories that emerge from experiences within the field have greater authenticity, validity and value.

Nevertheless, there are a number of difficulties with the approach. Ethnography is dismissed by those who favour a more positivist or scientific approach to educational research. Selected methods are generally flexible, open-ended and unstructured, making them open to the charge that they are unsystematic and lack reliability. Close engagement with small groups makes it difficult to claim that findings are representative. It is also more difficult to generalise claims to wider society – that is, findings from a detailed ethnography in one school might be very different to findings from another school.

Moreover, the ethnographer's approach is entirely at odds with scientific ideals of the detached and impartial researcher. She attempts to immerse herself within the culture of study, often reflexively introspecting on her own changing attitudes, behaviours and feelings. Many would challenge the veracity of the ensuing interpretation, questioning the legitimacy and validity of an account so dependent on the subjective experiences, choices and interpretations of a particular ethnographer. Others would challenge how ethical she is when she joins and then leaves the group she studies, suggesting that she is effectively using people as a means toward her own ends.

These difficulties make ethnography a non-starter for some educationalists. Nevertheless, it remains a very popular choice for research. Questions the education ethnographer might ask herself to ensure she has done a good job might include the following:

■   Does the account derive from direct contact with the group being studied?

■   Have aims and objectives developed responsively and flexibly?

■   Does the account generate or contribute to educational theory?

- Is the account open and critical about the author's identification and selection of 'relevant' data?

- Is the account reflexive – open and thoughtful about the ways that the researcher's personality and the research process have shaped findings and interpretations?

ACTIVITY

There are plenty of recent examples of ethnographic research with children and young people. Read the following two articles and consider the roles of children in educational ethnography:

- Levey , H. (2009) '"Which one is yours?": children and ethnography'. *Qualitative Sociology*, 32 (3).
- Christensen, P.H. (2004) 'Children's participation in ethnographic research: issues of power and representation'. *Children and Society*, 18.

Now have a look at the journal *Ethnography and Education*. Look at the most-read articles and draw a diagram identifying strengths and weaknesses of the approach.

One of the most influential recent educational ethnography studies was led by Andrew Pollard. Read the following article and consider the advantages and disadvantages of this longitudinal approach:

- Pollard, A. (2006) 'The identity and learning programme: "principled pragmatism" in a 12-year longitudinal ethnography'. *Ethnography and Education*, 2 (1).

Branches of ethnography

Earlier in the chapter we mentioned that there is no clear agreement in terms of how ethnography is defined. There are a number of branches within ethnography, each with their own contested meanings, definitions and uses. Three branches that have proved of interest to educational researchers are:

- Practitioner ethnography
- Critical ethnography
- Autoethnography.

Practitioner ethnography

Practitioner ethnography entails the researcher studying a cultural setting that they already participate in. Drawing from Stenhouse's influential call for 'teachers-as-researchers' (1975), it commonly involves the teacher conducting ethnographic research in the institution that she works in, working with the group she teaches. Alongside action research, practitioner ethnography is widely used by people who are studying as well as practicing – for example, working part-time in a school while completing their studies.

There are many advantages of this approach to ethnography. Problems associated with gaining and maintaining access are avoided – existing relationships facilitate integration and immersion within the site of study. Familiarity with the research site helps the ethnographer to collect and analyse data. As Griffiths has argued in relation to teacher-researcher studies, events that occur during fieldwork can be contextualised by pre-existing knowledge, and 'subtle and diffuse' links can be identified as well as more obvious ones (Griffiths, 1985: 212). Analysis can gain 'sureness' due to this 'subsidiary awareness' and 'tacit knowledge' (Pollard, 1985: 221) – the researcher and researched are 'people-who-know-each-other-and-have-experienced-the-same-experiences' (p. 226). This is especially true for research with children; as Pollard has argued, the teacher–pupil relationship is one of the only 'natural' relationships between adults and youngsters (p. 226).

While there are clearly benefits to this practitioner approach, there are also concerns. For example, Hammersley challenges the validity of the type of account provided by 'practitioner ethnography', arguing that the insider role is fraught with difficulties. In particular, he argues that a full grasp of an educational culture requires a wider understanding than simply that of the practitioner (1992: 144). Insider accounts are partial, limited and constrained by the viewpoint of one actor within a site (see Chapter 20 for a full discussion of the insider role).

Critical ethnography

As we have seen during this chapter, ethnography is concerned with developing descriptions of existing cultures and meanings. Over the last twenty years critical ethnography has emerged, which concerns itself with theorising about cultures as they *could be*. Drawing on critical theory and the work of Paulo Freire (1973) and critical pedagogy, critical ethnography begins with a moral or political commitment to tackle social injustice or unfairness. The critical ethnographer takes on the role of advocate, using ethnography as a tool for articulating the interests of a marginalised or disempowered group.

Critical ethnography entails:

- An explicit purpose to contest hegemonic oppression
- Perceiving cultures as positioned unequally within power relations
- Disrupting taken-for-granted assumptions
- Interrogating underlying discourses of power and control
- Challenging the status quo
- Developing emancipatory knowledge and skills
- Attempting to change the world for the group studied
- The researcher as an *activist*.

Critical ethnographers like Carspecken (1996) and Thomas (1993) argue that the approach offers the possibility to impact positively on the education system, making the lives of students and teachers more free, fair and equal. It moves from the description and understanding of culture to the challenge and transformation of it. Critics view the overt political nature of the approach as problematic, claiming that data collection is really a means to articulate and justify the pre-existing (left-wing) biases of the researcher.

Autoethnography

Autoethnography places the subjective experiences of the researcher at the forefront of the process. It is a cross between ethnography (exploration of culture) and autobiography (exploration of the self), starting from the perspective that the self is socially constructed within culture. A narrative is developed that critically reflects on the researcher's self as situated in relation to others and to social, political and cultural settings. Personal stories, feelings, experiences, anecdotes, observations and reflections become the means by which cultures are interrogated.

Autoethnography has been widely criticised for lacking any scientific credibility. Some claim it is not real educational research, being rather a self-indulgent activity. Others argue that the approach is very useful as a means of exploring the meanings and experiences of educational processes. Starr argues that autoethnography, like critical ethnography, offers the potential for educational transformation, suggesting that it is:

> a valuable tool in examining the complex, diverse and sometimes messy world within education where we stress cooperation, teamwork and distributed leadership but are mired in hierarchy and power tensions.

> (Starr, 2010: 7)

ACTIVITY

The following extracts are taken from Andrew Sparkes' autoethnographic account of an audit of university lecturers' publications. In this first extract, 'Jim' has just had a meeting with the Vice Chancellor to discuss the merits of his colleagues' work:

> After the three-hour meeting, Jim was drained, empty. As he walked back to his office, he went through a range of emotions – anger, disappointment, fear, helplessness, confusion, shame, insecurity, anxiety, determination, hostility. There was also a little bit of pride for a job 'well done', in that he had managed to get most of his staff successfully through the process for another year. But then he felt complicit, tainted by management speak and their business world ideology. He had played the game on their terms, not his. Had played a game that he did not believe in. Had played a game that made him despair, and feel sick inside. Bob Geldof would never have done that, Jim thought. He wouldn't have acquiesced and rolled over. He would have done something to challenge them. At that moment, Jim hated himself with a ferocious intensity.

> (Sparkes, 2008: 528)

The second extract is taken from later in the article – where Sparkes cites reviews of his account:

REVIEWER 1

I am usually not much of a fan of 'auto-ethnography' and 'fictionalized ethnography' but I must say that I resonated with this. More importantly, I find it an example of exactly where these approaches to research actually make something possible in terms of capturing more nuanced layers of experience. If the author had collected data more systematically as opposed to 'informal interviews' and 'selected personal experiences', the piece would not have the punch and resonance that it does. Hence, this is a case where these methods actually foster the project in capturing and communicating elements of the social that are more or less ineffable. To overturn and overflow the received idea of 'acceptable' scholarship in a largely social science arena, to escape the sort of 'oppressive empiricism' that is in rigid opposition to interpretation, to enact a 'generative undoing' of the standard 'boring' writing of the academy (in Richardson's straightforward terms) is a worthy goal IF the enactment allows something to be seen that could not otherwise be seen. Somewhere Foucault calls this 'increasing the circumference of the visible'.
    This piece does that.

(Sparkes, 2008: 541)

Consider the following:

1   What do you think of the first extract as a piece of academic writing?
2   Why do you think Sparkes includes a series of reviews as part of the final article?
3   What does Reviewer 1 regard as the value of the account?
4   What do you think the extracts (and the whole article if you are able to read it) say about the cultures of research in higher education?

Chapter summary

This chapter outlines the main characteristics of ethnographic research, providing examples of influential studies in the sociology of education that have utilised the approach. Ethnographers describe and explain the social and cultural lives of groups or institutions, uncovering the perceptions and interpretations of social actors within those settings. Three branches of ethnography that are commonly used in educational research are outlined – practitioner ethnography, critical ethnography and autoethnography. While there are many reasons to adopt an ethnographic approach to educational research, it may be difficult to uncover 'taken-for-granted' meaning, and over-familiarity can hamper validity. Most significantly, ethnographic researchers must be open, honest and reflexive with regard to their own values and assumptions and how these impact on the stories they tell.

Further reading

Peter Woods (1986) *Inside schools: Ethnography in educational research.* London: Routledge.

■ Woods' book provides an excellent starting point for students interested in undertaking an ethnographic study. It outlines and explores many of the strategies employed by teachers who utilise the approach.

Atkinson, P. and Hammersley, M. (2007) *Ethnography: Principles in practice* (3rd edition). London: Routledge.

■ Hammersley and Atkinson's work on ethnography and practitioner ethnography have shaped the landscape for many years. This third edition of their key introduction includes material on virtual approaches.

Carspecken, P. (1996) *Critical ethnography in educational research: A theoretical and practical guide.* London: Routledge.

■ The key book for students interested in critical ethnography.

11

Action research

Introduction

Action research refers to practitioners carrying out research on their own practice in order to enhance it. This typically involves classroom teachers testing and trialling changes to their pedagogic practice and evaluating the effectiveness of these changes. Arguably practitioners are the people who have the best understanding of *what* and *how* practice needs to be developed, and therefore they are ideally placed to do this. Because it is the teacher who generally decides what they wish to research and how they are going to go about it, action research can be seen as an empowering process for those involved since they are taking control of making the changes they perceive to be necessary.

This approach is quite different from a seasoned researcher arriving in a school to carry out a piece of research 'on' the teacher and their pedagogic practice. Lawrence Stenhouse (1975) was one of the key advocates for teachers to be actively involved in research. He claimed that it is not sufficient merely to study teachers' work; teachers also need to study their own work. There is a concern that not enough teachers are involved in research to improve teaching and learning (Hancock, 1997). This concern in itself is not new; Stenhouse himself conceded that 'it will require a generation of work ... if the majority of teachers – rather than only the enthusiastic few' are to be involved in research (1975: 142). This chapter will be split into three sections: first we will examine the cyclical nature of action research, followed by a discussion of different types of action research. Finally we will note a number of potential constraints to using this research strategy.

Cyclical nature of action research

The concept of action research can be explained by the notion of doing experiments in the field, rather than the laboratory. Its creation is attributed to the work of the social psychologist Kurt Lewin (1946), who discussed a model of action research in his article *'Action research and minority problems'* which addressed intergroup relations in some American communities in the 1940s. Following Lewin's ideas, action research involves a 'spiral of steps each of which is composed of a circle of planning, action and fact-finding about the result of the action' (Lewin, 1946: 38). According to Cousin (2009) the stages within the action research cycle are: reconnaissance, planning, preliminary research, formulating research questions, implementing, observing, recording and reflecting.

1   Reconnaissance

Reconnaissance can be described as 'fact-finding'. This process has four functions. Firstly, action needs to be evaluated to see if it has met expectations. Secondly, based on this evaluation the strengths and weaknesses of an action can be considered. This leads to the third step, using this information to plan the next steps, and finally the overall plan can be amended accordingly.

2   Planning

Planning is a key idea in all research practice, and it is not unique to action research. Nevertheless it is worth pointing out that it is necessary to move from a general idea of what the research is hoping to achieve to a series of stages which will enable this to be achieved. The actions that must be taken in order to achieve the aims of the research need to be identified. This may also mean that the original idea has to be modified to make it achievable or viable.

3   Preliminary research

Many pieces of research carry out a pilot study. This is often a small-scale piece of research to test the methods being used and to evaluate the impact or findings of the research. An example of this might be a school which decides to embed drama in all aspects of the curriculum. Rather than every teacher in the school trying to do this straight away, it makes more sense for one or two teachers in the school to trial the new approach by making changes to their planning and perhaps identifying key subjects where drama can be integrated. Once they have trialled the use of embedding drama in certain subjects within the curriculum, they will then evaluate the practice – has it improved the children's learning, engagement or confidence? Based on these findings the teachers are likely to make further changes to the ways in which they have embedded drama in the curriculum, and then they will be able to support other teachers in a school-wide initiative if this is deemed useful by the preliminary findings.

4   Formulating research questions

Based on the pilot research findings, the project may be implemented on a wider scale. It will be underpinned by research questions emerging from the preliminary findings; for example:

1   What is the impact of using drama on boys' motivation to write stories?

2   To what extent has the use of hot-seating encouraged children to become confident in asking and answering questions?

3   How effectively can drama techniques be integrated into cross-curricular planning?

5   **Implementing**
   Based on the planning and with reference to the research questions, the changes
   to pedagogic practice are made – in this instance, the development of the use of
   drama in the classroom.

6   **Observing**
   Different observational strategies are noted in Chapter 15. In the action research
   cycle the impact of the implemented changes needs to be observed. It is possible
   for the teacher/researcher to note these observations themselves simply by
   reflecting on the changes taking place – for instance, when marking literacy
   books they may note an improvement in the quality of the stories written by
   boys. Alternatively, they might wish to work with a colleague who may come
   in and make observations about how the classroom practice has changed.
   Alternatively, teachers may engage in discussions with each other about their
   experiences, or they may ask children for their views.

7   **Recording and reflecting**
   The changes that have taken place need to be recorded to aid further changes.
   This may mean writing field notes or recording interviews. The data can then
   be systematically analysed so that the changes that have been made can be
   further enhanced. This indicates the cyclical nature of action research, and it is
   not unusual to repeat each step in the process two or three times. The cyclical
   nature of this type of research offers opportunities for comparative data to be
   measured over time, giving a strong sense of reliability and validity within the
   research findings (Reason and Bradbury, 2006).

Practical example of the cyclical cycle

The cyclical nature of other pieces of action research can offer a practical illustration
of the different phases. Swann and Ecclestone (1999) clearly explained the stages of
action research which they undertook during their project. Initially they identified
two key issues with teachers' assessment practices: a lack of consistency in grading
students' assignments, and the fact that feedback comments were not effective in
improving students' learning. In an attempt to improve assessment practices they
went through a series of questions and statements to formulate each stage of their
action research.

■   What aspects of assessment do we want to change? (reconnaissance).
■   What seems to be preventing these desired changes? (reconnaissance).
■   Which impediments are within our control to change? (planning).
■   Formulation of tentative theories on how to make these changes (formulating
    research question).
■   Select a trial solution (implementing).
■   Decide how to measure success (or not) of trial solution (observing and
    recording).

- Carry out a review process. Any positive/negative effects on assessment? Any unintended consequences? Would other strategies have been more effective? (reflection).

(Adapted from Swann and Ecclestone, 1999: 69)

Different types of action research

Although all action research approaches follow these broad cyclical stages, there are different types of action research.

Emancipatory

Emancipatory action research aims to empower all the research participants. This is very much a 'grassroots' approach to the research, giving those involved the power and control to change their educational experiences for the better. Emancipatory action research encourages joint responsibility for the research from all parties, such as the practitioner, students and the facilitator (Carr and Kemmis, 1986). An example of emancipatory action research in practice is the work of Postholm, which involved all parties in the action research process. Postholm's (2009: 553) research took pupils' learning as a starting point to find out how teachers and researchers could cooperate to develop the school as a learning organisation. 'The aim of the work on which the teachers and I cooperated was not emancipatory from a societal perspective, but aimed to develop the teachers' awareness of their own teaching and the pupils learning as part of their professionalism.'

Reflective

Reflective action research is very much about the practitioner being in control and making changes to their own practice. The practitioner can then reflect on the impact of these changes for themselves and their students. An example of reflective action research is the work of Casey, Dyson and Campbell (2009). In Casey's role of teacher-as-researcher he sought to implement a new pedagogical approach to improve student learning when teaching physical education. Drawing on the work of Lewin (1946), his action research took three stages. 'The first aspect of the data analysis, due to the nature of teaching, was immediate and ongoing – allowing me to meet the "on the spot" learning needs of my pupils within the school context. At the second level, I systematically collected and organised data, and then the research team analysed it using inductive analysis and constant comparison (Denzin and Lincoln, 1994; Lincoln and Guba, 1985). Findings from this analysis were grounded in the tenets of the AR process; that is, if something needed changing or altering, I, as the teacher-researcher, was able to make changes' (Casey, Dyson and Campbell, 2009: 413).

Technical

Unlike emancipatory and reflective action research, technical action research is often instigated by a facilitator rather than the practitioner. Technical action research tries to improve the efficiency and effectiveness of practice. Furthermore, technical action research is often measured by the facilitator's criteria, tending not to involve the practitioner in this process. A popular action research methodology combines reflective and technical aspects (Torrance and Pryor, 2001; Munns and Woodward, 2006; Swann and Ecclestone, 1999). In this scenario a team of researchers works closely with a team of practitioners, enabling them to collectively identify where and how changes to practices could be made. After implementing these changes practitioners are then able to reflect on the effectiveness of these changes before implementing any additional alterations in the next cycle. Swann and Ecclestone (1999) and Munns and Woodward (2006) used a collaborative approach in their projects, recruiting several teachers from different schools to be action researchers on their project. The authors themselves acted as facilitators and co-ordinators within the project. It was hoped that all the teachers involved in the project would attend meetings, develop and test ideas within their own practice and contribute to guidelines and materials for other teachers. Sometimes researchers are not in a position to carry out research on their own practice and may ask practitioners to trial implementations to practice. The following vignette about technical action research highlights this particular issue:

VIGNETTE

I decided a technical approach to the action research would be most suitable for my project because this would allow me to suggest the lecturer make practical changes to her module, for example the lecturer could give verbal feedback instead of written, or she could change the style of feedback comments. I had anticipated that the data I collected at the preliminary research stage would provide a baseline from which I could then compare student engagement with feedback before and after the lecturer had implemented the technical changes. Therefore, I expected to assess the impact of changes on student engagement with feedback through my own criteria. So in my technical approach to action research I had taken away the opportunity for reflection by the 'practitioner as doer'. The action research cycle encourages the practitioner implementing change (in this instance assessment practices) to reflect on the effectiveness of these alterations and based on this further amendments may be made to the initiative. However, as a researcher working with a practitioner I was reflecting on the changes required and suggesting ways to implement improvements. This approach did not conform to the original ideals of action research in which practitioners are at the centre of reflecting on the initiative they have implemented. I was suggesting to the module leader a range of changes to be made to the assessment and feedback practices and I would then evaluate the impact of these changes. In this sense my use of action research did not conform to its traditional principles. Instead I was shaping the action research through collaborating with the lecturer to improve assessment practices.

(McGinty, 2011)

Potential constraints

If you are interested in carrying out action research with teachers or as a teacher yourself, it is worth reflecting on how to overcome potential barriers. There are several reasons why teachers may find it difficult to be involved in research.

The everyday business of teaching is not necessarily underpinned by the acknowledgement of how important educational theory is to practice. Teachers may not become actively involved in research – unless, for example, they are working for a higher degree, or they have been asked by a local university to be participants in a piece of action research. Indeed, the very intensity of a teaching day and the never-ending multitude of tasks that need to be done means that there is barely any time to eat a sandwich at lunchtime, let alone get involved in carrying out a piece of research. In addition, being involved in research requires an innate sense of confidence that your research is a worthwhile activity. For many teachers the continual erosion of their professional identities through frequent government interventions has meant that they do not feel that they can say anything worth saying, or any control in making changes to pedagogic practice.

One of the key problems is that research requires some level of objectivity to enable the researcher to reflect on what is happening, but when you are caught up with caring for the children in your class it becomes very difficult as an 'insider' to step away from this. There are good examples of teachers being involved in action research projects (e.g. the PALM project), particularly when they have been guided and supported by universities who have lent 'researcher expertise'. McNiff (1988: xiii) comments: 'Action research presents an opportunity for teachers to become uniquely involved in their own practice'.

Although practitioners have the opportunities to carry out reflective action research on their own practice, perhaps the most popular model within education research is a more technical approach. This often involves practitioners and researchers working together. Such a collaboration can undoubtedly be rewarding and fruitful for all involved. However, there are some key caveats that perhaps should be considered before working alongside practitioners to develop a piece of action research, and equally for practitioners it is important to consider the implications of this type of research. Implementing a methodology can be a complex process, and in the case of action research there are three issues – communication problems, differences in expectations and changing priorities – that may prevent successful implementation.

Communication

When using a technical approach to action research it is important to recognise the significance of communication between the practitioner(s) and the researcher(s) if the project is to proceed successfully.

Differences in expectations

For the researcher and practitioner to work effectively together on a piece of action research, clear expectations and guidelines are needed. At the outset of the project you need to give consideration to the importance of trust, respect and openness between the researcher and practitioner. It is important not to underestimate the issues of power, control and reputation that can make both parties feel vulnerable and exposed at times. Somekh (2006) reflected on this experience in her PALM (Pupil Autonomy in Learning with Microcomputers) project, whose original impetus did not come from the teachers with whom she was working, but rather from outside agencies. This created initial difficulties with her project because different parties had different expectations about the research. However, differences in expectations can emerge in any type of research; this problem is not specific to action research.

Changing priorities

When working with practitioners, changes in the priorities of team members can make it difficult to continue with a research project. Therefore it is important to consider how to communicate effectively and to ensure that expectations are aligned. The vignette below outlines the implications of changing priorities.

VIGNETTE

Around this point the situation was further complicated by a change in the module leader's priorities. She now wanted to join a different research team to redevelop her module for a piece of research focusing on blended learning, rather than use the module for action research on feedback practices. My original aim had been to advise the module leader on how the ways in which students received and are able to make use of feedback could be improved. This interpretation of action research can be likened to the example used by McNiff (1988) in which a lecturer in Education advised two teachers on implementing the use of historical artefacts in the classroom: 'The researcher's implementation is of his own solution to the problem of finding a demonstrably effective way of helping teachers to introduce innovation and to improve the quality of their pupil's education' (McNiff: 61). I too had aimed to improve the quality of learning through the development of feedback practices through a partnership between myself as an external researcher and the module leader.

(McGinty, 2011)

Chapter summary

A key tenet of action research is that it is not done *on* people, but *with* people (Cousin, 2009: 151). Action research is a cyclical process with each stage being visited and revisited two or three times. There are different types of action research: emancipatory, reflective and technical. A popular action research approach combines reflective and technical aspects. As with all types of educational research, good communication and trust among all those involved in the project are important to ensure success.

Further reading

Brydon-Miller, M., Kral, M., Maguire, P., Noffke, S. and Sabhlok, A. (2011) *'Jazz and the banyan tree: Roots and riffs on participatory action research'*. Chapter 23, pp. 387–414 in N.K. Denzin, and Y.S. Lincoln, (eds) *The SAGE Handbook of Qualitative Research*. Thousand Oaks, California: SAGE.

- An interesting chapter which explores the complexities of participatory action research and its importance in challenging existing structures of power.

Methods of data collection

12

Questionnaires

Introduction

It is easy to assume that questionnaire design is straightforward because we all have some experience of completing questionnaires, whether they are 'personality trait' quizzes in magazines, market research surveys on the high street or a medical questionnaire before starting a new job. In reality, however, there are many issues that need to be considered when designing a questionnaire to ensure a successful response rate and the collection of useful data. This chapter will be divided into four sections: advantages of questionnaires as a research method, designing questionnaires, response rates, and practical issues.

Advantages of questionnaires as a research method

The use of a questionnaire tool is supported by Kelly *et al.* (1994), who argue that participants may not wish to share their experiences in an interview. They also point out that questionnaires allow participants to respond to both closed and open-ended questions anonymously. There are several advantages in collecting questionnaire data:

- Collecting data from a larger number of respondents than you can interview
- Closed questions enable straightforward analysis
- Statistical tests can be applied
- Open-ended questions allow respondents to comment in their own words.

Due to the many advantages of using questionnaires in educational research it is relatively easy to find studies in all educational fields which have incorporated them into the design of projects.

ACTIVITY

Investigate what types of educational research have used questionnaires in your own area of interest.

■ Choose an education database such as Education Research Complete or ERIC and search using educational-related terms, e.g. 'questionnaire', 'cross-curricular', 'creativity'.
■ Scroll through the journal article abstracts to identify educational research in your area which has used questionnaires.

As you become familiar with other research in your area which has used questionnaire tools, if you decide to incorporate one into your own research you will need to start considering the questions to include in your own instrument.

Designing questionnaires

What questions should I ask?

A sensible starting point for deciding what questions to include in your questionnaire is to read relevant literature in your topic area. You may find it useful to focus on journal articles which have used questionnaires with the same research emphasis – for example, research on bullying (Maunder, Harrop and Tattersall, 2010), inclusion (Balfe and Travers, 2010), free play (King and Howard, 2010) and children's views on listening strategies in the classroom (Crosskey and Vance, 2011). Go back to your research questions or project aims and consider what issues you are trying to find out about, and then consider how you can formulate questions related to these issues.

Not only do you need to decide *which* questions to ask, you also need to decide *how* to ask the questions. There are several different types of questions. To illustrate these we will consider the practical example of a research project interested in the professional identity of newly qualified teachers. Two of the project aims were:

■ To explore the meanings that participants attach to 'professional' identity and how these shift from the time students achieve QTS to the end of their NQT year.
■ To identify the impact of the ITE context and the work environment on developing professional identity in relation to pedagogic practice within the classroom.

Your questions should be formulated based upon the aims of your research and the different types of questions you could use to do this will be discussed.

Question type

From looking at the project aims above it is clear that a variety of questions could be asked. Using the project aims, examples of the different types of questions and their relative advantages and disadvantages will be discussed below.

Closed question   Have you been offered your first teaching post? Yes/No

The advantage of closed questions is that it is easy to analyse responses – e.g. *67 per cent Yes* and *33 per cent No*. The disadvantage of closed questions is that the choices on the questionnaire may not allow participants to choose their 'real' answer because the researcher has made assumptions about the participants' answers through the choices provided. There are scenarios which closed questions may not cover. A trainee teacher may have decided to not apply for teaching jobs after completing their course, or they may have an interview tomorrow which could change their response! In addition, closed questions can only provide a limited amount of information – for example, we do not know from this question whether NQTs who answered 'no' have had any interviews, or if those who answered 'yes' have been offered fixed-term or permanent contracts.

Open-ended question   Why did you want to become a teacher?

The advantage of open-ended questions is that they can provide 'qualitative' data and let participants respond in their own words. The themes that emerge from open-ended responses can be followed up in interviews. The pitfalls of open-ended questions can include a lack of space provided for written responses, problems with reading handwritten responses and poor spelling and grammar, which can all make responses tricky to decipher. In addition, participants may not answer the question you have asked, writing about something else instead. Meanwhile, some respondents will leave this type of question blank. If you decide to use open-ended questions, read up on qualitative data analysis because this section of your questionnaire will require a specific analytical approach.

Multiple-choice questions   Please tick the year groups in which you undertook your three school experience placements:

Foundation   ☐
Year 1   ☐
Year 2   ☐
Year 3   ☐
Year 4   ☐
Year 5   ☐
Year 6   ☐

Multiple-choice questions are easy to analyse. Their drawback is that if the responses you provide are not relevant and do not cover all the options, your data will be skewed or incomplete. A good example of this is the fact that mixed year-group classes are not included in the options above. Therefore, potentially a different number of responses than the anticipated three might be picked. Responses of 'Year

5' and 'Year 6' would not tell us if the student was in a mixed Year 5/Year 6 class, or if these were two separate placements and their other selection was a mixed year-group class. Additionally, the specification of three choices would be problematic for a student who failed a placement and had to retake it, giving them four school placements. For these types of questionnaires it is useful to include an 'Other' option with a space for participants to provide information, which will allow participants to state their answer if it has not been included in the possible choices.

Likert scale questions   I feel well supported by my mentor as a NQT

1   Strongly agree

2   Agree

3   Neither agree nor disagree

4   Disagree

5   Strongly disagree

Likert scale questions are useful for finding out about perceptions, emotions and feelings. Traditionally five categories are used, but it is not unusual to see seven or even nine options to choose from. Arguably an even number of choices, such as 1 to 4, means respondents cannot choose the middle number (usually the neutral option). One problem with a Likert scale response is that sometimes respondents may circle two numbers, which is problematic in the analysis stage. In addition, Likert scales often encounter an 'end-aversion' bias among adults, where people tend not to mark the two extreme ends of the scale. Pantell and Lewis (1987) also identified a position bias among children's responses in questionnaires where they tended to choose the first answer among the response options.

Category questions   What type of teacher training did you undertake?

BA Primary Teaching with QTS

BEd

PGCE

SCITT

Category questions are useful for collecting demographic information. However, ensure that participants understand the categories available – for example, the initials above are only likely to be understood by those who move in educational circles. Also, be clear in your own mind about how demographic data collection is relevant to your research. Try not to make overly deterministic causal links between demographic data and other questionnaire responses, such as those with a PGCE have better relationships with their NQT mentor than those with BEd training.

Practical issues

Think carefully about how you want to analyse the data before sending out your questionnaire. The types of questions you ask will influence the type of data analysis you can do. Therefore, you need to know how you are going to process the results before you receive the completed questionnaires back. A closed 'Yes/No' question will allow you to give a percentage – *35 per cent of respondents said yes*. On the other hand, open-ended questions do not lend themselves to number-crunching and require a different type of analysis, but they may give you more in-depth responses.

Layout and sequence

1   Give the respondent clear instructions on how to complete the questionnaire, such as 'tick the box', 'circle all choices that apply' or 'if No, go to question 10'.

2   Keep the layout simple and use a font that is easy to read. Also think about the size of the font. It can be tempting to use a small font to get all your questions on one side of A4, which will make your questionnaire look relatively short. However, if respondents struggle to read the questions this will put them off.

3   If your questionnaire is for children you need to make sure that they are able to read the questions, or that an adult will be on hand to read the questions aloud.

4   Think about the number of questions you include. Respondents may suffer from 'questionnaire fatigue' if there are too many questions. Therefore you need to be realistic about the time and effort required to fill in a questionnaire. 'When designing a questionnaire, then, the researcher has to walk a tightrope between ensuring coverage of all the vital issues and ensuring the questionnaire is brief enough to encourage people to bother answering it' (Denscombe, 2003: 96).

5   Make sure that the printing or photocopying is of a good quality if you use a paper-based questionnaire. Alternatively, an online questionnaire may avoid prohibitive costs of printing and look more 'professional'.

6   The jury is out on the sequence of questions. Some researchers recommend putting the easy questions, such as gender and age categories, at the start to encourage the respondents to fill in the questionnaire. Others recommend putting the easier questions at the end when the respondent has already invested in the questionnaire and is therefore more likely to complete it. Whichever way you decide to organise your questionnaire, put questions of a similar theme together and try not to include too many open-ended questions.

7   A disadvantage of questionnaires is the lack of depth and detail that they can provide, but you can compensate for this by including open-ended question responses and complementing the questionnaire data with other research methods.

8   It is worth leaving space at the end of the questionnaire for respondents to include their contact details for a follow-up interview, or in case they have any further comments they wish to make.

ACTIVITY

As a starting point for considering the significance of questionnaire design for an effective piece of research:

- Think about a time when you have completed a questionnaire.
- What was good or bad about the questionnaire you had to complete?
- Compile a list and discuss with a partner.
- Now, use this list to analyse the strengths and weaknesses of the questionnaire you have designed for your own research project. Is there anything you need to amend before giving it to research participants?

It is important to be aware of the practical issues of administering a questionnaire. A questionnaire which was used with a group of pupils to evaluate the impact of teacher training in developing children's listening (Crosskey and Vance, 2011) will be used as an example of dealing effectively with consent, pilot testing and bias.

Consent

In the Crosskey and Vance (2011) study an information sheet and consent form were sent to respondents. As the questionnaire was for children, the researchers also sought permission from parents/carers and teachers. More information on informed consent can be found in Chapter 21.

Pilot testing

In the Crosskey and Vance (2011) study the questionnaire was piloted. Pilot testing is vital to check that respondents understand the questions, the questions are appropriate, and that the questionnaire is a reasonable length to encourage a good return rate. For example, you might discover that respondents' experiences may not be sufficiently described by the pre-set multiple choice responses, or the questionnaire may have little relevance or personal interest to respondents. You need to ensure that the questionnaire is completed by the target audience. Respondents may make up answers or leave out certain questions completely, and this will skew your data statistically. Through piloting your questionnaire you should be able to iron out any difficulties concerning the likelihood of respondents misunderstanding or misinterpreting questions.

Bias

If a questionnaire is being used to elicit the views of pupils about their own teacher then there is the potential for bias – for example, if pupils wish to answer positively to please their teacher. It is important for the questionnaire to be presented in such a way that pupils feel able to express their opinions safely and honestly. Identifying differences in pupils' responses to the same questionnaire at different times also controls for bias. For example, the Crosskey and Vance (2011) questionnaire was administered three times – before the teachers undertook the training in listening strategies in the classroom, during the training, and after the training. The use of an independent researcher should reduce any possible bias in terms of pupils responding to please their own teachers.

Questionnaire design checklist

- Have you piloted your questionnaire?
- Does the questionnaire give instructions for completion?
- Is the questionnaire a sensible length that will not require too much time to complete?
- Will the respondents understand the questions?
- Are the choices for response appropriate?
- Have you decided how you will analyse the data?

Response rate

Response rate is often the biggest issue with using questionnaires, making good questionnaire design crucial to increase participation. We've already highlighted the fact that asking too many questions can be very offputting for respondents, which will reduce your return rate. To work out how many questionnaires to send out, you need to decide how many questionnaires you need for analysis. Questionnaires, especially those administered by post, have a notoriously low return rate and this means you will need to send out a lot more questionnaires than you actually need for analysis. Broadly speaking, you can expect a response rate of about twenty to thirty per cent. This means that if you are hoping to have fifty questionnaires to analyse, you may need to send out at least two hundred questionnaires.

Questionnaires can be delivered to the respondents by various means including post, email or online. Postal questionnaires often have a low response rate, but they also have advantages such as wide coverage and eliminating any bias which may be introduced by interaction with a researcher. The advent of email and online questionnaire software may make the concept of a postal questionnaire seem quite dated; if you have access to the email addresses of potential respondents the questionnaire can simply be emailed out as an attachment, and you can then send email reminders to participants who have not returned the questionnaire. Alternatively there is some excellent software for designing and sending questionnaires, such as SurveyMonkey. Online software helps you design the questionnaire in a professional way and will let you send out a link to respondents. In addition, the software will collate the findings and allow you to perform basic statistical tests. Online software often has a subscription fee, but many institutions do subscribe. However, if this is not a possibility at your institution, online software often lets you have a free 'trial', sending a limited number of questionnaires without the need to pay for the service.

There are several strategies you can use to increase the number of responses – for example:

■ Offer a *suitable* prize, such as a book token, or say you will send out the results to interested respondents (but you must make it clear in your write-up that an incentive was offered).

■ Target your audience by name, such as Ms. Jones, rather than 'the head teacher'.

■ You may be able to get a 'captive' audience, for example by handing out your questionnaires at the beginning of a seminar and collecting them at the end.

■ Send email reminders.

■ If it is a postal questionnaire, include a stamped and self-addressed envelope.

■ Explain the purpose of the questionnaire and why the responses are important.

■ Structured interview questionnaires, where you read out the questions to respondents and complete their responses, can be effective but they are time consuming.

Dealing with problem responses

Most people will answer all the questions in the way that you have requested. However, some respondents may miss out a question. When coding your questionnaire responses it is better to record something on your grid rather than nothing, but you may want to differentiate the responses, for example between missing (M) and don't know (DK). This is important because when you are calculating your statistics at a later date it is important to know how many responses you are dealing with. For example, you may have 160 questionnaires returned, but perhaps only 143 people answered question 7. This means that if 87 respondents said 'yes' to question 7, you need to base your calculations on 87 out of 143, not 87 out of 160.

Chapter summary

Questionnaires are a useful tool for gathering responses from a large number of participants. The design of a questionnaire instrument can allow statistical analysis to be applied. It is crucial to pilot your questionnaire to ensure that respondents will be able to understand the questions and will not suffer from 'questionnaire fatigue'. There are lots of different types of questions, such as multiple-choice items, Likert scale questions and open-ended responses. However, do not worry about trying to include every possible type of question – this can be confusing for participants.

It is a good research method for ensuring anonymity and confidentiality, but you can ask participants who wish to be further involved in the research to leave their contact details voluntarily. There are also several disadvantages of using questionnaires, such as low response rates and the limited amount of information that can be obtained using this approach. Therefore, using questionnaires to complement other research methods in a research project can compensate for these drawbacks. For instance, your questionnaire may offer a broad overview of the research area, while other methods such as interviews or observations provide in-depth detail.

Further reading

Cox, J. and Cox, K. B. (2008) *Your opinion please! How to build the best questionnaires in the field of education* (2nd edition), Thousand Oaks, CA: Corwin Press.

■ This book is designed with the less experienced researcher in mind. It is sequentially laid out, taking you from your initial research questions through to phrasing your questions in the questionnaire. A self-evaluation resource for assessing the quality of questionnaire design is also included. This edition also discusses the use of the internet for online questionnaires.

13

Interviews

Introduction

> Interviewer: *So how do you feel about Chiltern now you've been here for a year?*
> Kirsty: *I feel quite alright now and it's not too bad. Like the kids we all get along nice and the teachers are quite friendly.*
> Interviewer: *You said before you came it was full of bad kids.*
> Kirsty: *(laughing) No there's quite a few good kids and lots in between. I don't want to move school anymore.*
>
> (Adapted from Reay, 2007: 1197)

The quote above is just one example of an interview that was carried out for educational research. Interviews are a popular research tool within education (for instance, lisahunter *et al.*, 2011; Ferguson, Hanreddy and Draxton, 2011; and Read, 2011 are all recent examples). An interview can broadly be defined as being conducted on a one-to-one basis, with a range of questions to be asked and answered. Some of these questions may be fairly straightforward and some will take a great deal of thought and consideration. Interviews generally fall into three main categories: semi-structured, unstructured, and structured (group interviews will be addressed in the next chapter). The type of interview that you conduct is dependent on your underlying methodology and the focus of your research (please refer back to the introduction for a discussion of these issues). After examining the different types of interview this chapter will discuss power dynamics in the interview process and illustrate how interviewing principles can mediate this, before exploring the practical aspects of interviewing.

Semi-structured interviews

These are perhaps the most commonly used type of interview within education research and in social science research more widely. The questions are pre-set, but do allow some flexibility into your schedule. If a participant starts talking about something which you had not previously considered, this is not generally thought to be problematic. In addition, this type of interview normally encourages participants to add their own thoughts – after all, this approach believes that it is important to identify what is most significant for the participants.

A good interview technique relies on 'rapport'. Rapport is the development of a sense of trust and empathy. This means that you will need to get the interview participant to 'like you' enough to give honest and detailed answers. In this type of approach it is okay to go 'off topic' or answer questions not directly pertaining to the interview questions, and this may partly facilitate the rapport-building process. Although it is not specific to education research, a seminal discussion on rapport in interviews can be found in Ann Oakley's work (2005).

Unstructured interviews

It may appear tempting to use an unstructured interview – after all, very little preparation is required beyond thinking about the broad themes you want to discuss and hoping the participant has something to say on them. If you have very chatty participants this type of approach may work. On the other hand, if your participants are less forthcoming you will still need a prepared range of probes to elicit the information. During semi-structured interviews it is not unusual to ask additional questions to subsequent participants if you feel that particular themes are emerging, but you may feel this is inappropriate if you are using an unstructured approach. Unstructured interviews are more likely to produce disparate accounts and themes, which may create difficulties in the analysis stage (although you may want to explore a grounded theory approach; see Strauss and Corbin, 1998 for more information).

Structured interviews

On the other hand, structured interviews require the same questions to be asked of each interview participant. The answers given tend to be very short and to the point – the questions do not allow for any flexibility. The focus is on the uniformity of question delivery, and in many ways a structured interview can be likened to reading out a questionnaire to a participant. This approach is underpinned by beliefs in objectivity and researcher neutrality. Interviewers who conduct this style of interview are less concerned about rapport. If a participant asked the interviewer a question, they are less likely to engage in a conversation and may respond with answers such as, 'Sorry, I'm just here to ask you questions'. Additionally, the interviewer is likely to be only concerned with answers to their pre-planned questions, and will not give opportunities for the participant to add additional information or thoughts. This type of interview may be used in survey research.

Interview participants and power dynamics

You may interview a range of participants within educational settings: teachers, senior management, governors, children, support staff and parents. It is important to reflect on your own identity and how this will influence the interview process. Deborah Youdell explores how interviews can be shaped by the identities of both the researcher and the participants. She gives a reflective account of interviewing students and teachers at an Australian high school (2006: 514–515). The range of possible participants is likely to shape the interviews, particularly in relation to the power dynamics involved in interview research. The power dynamics within the interview process can have a real impact on what questions you feel that you can ask, as well as the types of responses you are likely to get from participants.

ACTIVITY

These are a useful set of questions to consider before you start the interviews:

- Are you older or younger than the participants?
- Do you have more or less experience within the educational field?
- Do you have any 'common ground' with the participants? For example, are you a parent or a student teacher?
- Is your gender, ethnicity and socio-economic background the same or different?
- Do you see yourself as an 'outsider' or an 'insider'? Are you part of the educational community you are researching? Are you looking in on the educational community from the point of view of someone who is not closely aligned with this group?
- Do the participants see you as an 'outsider' or an 'insider'? How do you think this will affect the interview process?

Interviewing principles

The ways in which you deal with these power dynamics will be shaped by your own beliefs about research and how these translate into your interviewing principles. Oakley (1981) highlighted that interviewing is a masculine paradigm which does not include characteristics such as emotion and sensitivity. She was not inclined to continue interviewing women as 'objects', thereby not understanding them as individuals. Although this unwillingness arose from Oakley's moral and ethical convictions, it is also significant methodologically. Interviewing has been widely used by feminist researchers and has often been regarded as the most appropriate method for 'producing the kind of knowledge that feminists wish to make available as being more in keeping with the politics of doing research as a feminist' (Maynard and Purvis, 1994: 11). Ann Oakley moved away from traditions in interviewing which were seen as ways of avoiding bias – for example, not answering questions from interviewees or sharing experiences which would facilitate rapport-building (Oakley, 2005: 226). As Oakley states (1981: 49), there is 'no intimacy without reciprocity', meaning that unless the interviewer shares their own identity and experiences with the interviewee, it is unfair to expect participants to share such information about themselves. Oakley's research was about women becoming mothers, but her belief in a non-hierarchical, non-exploitative interviewing process lends itself to educational research.

The use of interviews in a non-hierarchical way does enable the development of a more democratised research process, and facilitate the formation of more reciprocal relationships between the researcher and the participants. The term 'conversational partner' (Rubin and Rubin, 2005: 14) allows for the interviewee to shape the topic and the direction of the research themes, suggesting ways in which the interviewer and interviewee may work together to develop shared understandings. The concept of a 'conversational partner' captures the idea of a non-exploitative, non-hierarchical relationship. The term 'conversational partner' also emphasises the uniqueness of each person with whom you talk, his or her distinct knowledge, and the different ways in which he or she interacts with you (Rubin and Rubin, 2005: 14). Sometimes principles of non-hierarchical and reciprocal relations can be difficult to apply, especially when this does not reflect participants' wider experiences within society. A case in point would be interviews with children.

Interviews with children

The idea that children should be given a voice is a relatively new one. Historically children have been subsumed within the 'family' in sociological research. However, a new sociology of childhood has emerged in the last thirty years, particularly through the work of Allison James, Chris Jenks and Alan Prout (James, Jenks and Prout, 2001). Based on this acknowledgement that children have their own voice, it is now much more common to see research which has explored childrens' perspectives. In addition, the advent of the United Nations Convention on the Rights of the Child (UNCRC) (1989) has meant that children have begun to be seen as individuals in their own right. However, adults clearly have more power in society than children, and this is particularly apparent within a school setting.

This power dynamic will have a significant impact when interviewing children (Eder and Fingerson, 2002). Experienced researchers are more likely to carry out interviews with children, so do not be surprised if your research supervisor is hesitant about you conducting interviews with children and advises against this. Nevertheless, if you do get ethical clearance to interview children there are a variety of strategies which can enable children to feel more comfortable:

- Interacting with children informally in a natural setting, such as the classroom, before carrying out an interview.
- Using language which children are familiar with, and avoiding technical terms.
- Pictures, toys and other practical resources are helpful in making young children feel comfortable and encouraging discussion.
- Draw on what children already know. For example, they may not be able to tell you their parents' occupations, but perhaps they can say where they work or what types of tasks their job entails.
- Be patient. It can sometimes take children a while to articulate what they want to say, especially with an unfamiliar adult.

ACTIVITY

A Masters student undertakes interviews with teaching assistants in their own homes, asking about their training and qualifications. The student is a young white female and the teaching assistants she interviews are also white females, but they are perhaps twenty to thirty years older. The student does not mention that she is also a teacher.

- Who do you think had the most power during the interviews?
- Why do you think the student did not tell the teaching assistants she was a teacher?

The view that researchers occupy a more powerful position than participants has long been a concern within research (Olesen in Denzin and Lincoln, 1994). However, this debate has evolved as researchers have looked more closely at the relationship between interviewers and participants. The image of the powerless respondent has been superseded by notions that power is only partial, transitory and often shifts between the researcher and the participants throughout the research process. Fine and Weiss (in Denzin and Lincoln, 2000: 115) suggest that 'they [the participants] recognised that we could take their stories, their concerns and their worries to audiences, policy makers and the public in ways that they themselves could not because they would not be listened to'. This highlights that it is possible that participants recognise and exploit power inequalities within the research process.

Practical aspects of interviewing

This section of the chapter will be divided into five subheadings:

- Interview questions
- Technique
- Location
- Recording
- Transcribing.

Interview questions

It is often a good idea to start with questions which do not put the interview participant under too much pressure – for example, some relatively straightforward introductory questions such as why they are studying this course, where did they do their teacher training or what is their favourite subject at school. You want your interview participants to answer your questions as fully and as honestly as possible. However, the way that you ask questions can influence their responses. For example, if you asked 'Why do you think boys present more challenging behaviour in the classroom?' this would tell us something about the attitude of the interviewer and the types of response they are looking for. This may put pressure on the interview participant to agree with the interviewer and say things that they do not necessarily believe. Therefore, when you are designing your interview schedule check that you are not unfairly influencing the responses of your participants.

Interview technique

Sometimes one of the hardest aspects of conducting an interview is not saying too much. It can be difficult because you often feel that you should not make the interview a one-sided affair, and that you want the interview participant to know that you are interested in what he or she is saying. However, when you are transcribing your interview data you do not want to find that you actually said more than the participant!

It is important to listen carefully, and perhaps listening is a skill that we often take for granted when in reality we are not always very good at it. There are lots of ways you can show the interview participant that you are listening and therefore that you are interested in what they are saying. This may simply be with the verbal cues you give them: eye contact, a nod of the head or an encouraging smile. Sometime you may ask them to clarify or expand a point. This is really important because the point may fit with the tentative themes that are emerging from your interviews. Alternatively, you may simply not understand what they mean, and if this is the case during the interview itself it is unlikely to be any clearer when you analyse the data. Therefore, do not be afraid to ask for clarification if needed. If you are interested in reading more about different interview techniques you may find the books by Lincoln and Guba (1985) and Rubin and Rubin (2005) helpful.

It is also useful to give the interviewee a bit of time at the end. Ask them if there is anything they would like to add – maybe something that they feel is important, but which they haven't had chance to raise during the interview. Often at this stage it is tempting to think that the participant is unlikely to have anything to add. Initially they may say 'not really, I can't think of anything'. However, given a brief pause to reflect, it is surprising how many participants have some additional information to impart. Don't worry if they haven't, though – if you use the 'member checking' procedure, participants often have something to add at a later date. It is also useful to give the interview participant your contact details in case they do remember something later.

Location

The ideal room for interviewing should be quiet and private. Hopefully this will provide a relaxed and informal setting in which to conduct the interviews. This is particularly important because you will wish to preserve your participants' anonymity and confidentiality. It is better to try and arrange a time for the interview when the participant has enough time to talk to you fully. It is good practice to reiterate why you are carrying out the research and what your research is about. It is also helpful to double-check that it is okay to record the interview. Also, from a practical standpoint it is very difficult to transcribe data when there is a lot of background noise – so shut the window! However, if you are interviewing children it may not be appropriate to be in an enclosed space alone with them, and you may wish to leave the door open and ensure that you are clearly visible. This contradicts our earlier advice about location, but it is certainly something you will need to consider in your research.

Recording interviews

Digital voice recorders (dictaphones) can be bought for approximately £30. However, if you have a smartphone it is worth looking to see if it has a voice recording facility. Test your digital recorder before you start the interview. Record yourself speaking – it is a little eerie listening to yourself saying 'hello, hello', but at least you can be confident that:

a   You know how to use the recorder

b   It is recording

c   The volume is correct.

There is nothing worse than finding out that the hour you have spent talking to someone has not recorded (it has been known to happen!), or that you can barely hear what is being said. In addition, check batteries and mains sockets. The advantage of having a plug-in recorder is that you know the batteries won't run out. The disadvantage is that you may not be in a location where a mains socket is readily available or accessible. The key message here is *be organised*. Preparation is everything to guarantee a successful interview recording.

Not all participants will feel comfortable being recorded, and it is important to double-check this before you begin the interview. If participants do not wish to be recorded you may be able to take notes during the interview (so remember to bring a notepad and pen). Once you have typed up these notes you can then ask the participant to confirm, amend or add to them.

Transcribing

Once you have recorded an interview it can then be transcribed. Transcription is the process of listening to a voice recording and typing the words verbatim (word for word). This can be a tricky skill to learn – it helps if you are a quick typist (or alternatively if you can slow the voice recording down to make it easier to type). Sometimes in bigger research projects a professional transcriber may be employed. However, in small-scale projects it is more likely that the person carrying out the research will transcribe their own data. The advantage of this is that you can often start to analyse the data as you go, as you think about what you are typing. It also ensures that you really 'know' your data.

It is also helpful to check the final transcript with the participant. Email the file to your participants and ask them to add or change any aspects that they are unhappy with. Alternatively, if you have conducted the interview with children it is worth sitting down and checking it through with them. The advantage of this is that you can be sure that the participant feels that the information is valid; they may want to add more detail, and perhaps most important, they are happy for you to use their words.

Chapter summary

Overall interviewing can be a rich way to gain insights into aspects of educational experiences and perspectives. To ensure that the interview process is successful you need to consider how to develop a rapport with your participants. The power dynamics within the interview process will play a large role in shaping the success of your interview and you need to minimise these power differentials as far as possible. Make sure you are really organised in terms of equipment and suitable locations. Most importantly, you need to be appreciative of the fact that participants are giving up their time and perhaps sharing very personal stories.

Further reading

Fontana, A. and Frey, J. (1994) 'Interviewing the art of science'. In N.K. Denzin and Y.S. Lincoln (eds), *The SAGE Handbook of Qualitative Research*. Thousand Oaks: SAGE, 361–376.

■　This is an excellent and accessible chapter covering in detail the fascinating history of interview research, the different types of interview and the power dimensions associated with interviews – well worth a read!

14

Focus group interviews

Introduction

Focus group interviews are a popular way of collecting qualitative data from a group of people in order to explore their perceptions, opinions, beliefs or attitudes. These interviews differ from one-to-one discussions (as discussed in Chapter 13) because the researcher asks questions in an interactive group setting and participants respond by entering into group discussions with one another. This chapter begins by looking at the nature and possible uses of focus groups and considering how they differ from one-to-one interviews. The chapter also looks at the advantages and limitations of focus group interviews. The practical and ethical considerations that need to be kept in mind when designing and conducting focus group interviews will also be explored. These include how to decide on the sample, the number of interviews and the size of the groups, deciding on the level of researcher involvement during the discussion, preparing the interview guide, and recording and transcribing the data. The chapter will also consider the issue of group dynamics and the public versus private aspects of group-based research.

What are focus groups?

Focus groups often get a bad press, with commentators lamenting the modern culture of opinion gathering, especially in the domain of politics. Focus groups may or may not be an ideal tool as a form of political representation and participation in democratic life, but their function as a mediating forum between citizenship and consumerism should not be confused with their role in educational and social research generally. Asking members of the public if a new washing machine is any good or whether a state allows too much immigration is a far cry from the role that focus groups can play in carefully planned and thought-out research.

As Morgan (1997: 4) helpfully points out, focus groups have been a part of social research for quite some time, with group interviews playing a notable role in applied social research programmes during World War II, including 'efforts to examine the persuasiveness of propaganda efforts and the effectiveness of training materials for the troops'. Morgan also goes some way to defining what a focus group is when he states that it is the 'researcher's interest that proves the focus, whereas the data themselves come from the group interaction' (Morgan, 1997: 6). Researchers use focus groups based on a desire to home in on a specific issue, case or instance – like a micro-version of the case study approach (see Chapter 9).

The use of focus groups

Litosseliti (2003: 18) provides a concise list of what focus groups are useful for (based on a review of other work on the subject):

- *Discovering new information* (for example about a new product) and *consolidating old knowledge* (for example, examining people's habits).

- Obtaining a number of *different perspectives* on the same topic, in the participants' own words.

- Gaining information on participants' *views, attitudes, beliefs, responses, motivations and perceptions* on a topic – *why* people think or feel the way they do.

- Examining participants' *shared understandings* of everyday life and the *everyday use of language and culture among particular groups.*

- *Brainstorming and generating ideas*, with participants discussing different angles of a problem and possibly helping to identify solutions.

- Gaining insights into the ways in which individuals are influenced by others in a group situation (*group dynamics*).

- *Exploring controversial issues and complex or sensitive topics* [emphasis in the original].

These are all excellent uses of focus groups, but it is important to highlight two other aspects that, perhaps more than the others, make the focus group an attractive option for researchers. These are the fact that *more* data can be gathered in *less* time (in comparison with interviews, for example), and the notion that the group aspect provides a potential basis for alternative viewpoints to be heard *at the same time* (more on these in the 'advantages' section below).

ACTIVITY

Think about the uses of focus groups mentioned above. Are you drawn to any of these in particular? For example, can you visualise the use of focus groups as a way of exploring a controversial issue in education? You may already have an idea in mind for your research, and it could be the case that this approach provides a close fit to your research objectives. If so, write down why this might be the case. Why would gathering people together in a group scenario work better than an alternative method?

Organisation of focus groups

When planning how to organise a focus group, the following should be considered carefully:

Sample   Take care over your choice of focus group participants. For example, if your groups are designed to explore issues previously identified in a set of questionnaires, the focus group participants should reflect the demographic make-up of your original sample as accurately as possible (if you want your focus group to be representative). Variables such as gender, class and race should normally be taken into account, alongside any other specific variables of significance to the research project.

At the same time, you may wish to focus purely on those who made similar remarks in relation to a specific question (why did you want to go to university, for example). It may be the case that full representation proves impossible. This is not unusual, but you should acknowledge the limitations that this places on the findings and analysis of your research.

Sample size   It is often tempting to include as many people as possible in a focus group, but care needs to be taken when deciding on the size of the group. Too many people can often prove intimidating for the members, reducing the chance that they will 'open up' and provide the kinds of data that you may be looking for. As the group's moderator it is also more of a challenge for you to control the group and steer it in the direction you want it to go – people can sometimes treat focus groups as either some form of therapy, or an opportunity to complain about whatever topic is under discussion. As Gibbs recommends (1997: 4), an ideal focus group size would be somewhere between six and ten participants.

How to conduct a focus group   It pays to think creatively when designing a focus group. Such groups do not simply have to take the format of question and response – there can be visual and aural elements as well, depending on the focus. This is particularly useful when working with children and when discussing more challenging issues (for example, relating to teaching performance). Creative ways of conducting focus groups include:

- Using artwork as a way of creating activities for people to collaborate on
- Presenting readings or asking the group to deliver them
- Using debating topics from recent newspaper articles
- Asking the group to complete an assignment before participation in the group.

So long as the participants know what they are to expect from the group, the possibilities are endless – so long as they are tailored to the aims of the research.

Don't forget to record the names of participants. It is essential that a note should be kept of the identity of each group participant. This information can easily get lost if names are not connected to voices during and immediately after the recording of the interaction. Also, ensure that you have the individuals' demographic details. When recording the group interaction, ensure that the microphone and recorder are positioned to capture the voices of all participants. It is also a good idea to use two devices to record. Name badges can also be useful – it might sound basic, but it will help you to recall who said what afterwards.

Advantages of focus groups

Data Capture   One of the obvious benefits of using focus groups is their capacity to gather together a large quantity of research data in a short period of time (Gibbs, 1997: 2). They are invaluable in this regard, since no other method can offer the same immediacy or the same potential for the researcher to influence the data collection as it happens. Although full control of this process is out of the hands of the moderator (see below), it is still the case that the focus group scenario can allow the researcher the opportunity to query and home in on particular aspects of the discussion, thereby making for a more effective 'focus' on the research topic.

Multiplicity of viewpoints   Questionnaires can provide multiple viewpoints, but never at one and the same time. One of the major advantages of focus groups is that several opinions can be publicly expressed at the same time. This means that focus groups have the added value of generating discussion, while also encouraging participants to critically assess the veracity of their own viewpoints. It also means that the researcher is in a unique position to gauge the validity of numerous arguments and opinions, thereby allowing for some distance to be maintained from the research focus. It may be the case that such a diversity of voices can result in an increase in the complexity surrounding the focus of the research, but this is generally no bad thing.

Critical engagement   Focus groups have been known to provide the basis for more critical engagement with the topic at hand. Of course, this may prove highly beneficial in a sector as politically and emotionally charged as education. As Kitzinger points out (1995: 300):

> A method that facilitates the expression of criticism and the exploration of different types of solutions is invaluable if the aim of research is to improve services. Such a method is especially appropriate when working with particular disempowered patient populations who are often reluctant to give negative feedback or may feel that any problems result from their own inadequacies.

Disadvantages of focus groups

Group bias   It may be the case that some participants monopolise the discussion, or they may be more dominant members of the group. This can result in the focus of the discussion shifting in their direction, meaning that the findings can be seen as skewed. This is a challenging scenario to manage, and it is up to the researcher to negotiate this situation. It is rare that you will get a group (in whatever context) in which some members are not more vocal or dominant than others. While you want these individuals to present their opinions and experiences, they are just that: personal opinions and experiences. In order for a focus group to be more than a glorified interview, its structure must allow for every voice in the group to be heard. Otherwise you are missing a valuable opportunity to gather information.

This is another reason why you should take care over who you have in the group, especially when it comes to their shared characteristics or their differences. As Gibbs (1997: 4) warns:

> if a group is too heterogeneous, whether in terms of gender or class, or in terms of professional and 'lay' perspectives, the differences between participants can make a considerable impact on their contributions. Alternatively, if a group is homogenous with regards to specific characteristics, diverse opinions and experiences may not be revealed. Participants need to feel comfortable with each other.

Loss of anonymity   It is also important to consider the 'public' nature of focus groups. Regardless of whether or not the participants know each other beforehand, the lack of anonymity in a focus group undoubtedly affects the behaviour and the attitudes of the participants towards the research process – a fact that could be considered to be one of the main drawbacks of this form of research. Care needs to be taken to steer the conversation away from conventional wisdom or opinions that are easily accepted by other members of the group. It should not be forgotten that people can be quite good at saying one thing while thinking something entirely different. The unfortunate truth is that, as the researcher, you may never be able to tell the difference. This is true also for individual interview scenarios, but it is arguably more the case for groups because of their public nature.

Singularity   Another drawback of focus groups is their singular nature. If you find that you did not collect the data you wanted, for whatever reason, it is very difficult to repeat the same focus group again. Even if it were possible to reassemble the group, the participants would probably not take kindly to the extra commitment (in any case, the cost of organisation and participation could act as a barrier). This is why it is vital that the design of the focus group is constructed with some care, especially concerning the kinds of outcomes that you desire from the research. All too often researchers can find that focus groups run away with themselves, leaving simple conversation or description in the place of decent research findings.

Examples of focus groups in educational research

Focus group example 1: E-learning and access to university

Source: Barraket, J. (2004) 'E-learning and access: getting behind the hype'. In M. Osborne, J. Gallacher and B. Crossan (eds), *Researching widening access to lifelong learning: Issues and approaches to international research*, pp. 191–202. London: RoutledgeFalmer.

Jo Barraket's study is a report on a federally-funded research programme in Australia. The objective of the research was 'to investigate the access and equity issues associated with the increasing use of ICT in learning programmes' at the University of Technology in Sydney (UTS). A major topic in Australia and elsewhere, Barraket's study set out to 'identify differences in access to, and use of, ICT between students from government targeted equity groups and a control group'.

There were two phases to the research, and it was in the first phase that the researchers conducted a series of focus groups with students from various equity groups. Student equity groups, as defined by the Australian government, include Aboriginal and Torres Strait Islander students, students with a disability, and several other groups. Twenty-seven students in total participated in the focus group phase. The information from the focus group study was used to 'develop an effective survey instrument for phase two, and to provide a rich "snapshot" of information on the ICT experiences of a small number of students'. Phase two built on the findings of the focus groups and consisted of a detailed survey administered to students in forty-four classes, which returned 1323 completed questionnaires. Overall, the study allowed Barraket and her team to conceptualise effective E-learning as 'part of a broader strategy of access'.

Focus group example 2: Researching the impact of accountability in schools

Source: Murphy, M. and Skillen, P. (2013) 'The politics of school regulation: Using Habermas to research educational accountability'. In M. Murphy (ed), *Social theory and education research: Understanding Foucault, Habermas, Bourdieu and Derrida*, pp. 84–97. London: Routledge.

This second example took a different approach to the first, in that the focus groups formed the second phase of the research in the light of the findings from an original set of interviews with teachers (as well as nurses and social workers) in the north of England. The aim of the research was to examine the impact of quality assurance on the work of professionals on the front line of public services. Specifically, the researchers were interested in how mechanisms such as audits and inspections impacted on the relationships between the public and public sector professionals. The research focused on the ways in which the teachers and other professionals perceived their work to be affected by the instrumental rationality at the heart of the new bureaucracy of quality assurance – a form of regulation that public-sector professionals, at least in the UK, are very familiar with.

In total, nine interviews and three focus groups were carried out, equally split between the three professions. The focus groups were organised after relevant themes had been identified in the individual interviews. All the interviews and focus groups were conducted in the same borough in the northwest of England. Given that three different professional groups were involved in the study, the research required different strategies to access the respondents. In order for access to be obtained to subjects who could provide adequate narratives around accountability and its consequences, more experienced personnel were recruited to take part. Focus groups as a data collection exercise proved invaluable in the research, since they were the perfect route via which some of the key themes arising in the original interviews – time management, interaction with pupils, the role of legislation – could be explored in much greater depth.

ACTIVITY

Consider the two examples mentioned above. Does the use of focus groups in these forms of research make sense? In particular, can you understand the reasoning behind the timing of the focus groups in the research design? Applying the points made earlier in the chapter, what kinds of benefits and drawbacks do you see being attached to these uses of focus groups?

Other issues to consider

The power of group dynamics: Group dynamics are a complex but fragile entity – the researcher must be on his or her guard when it comes to the invisible but potent strength of the group. There is also a danger that findings can be skewed to such an extent that they lack validity in the research process. Group dynamics must be considered alongside the demographic makeup of the group. Whether the group is comprised of professionals (such as teachers, support assistants, guidance counsellors etc.) or non-education professionals (parents, pupils) has a bearing on how focus groups should be conducted; it is not unknown for professionals in group settings to monopolise the conversation with concerns over current employment and working conditions, even when the discussion is in the context of pupil learning and the curriculum. These diversions may or may not have justifiable connections with the subject at hand, but the original purpose of the group (i.e. its focus) can sometimes get lost in the shuffle of argumentation.

The public and the private? The dilemma over the public nature of focus groups parallels to some extent the dilemma at the heart of the case study approach. Instead of the trade-off between depth and breadth, however, focus groups have a trade-off between the public and private – i.e. what you gain on one hand you lose on the other. At the same time, the boundaries between public and private are not so clear cut – an issue highlighted by Wilson (1997: 218):

> Is an individual in–depth interview a 'private' space inhabited by interviewer and respondent in which the latter may talk about private thoughts and behaviour? And in contrast must a focus group necessarily be construed as 'public' in which responses will be guarded, respondents circumspect and voices less authentic? Our evidence would suggest that there is no clear–cut answer: respondents and researchers do vary, as does the quality of data generated from both methods.

Chapter summary

This chapter has detailed the nature and the various uses of focus groups in research projects, and outlined some of the issues that need to be taken into account when organising focus groups. The chapter also examined some of the benefits and drawbacks of using focus groups in educational research settings, while also providing two examples of research projects that have made use of the method (in the contexts of e-learning and access to university, and the impact of accountability in schools). The chapter concluded by raising two other issues for researchers to consider when contemplating using focus groups: the power of group dynamics, and the 'public' nature of focus group research.

Further reading

Nestel, D. *et al.* (2012): 'Benefits and challenges of focus groups in the evaluation of a new Graduate Entry Medical Programme'. *Assessment and Evaluation in Higher Education*, 37 (1), 1–17.

- ■ This paper provides a good example of the use of focus groups in practice, the authors detailing the advantages and disadvantages of such an approach when it is applied to evaluation research.

Kamberelis, G. and Dimitriadis, G. (2013) *Focus groups: From structured interviews to collective conversations*. Oxon: Routledge.

- ■ George Kamberelis and Greg Dimitriadis's book *Focus groups: From structured interviews to collective conversations* (2013) is a conceptual and practical introduction to focus group research. It provides a comprehensive overview of the nature of focus groups, political and activist uses of focus groups, practical ways to run a successful focus group, effective analysis of focus group data, and contemporary threats to focus groups.

Liamputtong, P. (2011) *Focus group methodology: Principles and practice*. London: Sage.

- ■ Pranee Liamputtong's book *Focus group methodology* (2011) provides an introductory text which leads readers through the process of designing a focus group study, from conducting interviews to analysing data and presenting the findings. It is of particular interest to researchers who are working with different social groups, such as women, men, older people, children and ethnic minority groups, and anybody who is engaging in cross-cultural research.

15

Observations

Introduction

This chapter outlines and compares some of the distinctive forms that observation might take – for instance, participant and non-participant, overt and covert, structured and unstructured. It identifies some of the chief reasons for the popularity of observation as a method in educational research, and highlights some of the technical considerations that frame how observations are carried out. It goes on to consider different approaches to recording data from observations. Finally, the chapter discusses the main difficulties for the researcher who chooses observation – namely, issues of access, viability, visibility and the 'observer effect'.

What is observation?

Observation involves looking and collecting data by systematically recording interactions between people, patterns of behaviour, speech, rituals, routines and/or environments. Therefore, unlike other primary methods of data collection, observation does not depend on the respondents providing information to the researcher. Rather, the researcher gathers data from naturally-occurring situations, viewing social reality as it actually takes place. Many of the most influential pieces of educational research have utilised a variety of observational approaches to uncover characteristics of learning, culture and identity. For example, Paul Willis' exploration of 'the lads' in *Learning to Labour* (1978), Stephen Ball's *Beachside Comprehensive* (1981), Heidi Mirza's *Young, Female and Black* (1992) and Mairtin Mac an Ghaill's *The Making of Men* (1994) all used observational methods.

Why use observations?

Observations are an attractive method of data collection in educational research for many reasons. Among the three most important advantages are:

■ **Ecological validity** – observations provide the researcher with a direct view of behaviour in natural settings. The researcher can develop observations with little experimental control, so that what takes place would do so with or without the researcher's presence. This leads to high levels of ecological validity – the researcher can (quite) confidently claim a correspondence between what they observe and what really happens. For instance, a classroom observation is likely to provide a more accurate picture of the strengths and weaknesses of a lesson than an interview with a teacher or a survey of the pupils.

■ **Combines with other methods** – in the previous example, the classroom observation will almost certainly increase the validity of the survey or interview – the presence of the researcher can minimise exaggeration in subsequent responses. If observations take place prior to other methods, they can help inform the topics and structure of questioning. Used after other methods, observations can be used as a check on the validity of previous responses. Exploring the similarities and divergences between 'what you said' and 'what you did' are especially fertile grounds for the educational researcher.

■ **Uncovering the 'taken-for-granted' and 'unexpected'** – more than any other method, observations enable the researcher to enter the research site without prior classification or categorisation. This makes observations more likely to uncover the unexpected, which is especially beneficial in grounded theory. Likewise, much of our behaviour is habitual and involuntary, and therefore it is difficult to articulate or explain during an interview. Importantly, observations help the researcher to identify what is 'taken-for-granted', what 'goes-without-saying', or what an 'insider' knows.

■ **Gathering data that other methods cannot reach** – observations can enable the researcher to access settings, groups and events that other methods are unable to. For instance, very small children are unable to complete a survey and might be difficult to interview, but it is possible to observe them playing and interacting in playschool or nursery.

Technical considerations

Observational research takes a wide variety of forms, each producing very different data and each with its own set of strengths and limitations. Among the decisions which the researcher utilising observation must make are:

■ How to gain access to the research site

■ What, who and when observations take place

■ Finding the right place to observe

■ What and how to record

■ How to manage and handle data

■ How to leave the research site.

These technical decisions are largely shaped by the researcher's approach to observation, including the researcher's role, position and closeness to the research site, as well as levels of involvement, disclosure and structure.

Different roles in observation

Gold (1958) outlined an influential continuum that distinguished between observer roles:

- Complete participant
- Participant as observer
- Observer as participant
- Complete observer.

At one end of the spectrum is the *complete participant* – a total insider who conceals her identity from the other members of the group. One famous example of this approach was James Patrick's *A Glasgow Gang Observed* (1973), where the researcher became a full member to directly experience the language, rituals and behaviour of a gang. At the other end, the *complete observer* is entirely detached and unknown to the group. An example of this might be the researcher who places a video camera in a classroom to record interactions. In between, the *participant as observer* might normally have a connection to the group that exists outside the research. Theirs is a partial membership, like that of a classroom assistant who writes a fieldwork diary of her observations at the end of each week. Likewise, the *observer as participant* is also a partial member of the group, although this membership is not natural or normal. Typically this is the kind of role an Ofsted inspector might have within the classroom.

Gold's continuum starts to demonstrate that there are a number of alternative approaches you need to consider if you are to employ an observation method.

Participant or non-participant

Perhaps the most important decision is the extent to which the researcher takes part in the activities of the group or research site. Ethnographers, as we saw in an earlier chapter, believe in the value of full immersion within the group being studied, and the importance of experiencing the world as the group members do, so they tend to favour participant observation. This form of observation is commonplace in educational research, when researchers observe an educational setting they already inhabit as a teacher, classroom assistant, school manager or student.

Of course, there is a danger that by participating, the researcher might influence behaviour within the research site. Because of this risk, other educational research employs a non-participant approach, where the researcher observes behaviour but does not take part in it. In adopting this approach, the researcher might find it easier to record observations, but conversely she might find it more difficult to observe what she wants to.

Covert or overt

A second important decision is whether or not the group should be aware that they are being observed. If the group members are aware, the research is overt; if they are unaware, it is covert. Both approaches give rise to important difficulties. An overt observation is likely to impact on the group's behaviour – pupils and teachers are likely to alter their behaviour in response to the presence of an observer. A covert approach provokes ethical concerns such as deception and a lack of informed consent.

Naturalistic or artificial

In general, observations in educational research aim to look at interactions as they normally take place, i.e. as they naturally occur. Unlike other methods, observations allow the researcher to see activities and behaviour as they really happen, so researchers are likely to try to minimise the contamination of what they observe. Nevertheless, if a researcher is interested in a specific aspect of educational activity, she might attempt to contrive an artificial scenario to observe how different people respond. For example, a teacher-researcher might choose a particular educational resource to understand how different pupils respond to it. This approach blurs the boundary between observation and field experiment (see Chapter 2).

Structured or unstructured

As we saw in the previous two chapters, interviews might take either a structured, unstructured or semi-structured form. Likewise, observations might take various forms, from entirely unstructured on the one hand to fully structured on the other. Unstructured observations mean that the researcher starts with a blank sheet of paper and records what she observes, often in the form of a fieldwork diary. Structured observations generally use an observation schedule or a tally chart (see below) to identify pre-specified patterns of behaviour. Of course, there is a whole continuum in between, and many researchers who employ observations will combine a fieldwork diary with a schedule.

Gathering quantitative or qualitative data

While the famous educational research examples mentioned above used observations to produce qualitative data, the method is equally able to produce quantitative data. Close scrutiny of a group's behaviour can elicit rich, detailed 'thick' description. However, it is equally possible to use observations to identify trends, patterns and comparisons – for example, the number of times a teacher communicates with girls versus boys, or the number of 'positive' interactions compared with 'negative' ones.

Reflective or neutral

While the majority of current educational researchers would deny the possibility of researcher neutrality or objectivity, many observations will try to minimise the researcher effect − for instance, by specifying observational criteria or by using a number of different observers. Others will adopt a reflexive approach, considering the impact of their own values and positions on the patterns of behaviour they look for and the ways they interpret them. The latter approach will generally make use of reflective fieldwork diaries, where researchers record their observations and their thoughts on those observations.

Closeness or distance

Similarly, some observers will choose to maintain a detachment or distance from their observations, perhaps by making use of one-way mirrors, video cameras or other 'surveillance' technologies in order to minimise their impact on the research site. Others, believing in the significance of studying the minutiae of social interactions, will favour a mode of observation that gets them as close as possible.

ACTIVITY

Different approaches to observation are more suited to particular topics and sites of research. Draw out the following table and complete the boxes by identifying examples of educational settings and topics that would be appropriate in each case. Now identify one strength and one limitation of each approach.

	Example	Strength	Limitation
Participant			
Non-participant			
Covert			
Overt			
Structured			
Unstructured			
Quantitative			
Qualitative			
Naturalistic			
Artificial			
Reflective			
Neutral			
Closeness			
Distance			

Now think about your own research topic. If you were to employ an observational method, which of these options would you choose, and why? (Remember, in most cases this choice is a matter of degree rather than an either/or decision.)

Recording observational data

There are various ways a researcher might choose to record her observations, depending on her topic of research, her access to the research site, and the kind of data she intends to gather. If the researcher does not know what she plans to observe prior to commencing observations, she might use:

- **Video recording** – creates a permanent record of the observation, and can mean the 'observer' does not have to be present ('indirect observation') which might minimise the extent that the researcher contaminates the research site. However, the presence of a researcher with a camera can prove rather inhibiting, and a camera attached to a wall or tripod can only observe what takes place in front of it.

- **Audio recording** – again, this produces a permanent record and means the data collection is not limited to what the researcher can write during an observation or remember after it. A tape recorder might be less inhibiting than a video camera, but tape-recorded observations are unable to capture anything silent or visual, notably non-verbal communication.

- **(Reflective) fieldwork diary** – perhaps the most common means of recording participant observation and ethnographic research, fieldwork notes or diaries are written accounts of observations. These are likely to be detailed and include the viewpoints and feelings of the researcher, making them more subjective than either of the above. Non-participants might write their diaries during observations; participants might leave the research site at regular intervals to update their diary, or they might write at the end of each day or week.

If the researcher intends to develop a more structured and systematic approach to observation, she is likely to develop an observation schedule. This involves operationalising or 'coding' behaviour or events, specifically listing what to focus on and how to define it. An influential example of coding in education research was developed by Flanders (1970). His list of 'interaction analysis categories' was an observational tool to code or classify verbal communication among pupils and teachers in the classroom, with two main categories of 'teacher talk' and 'pupil talk' and ten subdivisions.

- **Event or interval sampling** – involves recording the number of times particular events take place, or making notes about observations at specific time intervals – for instance, every fifteen minutes. Event sampling might record 'critical incidents' such as examples of disruptive behaviour or pupils receiving negative feedback.

- **Checklists or tally charts** – event or interval sampling usually involves developing checklists or tally charts to produce quantitative data. The table opposite illustrates how a tally chart can help the observer identify patterns – in this case, to examine the use of questions in the classroom, see Table 15.1.

TABLE 15.1 Example of a tally chart

Teacher asks specific pupil a question	///////
Teacher asks question to whole class	//////////
Pupil asks teacher question	////
Pupil asks other pupils question	/

■ **Rating scales** – enable the researcher to make judgements about activities or events. For example, they might rate classroom behaviour on a scale from 1 to 5, with 1 being 'exceptional' and 5 'unacceptable'. Alternatively, as the example below illustrates, a ratings scale might allow the researcher to evaluate classroom activities across a continuum:

TABLE 15.2 Example of a ratings scale

	1	2	3	4	5	
Pupil-centred						Teacher-centred
Exciting						Boring
Active learning						Passive learning

ACTIVITY

You are going to conduct a non-participant observation of classroom behaviour, contrasting three approaches:

■ Event sample
■ Rating scale
■ Fieldwork diary.

Firstly, draw out your observation schedule and ratings chart (you need to consider what you will be looking for). Now, identify a film or TV programme set inside a classroom. Try out your three approaches to recording observations – each for ten minutes.

Compare the data you collect. How is it similar and different? Which do you prefer? Why?

Some difficulties for the observational researcher

Despite their obvious appeal to the educational researcher, observations carry with them a number of difficulties:

■ **Lack of reliability** – data gathered via observations is less reliable than many other methods. If a different researcher observed the same group on a different occasion, they would almost certainly collect different data. To maximise reliability, research might use more than one observer and/or repeated observations on a number of occasions.

- **Observational bias** – similarly, what a researcher 'sees', as well as how they interpret what they see, is inevitably partial and subjective. The researcher brings with them their own values and expectations, and these frame what, when, where and how they observe. To militate against this bias, some researchers develop systematic tools such as observation schedules to add scientific rigour to the method. They might focus on recording 'low-inference' behaviour (like occurrences of teachers asking open-ended questions or praising learners) rather than 'high-inference' behaviour (like instances of teacher kindness or learner creativity). Other researchers take the opposite approach, developing personal and reflexive accounts of their own position and the ways in which this impacts on their research.

- **Gaining entry, maintaining access and exiting** – one of the more difficult tasks for the observer is accessing the research site. This is especially difficult when attempting observation of a 'closed' group or space such as a school gang or a staffroom. Once they are in, the researcher needs to maintain their position, not causing any disruption or other adverse effects. In covert observation, this entails not arousing suspicion. Finally, they need to find a way to leave. Strong attachments might develop, and these can result in emotional discomfort for both the researcher and the observed participants as the fieldwork comes to an end. To avoid such difficulties, people who already occupy a position within the research site frequently undertake observations in education.

- **Observer effect** – anyone who has sat in a class during an Ofsted inspection will know that people behave differently when they are being observed. This change in behaviour is often termed the 'Hawthorn effect' after a famous study that found workers in an electricity plant became more productive because they were being observed. To minimise observer effects, researchers might communicate with people ahead of observations to assuage their fears, conduct observation over an extended period of time so that it becomes a normal part of daily life, or conceal observation by adopting a covert approach.

- **Balancing familiarity and strangeness** – in order to gain rich insights, the observer attempts to develop familiarity with the research site. The closer they can get, the greater the visibility of behaviour and events – although, of course, researchers can only view what happens in front of them. Especially in participant observation, the researcher risks 'going native', losing sight of the research as they become immersed within the group they study. Although observers require familiarity, they also need to maintain their distinct researcher identity, 'stepping inside and outside' of the research setting to uncover meanings and interpretations.

- **Ethical considerations** – observational research typically requires ethics committee approval. Covert observations are especially difficult to justify because they violate guidelines on informed consent and invasion of privacy. Observations, whether they are participant or non-participant, risk altering the natural setting. Without due care, they can impact negatively on the people who are observed. Before commencing observations researchers must consider how they will react if they witness bullying, illegal, abusive or violent behaviour. (See Chapter 21 for a full discussion of ethics in educational research.)

ACTIVITY

Read the following extract from a PhD student reflecting on her experiences of observations. Consider the following questions:

- What kind of observation techniques does Sarah employ?
- How do these techniques change during the fieldwork?
- What does Sarah identify as the main benefits of observation?
- What problems are implied in Sarah's account?
- How does Sarah's account suggest that observations work effectively when utilised alongside other methods?

Extract from Valerie Podmore and Paulette Luff's (2012) book *Observation: origins and approaches in early childhood* (p. 104):

> Having time to sit and watch children and adults go about their day-to-day play and work in a centre was a luxury. I remember the first day of observations – the clean notebook, the new document on the laptop and a sense of freedom, I suppose. I could observe what and how I wanted (within the bounds of the ethics agreement, of course). In a sense, it was overwhelming – where do I start? In the end, it began with who was in front of me, and I wrote and wrote and wrote some more.
>
> While they say first impressions count, I found that during the observation phase I had to revisit what I had noted. The longer you are in place, the more you understand why and how things happen the way they do. The reflective thinking about what I had seen and heard meant that I added both breadth and depth to the context of the observations. What seemed on the surface to be a very simple task – write down what you see and hear – I found myself immersed in asking more and more questions about why I saw and heard what I did – what other influences were there? And in that way, I found my field notes, which were initially running records, became a springboard for more ideas about what to look for. I would make a point of watching one thing for an hour, or being in a different place to watch things, or, as I became a familiar figure in the centres, interacting with children as part of observing, too.
>
> I loved observing children in my study centres, but I totally underestimated how exhausting it could be. After a day of writing down observations during the fieldwork stage of my data collection, I would arrive home, my head buzzing with impressions. Rather than the question of what to observe, at times it became a question of what not to observe. Everything seemed relevant en route to gaining a holistic understanding of the context. I realised, too, that this was not going to be possible in a month – you can start with observing the obvious activity in from of you, but the layers of complex interactions between people, places and things would take forever. The combination of photos, interviews, centre documents and the observations helped to reveal, partly at least, the complex mechanics of how centres function.
>
> Sarah Te One, February 2006

Chapter summary

Observations are the best way for a researcher to view educational activities as they actually take place, and they work especially well when combined with other methods of data collection, like interviews, documentary analysis and surveying. As we have seen during the chapter, there are a wide variety of approaches which the researcher might utilise to collect and record observations; the choice between these methods is dictated largely by practical constraints regarding the research setting, and the topic and types of data the researcher seeks. Each brings its own advantages and disadvantages. In general, observations have high levels of ecological validity and enable an 'insider' viewpoint on activities and behaviour. However, there is also a range of important limitations and difficulties, most notably in relation to bias and the danger that the observer might contaminate the research site. More than any method with the exception of experiments, the observer must be conscious of the ethical concerns that shape and constrain their practice.

Further reading

Papatheodorou, T., Luff, P. and Gill, J. (2011) *Child observation for learning and research*. Harlow: Pearson Education.

- A very readable book with useful vignettes, theory and key thinker boxes. The book makes a compelling case for the value of observation both as a research tool and as a way of enhancing our understanding of learning.

Podmore, V. and Luff, P. (2012) *Observation: Origins and approaches in early childhood*. Maidenhead: Open University Press.

- This is a great book for students interested in undertaking observation in early years settings. It provides an excellent overview of ethical considerations, relates theory to practice, and provides detailed advice on strategies and approaches.

16

Documents

Introduction

A wide variety of existing documentary materials can be obtained and analysed by education researchers, and documentary analysis can be used either as part of a research project (alongside other methods of data collection) or as the primary research tool. Analysing documents as a research tool is different to analysing documents for a literature review, which is discussed in Chapter 3. This chapter will look at a range of both written and image-based documents (such as records, government publications, diaries, photographs and drawings) and consider how and why they might be used and analysed by educational researchers. The advantages and disadvantages of using and evaluating documents will also be discussed.

What is documentary research?

Documentary-based research (sometimes called desk-based research) is just as valid as any other research method, so long as it fits the purpose of the study in question. It is an attractive method for those influenced by postmodern or poststructuralist approaches in understanding educational policy and practice, for example using the work of Michael Foucault and Jacques Derrida as ways to examine or 'deconstruct' government policy documentation. At the same time, documentary research tends to be underutilised in education and social science research generally (McCulloch, 2004). The relative invisibility of documentary research should not be taken at face value; just because other methods are currently more popular does not negate the potential that this form of research has for the modern researcher. The use of documentary research has a rich and productive history in the social sciences; as Ahmed (2010: 8) points out, it was a method greatly favoured by one of the most famous social scientists, Karl Marx:

> Marx made extensive use of documentary sources and other official reports, such as Her Majesty's Inspectors of Factories reports made between 1841 and

1867, reports by the Medical Officer of the Privy Council, Royal Commission and Inland Revenue reports, as well as reports on the employment of children in factories, the Banking Acts, the Corn Laws, the Hansard and Census Reports for England and Wales. He also referred to various Acts and Statutes, such as the Factory Regulation Acts of between 1833 and 1878. Marx also used newspapers and periodicals such as *The Times, Economist* and *New York Daily Tribune.*

The internet has made documentary research all the easier, and there are plenty of resources for your searches if you wish. What was once a sometimes laborious activity has now been made more manageable by the development of highly efficient search engines that can access documents instantly. As McCulloch (2004: 1) states, this major innovation 'has already helped to transform the nature of documentary studies and to extends its potential'. The rise of open access research, although it is still up against a firewall of 'closed' or privileged access rights, has helped to nudge documentary research ever closer to the heart of research methodologies. It should never be thought that desk-based research is in some way a poor cousin of 'field' work: oftentimes documentary research requires 'field' work anyway, in the shape of visits to museums, libraries, galleries, archive collections and so on.

So when you combine this technological revolution with its close cousin, the digital revolution, it becomes evident that the possibilities for valuable and exciting forms of documentary research are practically endless. The advent of the digital age with its capacity to shift and store documents and information means that the power of access gets combined with the power of analysis and storage. This is even evident in how we use and research via journal articles; where considerable amounts of time were once spent photocopying individual articles and painstakingly writing notes from them, now one can access these materials online in PDF form while note-taking digitally from the same sources.

Of course, none of this means that documentary research has turned into a failsafe approach to evidence gathering – the same historical caveats still apply. Digital and online access come with their own set of anxieties. While access, evidence gathering and storage have all become much more efficient, it is also wise to be aware of the potential downsides of this access – one of the key ones being plagiarism, especially of the unwitting variety. As researchers increasingly copy and paste excerpts from journals and online digital books, the chances are magnified that people will confuse someone else's work with their own. It is also much easier to lose track of the source for the documentary evidence you have accumulated – this is important for your evidence base, because you need to provide a source for all forms of evidence. More efficient access to documents also means that it is much easier to be in breach of copyright. Publishers take such breaches seriously, so be careful how you use copyrighted work, especially if you are looking to distribute it for research dissemination purposes.

ACTIVITY

Do a Google search on the internet for documents related to your chosen research topic. Keep a list of the kinds of documents you can find online, such as books and newspaper articles. What other kinds of documents exist relating to your topic? For example, can you access personal accounts related to the topic? Are there links to specialised databases and archives? As part of the list, keep a record of the amount of documentation that relates to each type of document – i.e. is there sufficient documentation to make documentary research viable in your topic area? Also, check Wikipedia entries to see the list of citations and where they originate.

What kinds of documents are there?

Documents come in all shapes and sizes, a fact reflected in the research that has used documents as a primary data collection method. It is rare that you will find a study that has not used some form of documentary analysis as part of its research design, given that sources come in formats such as:

- Newspaper articles – the way that educational issues are reported in the paper can say a great deal about the attitudes and values associated with education at any one time among the public.

- Biographies – these can be an excellent source of historical information, and not just in the traditional published format – they can also come in the form of individual life histories, career biographies, etc.

- Field notes – these notes are taken at the site of the research project, whether it is a school or a playground, libraries or community groups.

- Diaries/log books – see Jerry Wellington's chapter on documentary research (2000, Chapter 8), which includes an excellent account of the use of diaries in research.

- Journals – Duncan Mercieca used the reflective journals of student teachers to help explore the ways in which novice teachers understood what reflective practice was all about (Mercieca, 2013).

- Minutes of meetings/memos/emails – as most organisations are required to keep records of their activities and their decision-making processes, minutes can prove a powerful and also a reliable source of research data. They are particularly useful if the research relates to issues such as organisational change, institutional culture and/or educational management and leadership. Caution should be taken with minutes, however, because they are always intended as both an accurate and a formal record of the issues discussed and actions taken. Much tends to be left out of the formal record for the sake of both efficiency and diplomacy. This is often not the case with emails, but caution should be adopted here too, given that the use of email (which is nearly always a personal form of communication) highlights ethical as well as privacy issues. Memos, still used in some organisations (and some more private than others), have been used to good effect in various types of investigative forms of research, especially in relation to the machinations of government and the civil service.

- Books/articles – many researchers use previously published academic papers, including books, as an evidence base for their research questions, and it is not unusual for whole research projects (at both UG and PG level) to be entirely based on desk-bound academic research. This is particularly true in research on the philosophy of education.

- Policy documents – the use of policy documents as a device for gathering evidence is a common approach for researchers who are interested in how educational arguments are presented via official statements. This is a popular method for those who value research as a form of interrogation (see Chapter 1). For researchers of this persuasion, much can be gained by critically analysing the discourses that are at play in official papers, which makes sense because much of this form of documentation is a text-based version of an argument – for example, about the need for curriculum change, transformations in pedagogy, etc. As such, these arguments can be revealing as to the intentions (hidden or otherwise) behind the development of such policies (see the examples presented later in this chapter).

Advantages and disadvantages of documentary research

There are a range of advantages to documentary forms of research:

- **Scope** – engaging in documentary research means that you can physically 'access' your database much more easily than in observational research, for example. Although researchers often need to visit libraries or archives to access such material, the scope of their documentary research is limited only by the availability of the documents themselves – as Cohen *et al.* state (2007: 201), documentary research 'can enable the researcher to reach inaccessible persons or subjects'.

- **Lack of bias** – as Ahmed points out (2010: 10), documentary records tend to be 'unbiased as the documents are collated usually for other purposes ... the researcher is not in a position to bias subjects and the authors of documents are unlikely to assume their future use in research fields'. While the documents can be interpreted in different ways by different researchers, whatever bias exists reflects the researcher/interpreter rather than the document itself. As such, the research subject is not an active part of the research process – more a passive entity, a fact that offers at least some form of 'objectivity' in the research.

- **Ease of use** – for most forms of document there tends to be a finished product in existence that states the case for whatever is under discussion. This may be a biased and partial statement, but it is a statement that serves a particular purpose. The researcher can use this to his or her advantage and 'manipulate' the data in various ways until they are convinced that there is an appropriate fit between the documents, the research objective and the argument built on the available evidence. As the evidence comes mostly from static entities, this is for the most part doable, which is not the case with human subjects – the research site cannot be visited continually to gather more and more data and/or to view the research subject from other angles or interpretations. Of course, this is only true up to a point, since there is a limit to all forms of manipulation (regardless of form), but suffice it to say that such manipulation is much easier with documents than with humans.

- **A window onto the past** – while the memories of individual people can tell us a great deal about the past, documents extracted from historical situations are arguably a more effective way to take a longitudinal view of a research question. As Cohen *et al.* (2007: 201) argue, documents can show how situations have evolved over time:

> Documents, many written 'live' and in situ, may catch the dynamic situation at the time of writing. Some documents, particularly if they are very personal (e.g. letters and diaries) may catch personal details and feelings that would not otherwise surface.

Disadvantages

- **Authenticity** – it can sometimes be a challenge to gauge the authenticity of the documents themselves. Are they based on actual events, are they factually correct, or are they opinions masquerading as fact? There is always the danger that your interpretation of documents may be an interpretation of an interpretation, making the connection between the 'truth' and your research even more obscure – a case of Anthony Giddens' 'double hermeneutic' at its most damaging (Giddens, 1987).
- **Context** – historical context is crucial. Cohen *et al.* (2007: 202) argue that documents should be understood 'within the context' in which they were written; otherwise they tend to lose whatever meaning they had in the first place. For example, there's not much point in examining the discourse of education policy documents from the late nineteenth century without taking into account the nature of current social mores, increasing industrialisation and urbanisation and a national culture which had only recently come to terms with the idea of a 'national' education system.
- **Primary/secondary distinction** – it is important to make a distinction between primary and secondary sources when it comes to documents. As Duffy points out (1999: 108):

> Primary sources are those which came into existence in the period under research (e.g. the minutes of a school governor's meeting). Secondary sources are interpretations of events of that period based on primary sources (e.g. a history of that school which obtained evidence from the governor's minutes).

However, Duffy also makes a good point when he indicates that this distinction isn't as simple as it appears, since notions of primary and secondary are also open to interpretation: 'if the author of the school history was the subject of research, for example, her or his book would become a primary source for the researcher' (Duffy, 1999: 109).

ACTIVITY

Think of a research topic that you would like to study. Is the use of documents to gather evidence a viable research tool? Make a list of the benefits and disadvantages of using documentary research in your chosen area, based on the points mentioned above. Do the advantages outweigh the disadvantages? If not, can you adjust the topic so that there are fewer limitations to the study? This is a useful device for any method that you may choose.

Examples of documentary research in practice

Example 1: Quality and equality in UK education policy

Source: Gillies, Donald (2008) 'Quality and equality: the mask of discursive conflation in education policy texts'. *Journal of Education Policy,* Vol. 23, No. 6, pp. 685–699.

This paper, drawing on a critical discourse analysis of policy texts in the UK over the past decade, explores the ways in which a dual political commitment to quality and equality has been manifested, probing the related ideological tensions evident within education policy discourse. Donald Gillies bases his argument on a study of thirteen key policy texts published in the countries of the UK in the years 1997–2006. Most of his attention is focused on the ways in which the discourse of quality management is allied to egalitarian discourse in these policy texts. Gillies chose to focus his documentary research on the ministerial forewords, a method he chose for two reasons.

> First, this concision allowed for the study to be manageable; second, forewords often summarise the key points within the policy documents and highlight the political priorities and expected results. This is not to ignore the issue of policy refraction or indeed of 'policy as text' (Ball, 1994), but since the focus was on government rhetoric, it seemed sensible to centre the study on government ministers' words as opposed to the complete policy texts.
>
> (Gillies, 2008: 688)

The texts were a combination of Green and White papers, speeches and a document from Her Majesty's Inspectorate (HMI). 'All of the texts could be seen as linked by two common themes in the recent UK education policy: a demand that standards should rise and a concern that this should be for the benefit of all learners.' Gillies argued that this form of documentary approach was important in that it did not simply illustrate the significant recurrence of terms associated with quality and equality, but also showed how the two discourses shared certain terminology and that 'determining precise usage of particular words was by no means simple or obvious. It was this phenomenon which triggered the analysis reported in this paper'.

Example 2: Special education policy in Cyprus

Source: Liasidou, A. (2011) 'Unequal power relations and inclusive education policy making: a discursive analytic approach'. *Educational Policy*, Vol. 25, No. 6, pp. 887–907.

In her research on Cypriot education policy, Anastasia Liasidou aimed to critically examine the ways in which 'power manifests itself through language and bears a prodigious effect on the ways in which discursive binaries of "normality" and "abnormality" are construed and reified'. Her argument centred on the notion that notions of normalcy are socially and culturally mediated ideological constructs 'implicated in an array of unequal power relationships and vested interests aimed at safeguarding the institutional and ideological status quo'. Using critical discourse analysis (CDA) she aimed to explore the linguistic subtleties of certain texts and make transparent the unequal power relationships inscribed in them. Using this form of documentary research, she was able to address the following questions:

- What are the dominant discourses endemic in the Cypriot special education policy context?
- In what ways are special education imperatives consolidated and perpetuated, albeit with ample rhetoric advocating greater inclusive policy and practice?
- In what ways is the "othering" image of children with presumed SEN construed and depicted?

Chapter summary

This chapter began by providing a brief historical overview of documentary research, pointing out that even before the advent of the internet, influential social theorists such as Karl Marx were busy using documentary records to develop their ideas. The chapter then detailed the different kinds of documents that can be used in this form of research (policy documents, archives, minutes of meetings and so on). The discussion outlined some of the advantages and disadvantages of this form of research, while also including two examples of research that have used documents to gather evidence.

Further reading

Laugharne, J. and Baird, A. (2009) 'National conversations in the UK: using a language-based approach to interpret three key education policy documents (2001–2007) from England, Scotland and Wales'. *Cambridge Journal of Education*, 39 (2), 223–240.

- This is a strong paper that takes policy documents as its mode of evidence gathering and as a way of understanding UK policy conversations.

McCulloch, G. (2004) *Documentary research: In education, history and the social sciences*. London: Routledge.

- Gary McCulloch's book *Documentary research* (2004) provides an overview and examination of how to research and use texts from the past and present, considering sources ranging from personal archives to online documents and including books, reports, official documents, works of fiction and printed media.

McCulloch, G. (2000) *Historical research in educational settings (Doing qualitative research in educational settings)*. Buckingham: Open University Press.

- Also useful is McCulloch's book *Historical research in educational settings* (2000). This book explores how to set about historical research in education, and gives practical advice for getting started and for suitable research methods in different kinds of projects. It includes case studies on topics such as curriculums and classrooms; literacy in the nineteenth century, and the university history curriculum.

17

Using the internet

Introduction

The internet provides a fruitful source of data collection nowadays. Digital technologies, like social networking sites, can put the researcher in contact with large numbers of respondents very quickly and easily. Correspondence can take place without conventional time and space restrictions. Quantitative data can be gathered through the use of online surveys. Qualitative data can be collected through settings such as chat rooms, emails or discussion boards. Many online methods of data collection are new and innovative – and consequently there is much debate about their relative merits and models of best practice. This chapter outlines various approaches that the educational researcher might adopt, and discusses their associated strengths and limitations.

New fields of educational enquiry

Advances in online technologies impact significantly on educational theory and practice – on what, how, when and where we learn. The development and rapid expansion of the internet have brought about a sea change in the ways we access, share and experience information. Recent developments of web 2.0 technologies – social networking, podcasting, blogging, wikis and so on – have changed our relationships with knowledge and with one another. Such technologies *democratise* information, providing us with the opportunity to participate in knowledge generation by authoring a blog or posting a video on YouTube. Subsequently, the last few years have seen considerable interest in exploring potential applications of online technologies in education on the part of both practitioners and educational researchers. There are numerous education journals dedicated to the exploration of technology and technology-enhanced learning. Organisations like *Society for Information Technology and Teacher Education* (based in the US) and the *Association of Learning Technology* (ALT) and *Jisc* (both based in the UK) exist to promote innovation and excellence in the application and use of new technologies in education. Vast new areas of research have emerged, offering tremendous scope for empirical study. Potential research topics include:

- The use of *Facebook* on university courses.
- Learning through multi-user game-based learning.
- Experiences of studying via MOOCs (massive open online courses).
- The use of the internet within the primary classroom.
- Impact of virtual learning environments (VLEs) on retention/attainment/ student experience.
- The use and non-use of mobile phones to access online information in the classroom.
- Students' experiences of e-assessments (wikis, blogs, discussion boards).

ACTIVITY

Look at the list of potential topics above. Choose the two you find most interesting and develop a research project outline for each. Try to develop clear aims and objectives and an outline of your proposed data collection methods.

In either project, is it possible to make use of any online methods of data collection? If so, how would this enhance the research project? Are there any drawbacks?

Different uses

Developments in online technologies also impact on educational research, creating new ways for researchers to access information, recruit respondents, collect data, communicate with one another and present their work.

- **Accessing information** – online databases give researchers access to published work on their desktop computer. As a result, it has become far easier to access material, refine searches, and manage and store literature.
- **Recruiting respondents** – researchers can use the internet to advertise their studies and recruit potential participants. They can use existing mailing lists to send out mailshots or provide contact details and ask potential recruits to make contact. Likewise, researchers can use online strategies for maintaining contact with existing participants. Online tools facilitate communication especially for longitudinal research, thereby offering the potential to minimise attrition rates.
- **Collecting data** – much of this chapter is concerned with how the internet can be utilised as a tool for gathering data. Most commonly, researchers make use of online surveys. Other strategies include conducting online interviews or observations utilising 'web 2.0' tools, including social networking, virtual environments and multi-user gaming. Respondents can provide data by completing blogs or podcasts. Virtual ethnography has become a more commonly used approach in recent years.

- **Communicating with other researchers** – various online tools enable educational researchers to collaborate with one another without the physical constraints of time and space. For instance, Young and Perez (2011) make a convincing case for the use of wiki tools as a means of enabling international and collaborative 'eco-research', with contributors working together without needing to travel.

- **Publishing work** – many of the stages of academic publishing are now conducted electronically. The main characteristic of journal publications is the peer review process, and in most cases this now takes place entirely online. However, the most significant change is in the ways that academic work is published. Online publications – e-books and e-journals – have become increasingly widespread. Recent years have witnessed the proliferation of open access research outputs, with articles freely available online via repositories or online journals. This is a substantial alteration to the established publishing system that has been in place for hundreds of years.

ACTIVITY

Open access will transform academic publishing over the next few years. Already many institutions insist their academics publish their work in openly accessible repositories, and much academic work is published under a Creative Commons license. There is considerable debate at present about what open access will look like in the future. The Finch Review (2012) considered two potential open access models for publically funded research – the 'green route' and the 'gold route':

Gold route

Considered to be the most sustainable method in the long term, and recommended by the Finch report, the gold route involves publishing in a fully open access journal or website.

Subjected to the same peer-review procedures as a traditional journal, the open access journal will usually be available online. Authors may need to pay for their work to be published, although this is very rare as it is often provided for by the research grant. Some institutions even pay these fees out of a central fund to account for the differences between research councils.

Green route

Self-archiving in a repository is a concept that is gradually gaining ground. There are risks, as this process relies on researchers uploading their own papers. To counter this, some institutions have made it compulsory for all published work to be added to their respective repositories.

Repositories offer a number of benefits. They increase the availability of some published journal works with restrictions on reprinting or text mining, and may enable work to be propagated across the internet and used for novel applications. Repositories also allow authors to keep track of who is downloading their data.

[Extract from: http://www.jisc.ac.uk/whatwedo/topics/opentechnologies/openaccess/green-gold.aspx]

Consider these two open access models.

1   How do you think they will change the ways that educational research is published and accessed?
2   Which route is preferable?
3   Are there any concerns associated with the shift towards open access?

Online research tools

As the internet develops and expands, numerous new ways of gathering data are opened up to the educational researcher. Social media, developed for a wide range of purposes, provide access and tools to enable researchers to gain entry to groups, simulate educational situations, engage in dialogue and elicit responses. Among the tools educational researchers can utilise are:

- **Virtual environments** – most university courses now make use of a virtual learning environment like *Moodle* or *Blackboard*. These provide access to potential 'target' groups (that is, people studying on a specific course or module) and they contain a range of tools such as wikis and discussion boards. Virtual environments designed for non–educational purposes, like *SecondLife*, can also be used to gather data. Avatars (virtual characters) can be created to interact with others in order to conduct 'virtual interviews' or set up virtual experiments or simulations.

- **Online multi–user gaming** – online games have been used for educational purposes for many years, with Harvard University's *River City Project* a prime example of enquiry-based learning via internet gaming. The project, where learners use scientific enquiry to identify the cause of disease in a simulated town, has used the game in research to explore situated learning and strategies for engaging 'hard to reach' learners, among other things (River City Project, 2013).

- **Email** – email is a particularly effective way of maintaining contact with respondents in longitudinal research. It can also be a tool for conducting interviews, especially with people who may be in different locations or who may be unable to travel. Email is asynchronous communication – meaning that respondents have time to consider and edit their answers, rather than having to respond instantaneously. Mastermann and Shuyska used email interviews to examine postgraduate learners' digital literacies, finding what they termed a 'pen-pal' technique an effective way of gathering data from busy students (2012: 341).

- **Social networking** – sites like *Facebook* provide instant access to more than 850 million users worldwide. This makes *Facebook* an especially effective tool for recruiting participants. It is also an excellent vehicle for gaining insider access to individual and group behaviour, observing people interacting in naturalistic settings. Consequently there has been considerable research on *Facebook* use in recent years (see Wilson *et al.*, 2012). While *Facebook* does enable researchers to access special interest groups, other social networking sites (like *Yammer* or *LinkedIn*) serve more specific 'closed' networks, thereby allowing researchers to specify their sample.

- **Chat rooms** – likewise, online chat rooms provide virtual spaces for communication. Educational researchers can identify specific interest groups that correspond with their research. In open chat rooms they can 'lurk' – meaning that they observe what takes place without participating. This means they can observe naturalistic behaviour without interfering. They can also participate by introducing new material or asking specific questions.

- **Podcasting, vodcasting and blogging** – new tools also provide opportunities for respondents to become authors. Blogs, podcasts and vodcasts enable respondents to produce data for a researcher written, oral or video form. Gray *et al.* (2010) identify a wide range of online tools to enable students to become authors.

- **Wiki** – as discussed earlier, wikis provide a collective workspace for researchers to work together. As Young and Perez (2011) demonstrate, they also provide an excellent repository for respondents to submit 'multi-modal' data – their videos, digital photographs or text.

- **Surveying tools** – online tools like *SurveyMonkey* and *SurveyGizmo* make writing and distributing surveys fast and cheap. Researchers are able to reach an extensive (worldwide) audience immediately, and computerised data transfer means that responses are easily collected and analysed.

ACTIVITY

Imagine you are interviewing parents about their children's experiences of sports in school. You need to choose between:

- Online synchronous interviews (via a chat room or conferencing site)
- Online asynchronous interviews (via email or discussion board)
- Online video conferenced interviews (via Skype or Lync)
- Offline face-to-face interviews.

To help you decide, draw out the following table, identifying advantages and disadvantages of each approach. Complete the final column by identifying how each approach might impact on the type of responses you would be likely to receive.

	Advantages	Disadvantages	Impact on data collected
Chat room			
Email			
Skype			
Face-to-face			

Virtual ethnography – 'netnography'

Virtual ethnography, or what Kozinets refers to as 'netnography' (2010), entails the detailed and naturalistic study of online cultures. Researchers immerse themselves within the online communities – chat rooms, social networking sites, virtual environments and so on. While some virtual ethnographers focus entirely on online spaces, others examine a combination of online and offline, claiming that:

> Online interaction cannot be understood in isolation from the physical contexts in which participants are located and the 'real-world' social networks in which they are embedded.
>
> (O Dochartaigh, 2012: 186–187)

Virtual ethnography shares many of the qualities of in-person ethnography (see Chapter 10). Since the ethnographer does not have to immerse herself physically in the cultures she studies, virtual research is far less intensive in terms of time or resources. By 'lurking', researchers can observe online communities in an unobtrusive manner, and then develop further analysis by conducting surveys and group or individual interviews.

Advantages of online methods

The internet provides many opportunities to enhance educational research:

- **Scope and scale** – perhaps the main attraction of online methods is the capacity for the researcher to access vast audiences with great ease. Traditional constraints of time and space are largely resolved. Online surveys can be distributed worldwide at the click of a mouse, and interviews can be conducted via *Skype* or email, making them far easier to arrange and conduct.
- **Affordability** – online data collection tools are far cheaper than traditional approaches. There are none of the associated costs of travel or printing. Email interviews avoid the costs of transcription from face-to-face recordings, and online surveys avoid costs usually related to administering, distributing and collecting questionnaires or structured interviews.
- **Recruiting participants** – mailing lists or internet adverts make it far easier to identify and specify characteristics of research participants.
- **Higher response rates** – online tools provide greater flexibility, allowing respondents to complete a survey in their own time and, if necessary, over a number of sittings. They can participate from home. This tends to result in higher response rates.
- **Multiple engagements** – online tools mean that respondents are far more likely to agree to participate in a number of ways and on a number of occasions. Participants might be identified via a chat room or social network and asked to write a blog, complete an online survey and take part in an email interview – all without leaving their home.

- **Engaging digitally literate young people** – as children and young people are 'digital natives' (born and raised in a digital world), they are generally very comfortable communicating electronically. Online methods allow respondents to participate in ways in which they are confident and knowledgeable.

- **Exploring sensitive issues** – because respondents are able to participate in online research from their own homes and without disclosing their identities, they might be more likely to divulge a greater depth of personal information. This can make online approaches more effective for exploring sensitive issues like school bullying, characteristics of poor teaching or educational failure.

- **New research directions** – as Hine (2005) has argued, the digital age has bought with it new ways of communicating and sharing information. This opens up all sorts of new research fields, approaches, topics and processes, enabling research innovation and experimentation.

- **Minimising 'researcher effect'** – online tools can enable research to be conducted in more naturalistic settings. As noted above, internet research facilitates anonymity, and this can include the anonymity of the researcher as well as the respondents. In some instances data can be collected without involvement from participants. 'Data crawling' or 'data mining' entails gathering data from respondents' online profiles. When this data is public, as it often is on social networking sites, data can be gathered without respondents' active participation.

Disadvantages

- **Verifying online identities** – it can prove especially difficult to confirm that online respondents are accurately presenting their age, gender, ethnicity, and so on. This is particularly problematic for research with avatars, where respondents might have entirely different characteristics to their online representation, or they might have multiple avatars.

- **Digital divide** – while a key advantage of online methods is their scope to reach a massive audience, there is a danger that data collection will be limited to people who have internet access or people who are confident using social networking tools. This has the potential to distort samples, for example by under-representing responses from economically disadvantaged nations, communities or individuals. Moreover, research focused on the educational value of online tools might be biased in favour of positive perspectives.

- **Keeping control** – in common with other research methods where the researcher is not physically present, it is more difficult to ensure validity and reliability. As Denissen *et al.* (2010: 566) point out, where online surveys or interviews are completed at home, researchers are unable to ensure that conditions are appropriate (e.g. that there are no distractions), or that respondents do not cheat. Moreover, the researcher is unable to respond to queries or offer support, an issue which is likely to be more pertinent when children are completing surveys or interviews. Synchronous communications can be difficult to facilitate, with the pace of chat room dialogue meaning the researcher might need to type fast to keep up.

■ **Lack of online rapport** – it can be more difficult for a researcher to gain trust and rapport with respondents without face-to-face contact. A lack of presence or face-to-face communication might hinder the development of positive relationships.

■ **Missing out on face-to-face clues** – when conducting interviews or observations 'in person', a researcher draws from non-verbal responses (body language like eye contact, appearance, muscle tone) to add a further layer to analysis. Clearly, this is not possible when interactions are remote.

■ **Researcher anxiety** – one of the main obstacles to the use of online methods is anxiety about their efficacy and the researcher's technical skills and experience. Because these methods are relatively untried and untested, researchers might be reluctant to employ them, favouring more traditional face-to-face methods instead.

■ **Interpreting responses** – online communications are quite distinct from face-to-face interactions. Researchers might have difficulty interpreting colloquial online speech, shorthand, symbols or silences in responses.

■ **Ethical issues** – online methods share many of the same ethical issues as face-to-face methods. However, as Gaiser and Schreiner argue, these issues need to be understood within the context of online spaces:

> Informed consent, confidentiality, anonymity, privacy, the nature of what constitutes private and public spaces, virtual personae, copyright, and more, take on new meanings and require fresh insights when you are conducting research in an online environment.
>
> (Gaiser and Schreiner, 2009: 27)

■ For instance, Solberg (2012) explores the ethical and legal issues associated with 'data mining' from social networking sites, raising questions about the extent that using publicly accessible information requires consent. Like the physically-present covert observer, a researcher 'lurking' on a chat room site must consider how ethical data collection is when contributors are unaware of their own participation.

Mixing methods – combining online and offline

It is relatively uncommon for educational research to be conducted entirely online. It is far more likely that a researcher will employ a mixed methods approach, using online methods to complement face-to-face data collection techniques. For instance, an online survey will enable the researcher to elicit responses from participants in dispersed geographical areas, in conjunction with face-to-face interviews with more accessible participants to gain depth and detail. Alternatively, face-to-face interviews can be followed up by email questions, enabling the researcher to raise further questions or points of clarification. By examining case studies and reviewing existing literature, Hesse-Biber and Griffin (2012) identify a number of advantages of an online/offline mixed methods approach, including locating and 'studying up' about 'hard to reach' populations. By triangulating online and face-to-face methods of data collection, the researcher can gain the advantages of online research and overcome many of the disadvantages.

Chapter summary

This chapter has outlined some of the ways in which online technologies are transforming the focus, practice and dissemination of educational research. Online surveys and interviews are increasingly utilised, either alongside or as an alternative to face-to-face research methods. The chapter has considered virtual ethnography and ways in which the educational researcher might employ 'web 2.0' tools to gain an understanding of educational processes. While such tools offer many new and exciting opportunities for the researcher, they also give rise to a number of difficulties, especially in terms of ethical concerns and the capacity to maintain control. Researchers can reach a far wider research community, but their research may be hindered by the lack of face-to-face interaction.

Further reading

Hine, C. (ed.) (2005) *Virtual methods: Issues in social research on the internet*. Oxford: Berg.

- Christine Hine has written extensively in this area, and this book is an ideal collection of essays on virtual methods containing lots of ideas and critical engagement.

Fielding, N., Lee, R. and Blank, G. (eds) (2008) *The Sage handbook of online research methods*. London: Sage.

- The book includes twenty-nine chapters on online research methods, covering a wide range of issues and approaches. The final section on the future of online research is especially interesting and thought-provoking.

Theorising research

18

Using theories and concepts in research

Introduction

In planning a research project it is vital that key concepts associated with the topic of the research are adequately explored in the literature and defined by the researcher undertaking the project. Concepts are slippery and do not have clear or fixed meanings, and often researchers and others understand things in different ways. Therefore, it is critically important that key concepts are clarified. This also makes it more straightforward to plan the research. In addition to clarifying key concepts, it is important to draw on theories that have already been established and to relate these to your own research in order to ground the study in what is 'already known'. This chapter considers what 'theory' is, and explains why it is important to explore theories that are relevant to one's research. As the field is so vast, this chapter will concentrate on the use of *social* theory in educational research.

The place of theory in education research

It is often the case that books on educational (and others forms of) research emphasise the correct approaches to using specific types of research tool, such as interviews and questionnaires, or focus on the construction of a dissertation or research report and set out how the constituent parts are assembled to construct the finished product. Of course, this is invaluable guidance, and it is an essential aspect of any text that aims to educate those undertaking research in educational settings. It is a form of knowledge that is well catered for in the literature, which has expanded to keep up with the increasing demand for applied research.

Nevertheless there is a tendency to pay less attention to the role of theory in the construction of such projects, and the various ways in which theories generated in the social sciences in particular can be used to extract *meaning* from the research site under examination. As attested by the variety of publications that link social theory and educational research (see Murphy, 2013a), it is a tremendously worthwhile activity to engage the two concepts, so long as the researchers themselves come armed with an understanding of the challenges that await them.

What the published research illustrates is not just the complexity of concepts in social theory, but also the varied sets of issues that may be faced when applying such ideas in educational research contexts, which is a field of complex interwoven imperatives and practices in its own right. These challenges – epistemological, operational, analytical – can be seen to impact on researchers and their attempts to make sense of educational questions, whether of governance and management, inclusion, teaching and learning or professional identities. Previously published research indicates that the application of a challenging set of ideas onto a challenging set of practices should be treated with care and a strong consideration for intellectual arguments as well as the concerns of the professional researcher.

There is much to be gained for the educational research community generally from taking advantage of the originality, rigour and intellectual insight of ideas from the social sciences. The work of theory – about power and control, democracy, social organisation, language and communication, selfhood and subjectivities, the state and the economy, offers an excellent source of ideas, and can, when implemented effectively, contribute to the delivery of higher quality educational research.

What is social theory?

Broadly speaking, social theories are analytical frameworks or paradigms used to examine social phenomena. The term 'social theory' encompasses ideas about 'how societies change and develop, about methods of explaining social behaviour, about power and social structure, gender and ethnicity, modernity and "civilisation", revolutions and utopias' (Harrington, 2005: 1). In contemporary social theory certain core themes take precedence over others, such as the nature of social life, the relationship between self and society, the structure of social institutions, the role and possibility of social transformation, and themes such as gender, race and class (Elliot, 2008). Alongside the existence of this broad range of issues, there is also a large number of what could be termed social theories – feminist theories of various persuasions could be labelled as such, likewise critical race theories. Space precludes a more detailed examination of the field of social theory – there are other sources that offer such an overview (see Elliot, 2008 and Callinicos, 2007 in particular).

Issues to consider in theoretical application

■ **Moving from practice to theory** – the application of concepts from social theory brings its own set of challenges. Some of these reflect issues of design, including the development of tools such as data measurement and analytical criteria. Just as significant are the difficulties faced when grappling with the core concepts of social theory, which themselves already come with a range of contradictory meanings. Notions of 'power', 'culture' and 'practice' are challenging at the best of times, but such challenges are compounded when they are aligned with the core educational concepts of teaching, learning, assessment and curriculum. All forms of research, regardless of subject, come with a set of issues that need addressing in practical settings. Educational research is no different, and the fact that it is most often embedded in forms of professional practice merely adds further challenges. As a result, it should be emphasised from the outset that the movement from practice to theory is as challenging an intellectual journey, if not more so, than the journey from theory to practice. While the latter can often confound researchers who face difficulties in applying theoretical models and principles in other contexts, the former can often compound the situation for the educational researcher. Many of those engaged in educational research tend to arrive at this research topic via the linked but distinct field of professional practice. While this can have certain advantages in terms of insight, providing a level of insider knowledge that is unavailable to the non-professional, it can also mean that intellectual judgement may be clouded by immersion in the hothouse of educational politics.

- **(Inter)disciplinarity** – this scenario is also compounded by the nature of professional training. Educators may be well versed in the application of educational theory to educational practice, but rarely are they required to apply theories from other disciplines in any meaningful way. This is both a blessing and a curse of being an educational researcher – an *un*disciplined approach to the field of research can have drawbacks as well as benefits, providing professionals with a multidisciplinary grounding while also bringing a disinclination to belong to and work within the parameters of any specific disciplinary paradigm.

- **Theoretical 'authenticity'** – when applying theory to research it is often tempting to try to stay true to the 'authentic' version of the theory being applied. However, nowhere is it written that researchers may not choose how and in what contexts they apply the work of theory. While the overzealous might demand the 'pure' use of someone's work, regardless of context, it should not be forgotten that all theorists have, at various stages in their careers, cherry-picked from the work of those who have influenced them. To suggest that there is a 'right' and a 'wrong' way to understand and apply educational or social theorists is to misinterpret the role of theory in research – the latter should never be made to bow down to the former. If anything, cherry-picking and cross-pollination should be positively encouraged, for how else do we arrive at original and innovative forms of knowledge, which can help us progress through the world of often stale and moribund arguments and paradigms in educational policy and practice?[1]

- **The concept of power** – another issue in educational research relates to the special status assigned to the concept of power in social theory and also in educational research. However, given this close relationship between power and educational research, one needs to be even more careful in the pursuit of research objectives. One doesn't need to be a Foucauldian to understand that power is omnipresent, and that power and knowledge have a tight bond that is not easily broken. Nevertheless, the workings of power in educational settings should never be taken lightly or over-simplified, given that educational institutions and their assorted sets of practices provide ideal environments for the interplay of multiple forms of power – cultural, social, structural – which in many cases are irreducible to each other. Power is a notoriously difficult concept to pin down, and the researcher can all too easily fall into the trap of looking for power in the wrong places – or worse still, misrecognising their own capacity as power brokers in educational research settings. It is important for the researcher to recognise their own powerful presence in educational settings, while also accepting the fallibility of one theory of power in the face of complex and highly differentiated institutionalised arrangements. Erring on the side of intellectual caution does not do the educational researcher any harm, especially when combined with a recognition of the unfinished debates in social theory that form the backdrop to such forms of research in the first place (Murphy, 2013b).

The application of theory in educational research: some examples

Theories are flexible enough to be applied in a diversity of educational contexts. Alongside this diversity of context there is also an evident diversity of research *design* at work in the field of theoretical application. Theories are applied for a variety of reasons, which can only impact on the application itself and the ways in which theories are used both to examine the findings of the research and to draw out implications and recommendations for future studies. For the purposes of clarity, below we have included some examples based on the five approaches to research outlined in Chapter 1.

Example 1: Using theory in research as *exploration*

Source: Connelly, P. and Healy, J. (2004) 'Symbolic violence and the neighbourhood: The educational aspirations of 7–8 year old working-class girls'. *The British Journal of Sociology*, Vol. 55, No. 4, pp. 511–529.

A number of authors have used the ideas of Pierre Bourdieu to carry out exploratory research on a variety of topics (see Grenfell and James, 1998), one of these being the nature of learner identities. In their article Paul Connelly and Julie Healy aim to understand how the girls' local neighbourhood in Belfast, Northern Ireland influences these aspirations and identities. In order to do so they employ Bourdieu's concepts of *symbolic violence* and *habitus* to illustrate how the local neighbourhood 'represents the parameters of the girls' social worlds'. According to their research, the local neighbourhood 'provides the context within which the girls tend to develop strong interdependent relationships with their mothers that also tend to encourage and reinforce the girls' particular gendered identities'.

Example 2: Using theory in research as *interrogation*

Source: Douglas, P. (2010) "Problematising' inclusion: Education and the question of autism'. *Pedagogy, Culture and Society,* Vol. 18, No. 2, pp. 105–121.

Source: Liasidou, A. (2011) 'Unequal power relations and inclusive education policy making: A discursive analytic approach'. *Educational Policy*, Vol. 25, No. 6, pp. 887–907.

Source: Morgan, A. (2005) 'Governmentality versus choice in contemporary special education'. *Critical Social Policy*, Vol. 25, No. 3, pp. 325–348.

The work of Michel Foucault has been used extensively in education research (Besley and Peters, 2007). One particular area of investigation in which his ideas are prevalent is the field of *special education needs* (SEN). Patty Douglas's paper on autism is a Foucault-inspired critique of Ontario's policy of special educational transformation in schools. Douglas' desk-based research using government documentation suggests that Foucault's notion of governmentality can help to build a critique of power relationships at the heart of policy, and also suggests ways this culture might help to 'inform new ways of thinking and practising' inclusion. In a similar fashion to Douglas, Anastasia Liasidou takes a Foucault-inspired discourse analytic approach to special educational needs, challenging what she calls binary and deficient narratives of normality and abnormality. She uses critical discourse analysis to 'expose the ways in which children with presumed SEN are disempowered by the policy framework of a particular sociopolitical context', bringing into focus the ways in which language helps fabricate notions of 'normality' and 'special educational needs' (see also Chapter 16 for a description of her methodology). Angela Morgan also applies Foucault to SEN, specifically his work on governmentality, and exposes the power relations behind special educational needs policy. Her area of focus is somewhat different, however, in that she is more interested in how power within the special education system impacts on the nature of parental 'choice'. Her analysis 'unmasks the disciplinary power operating within the special education system and explores the manner in which such power affects choice for parents'.

Example 3: Using theory in research as *reconstruction*

Source: Fryer, M. (2012) 'Facilitative leadership: drawing on Jürgen Habermas' model of ideal speech to propose a less impositional way to lead'. *Organisation*, Vol. 19, pp. 25.

Mick Fryer's article is an example of research that uses social theory to recommend a case for an alternative or innovative method – this time terms of the German sociologist Jürgen Habermas and the concept of leadership. In using Habermas' concepts, Fryer joins an ever-growing band of researchers keen to utilise his theories (Murphy and Fleming, 2010). Fryer's research draws on Habermas' notion of ideal speech, along with some commentaries on Habermas' work, to propose an outline for a model of leadership as the facilitation of ideal speech. It also considers the practical feasibility in contemporary organisations, of leadership that facilitates ideal speech, 'identifying some aspects of organizational theory and practice that may offer nourishment to such an approach'.

Example 4: Using theory in research as *testing*

Source: Barone, C. (2006) 'Cultural capital, ambition and the explanation of inequalities in learning outcomes: a comparative analysis'. *Sociology*, Vol. 40, No. 6, pp. 1039–1058.

Source: Jæger, M. M. (2011) 'Does cultural capital really affect academic achievement? New evidence from combined sibling and panel data'. *Sociology of Education*, Vol. 84, No. 4, pp. 281–298.

Source: Zimdars, A., Sullivan, A. and Heath, A. (2009) 'Elite higher education admissions in the Arts and Sciences: is cultural capital the key?' *Sociology*, Vol. 43, No. 4, pp. 648–666.

One theory that has particularly attracted the 'testing' approach in research is Pierre Bourdieu's notion of *cultural capital*. Its status as a key concept in understandings of inequality and as a mediator of power differentials makes it the ideal candidate for such research. Carlo Barone's paper aims to explore the significance of cultural capital in educational settings, specifically the relation between social origins and student achievement. Using data from the *Project for International Student Assessment on 25 Nations* (PISA), Barone's findings suggest that cultural capital provides a 'relevant, but far from exhaustive, account of schooling inequalities'. He argues that in order to elaborate a more satisfactory explanation, two more factors need to be taken into account: occupational aspirations and economic resources. He also discusses whether these factors can be integrated into a coherent theoretical framework to achieve a better understanding of educational inequalities. Anna Zimdars *et al.*'s paper does something similar, but this time in relation to access and admissions, examining the extent to which cultural capital helps to explain the link between social background and gaining an offer for study at the University of Oxford. Their findings only partly support Bourdieu's 'postulation of cultural capital as the main differentiator between fractions of the middle class'. Interestingly, this tallies with Mads Meier Jæger's findings in the third paper on the same theme. Testing the hypothesis using new evidence from 'combined sibling and panel data (longitudinal and qualitative)', Jæger found that the effects of cultural capital are 'smaller than previously reported', its effect varying in high and low socioeconomic status environments.

Example 5: Using theory in research as *critique*

Source: Gouthro, P. (2009) 'Neoliberalism, lifelong learning, and the homeplace: Problematising the boundaries of "public" and "private" to explore women's learning experiences'. *Studies in Continuing Education*, Vol. 31, No. 2, pp. 157–172.

Patricia Gouthro uses her paper to highlight what she sees as deficiencies in Habermas' theoretical construction, which come to light in her research on the boundaries between the public and private in Canadian women's learning experiences. Her article is less of an application of Habermas and more a critique of his theoretical shortcomings and how these have transferred into Canadian critical education. While she is sympathetic to the work of critical theory, Gouthro claims a Habermasian analysis is insufficient for explaining the persistence of gender inequalities within adult education, her argument being that critical theory 'does not adequately take up other "medias" of power, such as patriarchy'.

[See the website www.socialtheoryapplied.com for more information on the use of theory in educational research].

Chapter summary

This chapter has explored the place of theory in educational research, especially that branch known as 'social theory'. It defined what this is, before considering some of the issues faced in applying social theory in research (including moving from practice to theory, interdisciplinarity, the nature of theoretical authenticity and the challenges of using power as a concept in educational research). The chapter also provided a range of published examples of research that have applied social theory in their design; these examples were aligned to the five key approaches outlined in Chapter 1.

Further reading

Hammersley, M. (2012) 'Troubling theory in case study research'. *Higher Education Research and Development*, 31:3, 393–405.

■ A paper that asks interesting questions about the need for, and value of, theory in educational research.

Murphy, M. (ed.) (2013b) *Social theory and education research: Understanding Foucault, Habermas, Bourdieu and Derrida*. Oxon: Routledge.

■ Mark Murphy's edited collection *Social theory and education research* (2013b) brings together a set of case studies that have applied either Foucault, Derrida, Bourdieu or Habermas in educational research contexts. These contexts include academy schools, school surveillance, the geography curriculum and school regulation. An introductory chapter provides a useful context within which the ideas of these four social theorists is situated.

Dressman, M. (2008) *Using social theory in educational research: A practical guide*. Oxon: Routledge.

■   A practical 'how-to' guide to applying theory in research is provided by Mark Dressman in *Using social theory in educational research: A practical guide* (2008). It includes sections on 'getting theoretical', 'an illustrated tour of how theory works (and doesn't work) in educational research', and 'framing research theoretically'.

Note

1   Examples of such cross-fertilisation of ideas do exist – for instance, see the journal *Studies in Philosophy and Education*, a special edition of which explored Habermas 'in conversation with others' including the likes of Derrida and Lacan (Murphy and Bamber, 2012).

CHAPTER

19

Evaluating methods

Introduction

'As with any kind of research, the methods and conclusions need to be justifiable. Such justification cannot be assertion or an act of faith, but must rely on demonstrating to the reader the nature of the decisions taken during the research and the grounds on which the decisions can be seen as "reasonable"' (Denscombe, 1998: 212). To ensure that your research findings are viewed as credible – that is, 'true' and worth taking notice of – a series of evaluative measures must underpin your design. The types of evaluation will depend on whether your research aligns itself most closely with the interpretivist or positivist paradigm. The reader requires several pieces of information before they can evaluate whether research findings are credible. This chapter will discuss the approaches for evaluating both positivist and interpretivist research. First, however, key factors that enable the evaluation of *all* research will be discussed.

Evaluating all research

Regardless of which paradigm your research fits into, there are elements which should be included so that your results can be evaluated by others. These are:

- Inclusion of your research questions or hypothesis.
- Inclusion of your research design.
- Explanation of the reasons for your choice of design.
- Explanation of how you analysed your findings.
- Sufficient evidence from your findings to demonstrate that this is an accurate representation of your analysis.

Contextual information is useful in all types of educational research and generally includes:

■ The number of participants
■ Data collection methods employed
■ Number and length of data collection sessions
■ Time period over which the data was collected.

ACTIVITY

An empirical study explores students' experiences of engaging with formative feedback in a post-1992 university. Participants were from two first-year undergraduate modules which provided formative feedback on assignments. Qualitative research methods were used: twenty-four semi-structured interviews, fifty reflective writing documents and eighty-three questionnaires were collated for open-ended responses and descriptive patterns. Newcity University is a widening participation university which is drawing students from sectors of society that have traditionally been under-represented in higher education. Of the twenty-four students I interviewed for the main study, ten were from a minority ethnic group and eight were twenty-one years old or over when entering the university. Twenty out of the twenty-four students were the first person in their family to go to university. Newcity University operates a two semester structure. I interviewed students in late January/early February after they had received feedback from their semester one modules. I also interviewed students at the end of May after they had received their semester two feedback. All interviews were digitally recorded with the participants' permission. I transcribed each interview myself using Olympus Digital Recorder Software. Interview times varied between thirty minutes and one hour. The data collection was carried out over a period of eighteen months (McGinty, 2011).

■ Make a list of the contextual information provided
■ Compare your list with a partner
■ How does this information enable you to evaluate the credibility of the research?

Evaluating positivist research

Evaluation of positivist research is based on the extent to which the methods used can be seen as an objective way of understanding the laws of human behaviour. This is because positivism tries to replicate the natural sciences. Therefore, the way in which this type of research is evaluated reflects this premise. According to Denzin and Lincoln (2011: 108–109), positivists focus on 'rigorous data produced through scientific research ... Value is found in the scientific method. Gold standard is scientific rigour'. This enables researchers to verify 'hypotheses established as facts or laws' (Denzin and Lincoln, 2011: 101). Table 19.1 gives some key terms and definitions for evaluating positivist research.

TABLE 19.1 Reliability and validity in positivist research

Reliability and validity in positivist research	
Internal validity	Demonstrating validity is about showing how 'truthful' your research findings are. In positivist research this means seeking to ensure that the study measures or tests what is actually intended.
External validity	Merriam (1998) suggests that external validity is concerned with the extent to which the findings of one study can be applied to other situations. In positivist research the concern often lies in demonstrating that the research findings can be applied to a wider population.
Reliability	Positivists use techniques to show that if the work was repeated, in the same context with the same methods and using the same participants, similar results would be obtained.
Objectivity	The basic issue here can be framed as one of relative neutrality and reasonable freedom from unacknowledged researcher biases (Miles and Huberman, 1994).

Positivist research evaluation

In a positivist research project testing the hypothesis that the fitness level of an average ten-year-old boy is higher than that of a ten-year-old girl, you would need to ensure that the variables are carefully controlled. For example, the variables may be when and how heart rate is measured, and the type and duration of exercise. The researcher would be neutral and objective and would give exactly the same instructions to each participant. If a different researcher repeated this experiment the findings should be largely replicated based on children of the same age, gender and height/weight ratio. To demonstrate the reliability of this experiment you would have to explain how all the conditions were kept constant so that it would be possible for another researcher to conduct exactly the same experiment with a different class of children.

If you consider the information required to repeat the research it will help you think about the level of detail you need to convey to the reader. The results of the experiment are discussed in relation to your hypothesis. The results are likely to be in the form of a statistical analysis. Appropriate statistical tests can be conducted, such as a chi-square test to compare the average fitness levels of boys and girls. The checklist below recaps on the information you need to include indicating the validity and reliability of your positivist research project.

Checklist for indicating the validity and reliability of positivist research:
✓ State the hypothesis clearly
✓ Explain the variables in the study
✓ Describe the characteristics of the population
✓ Explain how the sample was selected
✓ Include the research design and justification of research instruments
✓ State the criteria for dealing with identified missing data
✓ Use appropriate statistical techniques
✓ Discuss results in relation to the original hypothesis
✓ Acknowledge the limitations of the study

Evaluating interpretivist research

'Qualitative research involves an interpretive naturalistic approach to the world. This means that qualitative researchers study things in their natural settings, attempting to make sense of, or interpret phenomena in terms of the meanings people bring to them' (Denzin and Lincoln, 2011: 3). Interpretivist researchers want to ensure that they can demonstrate the validity and reliability of their research, but they acknowledge that they are not neutral and objective researchers and that research with humans is not the same as a scientific experiment with chemical compounds. The language and processes used in interpretive research are different from the evaluation of positivist research. This can be confusing because different words can refer to the same concepts and sometimes the same approaches can overlap when being used to indicate validity and reliability. Generally validity is about 'truth', and the terms *credibility, trustworthiness* and *transferability* are associated with this concept. Reliability is about how carefully the research was carried out and the likelihood of the same findings emerging if the study was to be replicated. Words associated with reliability in interpretivist research are *dependability* and *confirmability*. Table 19.2 summarises the definitions.

TABLE 19.2 Reliability and validity in interpretivist research

Reliability and validity in interpretivist research	
Credibility	*Credibility* refers to sufficient illustration of the social reality being studied. Lincoln and Guba (1985) recommend a set of activities that help to improve the credibility of research results: prolonged engagement in the field, persistent observation, triangulation, negative case analysis, checking interpretations against raw data, peer debriefing, and member checking.
Transferability	Lincoln and Guba's (1985) notion of 'transferability' is a useful technique to support the trustworthiness of the data. They suggest that a rich enough depiction of the data should be presented so that the reader can make comparisons to another setting.
Dependability	Lincoln and Guba suggest that in order to assess the dependability of a study, the researcher should consider the question 'How can an inquirer persuade his or her audience that the research findings of an inquiry are worth paying attention to?' (1985: 290).
Confirmability	Confirmability means that steps must be taken to help ensure that as far as possible the findings of the study are the result of the experiences and ideas of the participants, rather than the subjectivity of the researcher. Reflexivity and the triangulation of methods can promote confirmability since these indicate how researcher bias has been addressed.

Credibility and transferability

The notion of validity, literally meaning truth, identifies how accurately an account represents participants' realities of social phenomena (Cresswell and Miller, 2000). Interpretivist researchers often acknowledge that all knowledge is relative to the context in which it is situated, and because of this there can be no 'truth' because reality is socially-produced knowledge. So while researchers may believe that no individual participant's account can represent reality as other people see it, they nevertheless believe they have a duty to provide 'truthful' representations of the participants' voices. There are several strategies you can use to increase the credibility of your findings, such as member checking and reflexivity.

Member checking

- Give each participant a copy of their own transcript for 'member checking', to ensure that participants agree that the transcript is an accurate record of what they said. Give participants the opportunity to add to or amend any of their comments.

- Additionally it is worth sharing your analysis with participants to see if this resonates with them. They may be able to shed additional light on your interpretations. By asking participants to discuss the extent to which your analysis resonates with their perceptions you are increasing the validity of your research (Lather, 1986). They may also be able to explain any quirks or discrepancies in your data.

Reflexivity

- Interpretivist researchers often explain their own personal beliefs and biases to ensure the validity of their work (Cresswell and Miller, 2000).

- Lather (1993) uses the term 'construct validity' to indicate reflexivity. This approach suggests that the researcher should consistently explain all the steps taken in the research process and evaluate how she has influenced the process of the research.

- Following Oakley (2005: 226), it is worth commenting on 'The social/personal characteristics of yourself as the interviewer, the quality of the interviewer–interviewee interaction, hospitality offered, attempts by interviewees to use interviewers as sources of information, and the extension of interviewer–interviewee encounters into more broadly based social relationships'. By doing this the reader can judge the research in light of your position and any circumstances influencing your research.

Example of a reflexive account

Many of my interviews took place in the pseudo sitting-room (used by the university mentoring team) complete with sofas and a coffee table. I was able to book this room in advance with relative ease. This provided a peaceful and informal setting in which to conduct the interviews and I'm sure that this ambience helped to contribute to the depth of emotion portrayed in some of the interview data. I used personal disclosures about my own experiences of feedback as a way of developing rapport with students. Therefore, by exposing my own vulnerabilities and weaknesses, I deflected from my 'authority' as a researcher. However, as a postgraduate student receiving feedback, I could not pretend that my current life experience was the same as a first-year undergraduate grappling with academic requirements. Consequently, it may be misleading to compare our life experiences as similar and the extent to which a relationship based on equality could really emerge. Students asked me questions, my opinions about the meaning of feedback comments and asked me to help decipher written comments. I was confused as to whether the students viewed me as an expert with the knowledge to respond or as a friend helping them out.

(McGinty, 2011)

Transferability

Your analysis needs to be credible, and this means that enough of the data needs to be present in order for the reader to be satisfied with the trustworthiness of the analysis being claimed. Lincoln and Guba's (1985) notion of 'transferability' is a useful technique to support the trustworthiness of the data. They suggest that a rich enough depiction of the data should be presented so that the reader can make comparisons in another setting. Geertz (1973) also argues that the validity in your research comes from context–rich, meaningful and 'thick' descriptions. The interview quote below is an example of 'thick' description:

> When I can't read it, some of my lecturers have really bad handwriting and I just can't read their writing I haven't got a clue what they have said and it doesn't help me in the slightest, particularly if they are going into detail and they are writing all over my work and it is like mangled up and most of the lecturers use red pen and I don't know it kind of gets to me if I open it up and its covered in red crosses and marks and it's horrible it's like my work is bleeding it just puts me off from even reading it.
>
> (Josie, interview from McGinty, 2011)

The data you use should be rich examples of the points that you wish to convey. When writing up your findings you may choose to use one or two excerpts for each point and then explain the significance of these. In an interpretivist paradigm, one of the best ways to consider how to write up your findings so that the reader can evaluate your research is by looking at journal articles which have used qualitative data analysis in educational research. Good examples will be found in journal articles written by Stephen Ball and Diane Reay. Like other qualitative researchers, you are not claiming that your research design will allow for generalisable findings. Rather, you hope that aspects of the narrative or 'story' (Tesch, 1990: 2) that emerges will resonate with others.

Dependability and confirmability

The term 'dependability' is often used by interpretivist researchers, rather than 'reliability' which has more positivistic associations (Lincoln and Guba, 1985). Dependability requires the researcher to take into account any issues of instability, as well as changes that may be induced by the research design. Dependability is often described as a consideration of the extent to which the process of the study, including the research methods and researcher, are consistent over time (Miles and Huberman, 1994). You can address the issue of dependability through consistency in the research process – for instance, using the same interview questions, digitally recording all interviews and transcribing all the interviews yourself. Reporting an audit trail is perhaps one of the best ways to indicate dependability, for example by providing the reader with copies of questionnaire designs and interview transcripts. Including copies of this information in your appendices, so the reader can 'audit' the dependability of your research, is also helpful.

- An audit trail (Lincoln and Guba, 1985) is a map for the reader detailing the key decisions taken from the conception of the research question through to the findings derived from the research. 'An inquiry audit cannot be conducted without a residue of records stemming from the inquiry, just as a fiscal audit cannot be conducted without a residue of records from the business transactions involved' (Lincoln and Guba, 1985: 319).
- Diachronic reliability is the stability of an observation over time. Collecting your data over a period of time ensures the findings are consistent over a prolonged period.
- Triangulation is the use of a variety of research methods to enhance the validity and dependability of the findings, since the same findings may be identified regardless of the method.
- Synchronic reliability is the similarity of observations within the same time period, for example through the triangulation of research methods.

Checklist for indicating the validity and reliability of interpretivist research:
✓ State your research questions clearly
✓ Explain and justify your choice of research design
✓ Describe the characteristics and selection of your participants
✓ Explain how the research was conducted
✓ Explain how you developed the validity of your findings
✓ Justify the dependability of your research
✓ State your analytical processes
✓ Include sufficient original data to support your interpretation
✓ State how your own subjectivity and identity influenced the research
✓ Include copies of interview schedules, transcripts, etc.
✓ State discrepancies in the data
✓ Discuss findings in relation to similar research
✓ Acknowledge limitations of the research and areas for future research

Chapter summary

In summary then, providing the reader with enough information about your research is important to enable them to evaluate your findings. This means incorporating sufficient information about the research design, the research questions and how the findings have been analysed. It is also important to include information about the context, such as participant numbers, participant demographics, the length of data collection sessions and the time period in which the whole data collection phase took place. The way in which your research is evaluated will depend on whether your research aligns itself with the positivist or interpretivist paradigm. The language used for evaluating research also depends on the research paradigm. Essentially, research needs to be evaluated on the extent to which the findings can be deemed accurate and truthful. The terms often used for this are validity and reliability. However, it is not unusual within interpretivist research to see the terms dependability and confirmability.

Further reading

Denzin, N.K. (2011) 'The Politics of Evidence.' Chapter 39, pp. 645–657 in N.K. Denzin and Y.S. Lincoln (eds) (2011) *The Sage Handbook of Qualitative Research*. Thousand Oaks: California (4th edition).

■   This is a thought-provoking chapter which explores the tensions between positivist and interpretivist research. Suggestions are made for how interpretivist research can be evaluated in its own right.

20

The position of the researcher

Introduction

One of the most important considerations for the educational researcher is the position they occupy in relation to the research setting, the participants in the research and the data analysis and presentation. For some, researchers are 'experts', removed from the site of study and capable of theorising from an objective standpoint. For others, the researcher is bound up in the research itself and incapable of presenting anything other than a partial and subjective account – personal judgements defining the topic of study, the methods used, the analysis and presentation of data and so on. Given the current prominence of this second position, strategies for dealing with the inherent subjectivity of research should be considered – most notably, the quality of reflexivity. Much educational research today is 'practitioner' or 'insider' research, and this chapter considers the benefits and problems associated with the role of the 'insider researcher' – issues such as friendship, familiarity, shared histories and futures, over-rapport and taken-for-granted 'truths'.

What does it mean to take a position?

Meighan and Siraj-Blatchford (1997: 289) talk about taking a 'stance' in education research, and how important it is to understand what this stance means in relation to our research outcomes:

> Each and every one of our daily interactions is fundamentally dependent on our subjective understanding and interpretations, our world-view. ... it is difficult to imagine how we could engage in social interaction at all without constant recourse to the various views, definitions and motives we hold, to the personal beliefs and assumptions, hopes and fears we cling to and which we use to make sense of our experiences and to direct our behaviour. In interaction, then, we constantly theorise about social life ... and as we theorize, we develop a stance.

They go on to argue that because subjective understanding is so important, research can be made difficult in two ways:

- There is a danger of 'substituting our (observer) versions and interpretations of what we see happening for those accounts and evaluations held and acted upon by those (insiders) who are making it happen'.

- Both researchers and the researched 'cannot suddenly switch off their personal predilections and purposes and stop being human in the name of "objective" research' – i.e. research is a social act, and it therefore has unavoidable limits to objectivity attached (Meighan and Siraj-Blatchford 1997: 228–9).

These dilemmas rightly receive a good deal of attention in the current research literature, usually in relation to the notion of research 'positioning'. Originally the term 'positioning' derived from Davies and Harré's (1990) work, who later described positioning as the 'discursive practice whereby people are located in conversations as observably and subjectively coherent participants in jointly produced storylines' (Davies and Harré, 1999: 37). The implications of such a positioning approach for education researchers is that 'no longer is it appropriate for the researcher to let the "data speak for themselves". Instead, interpretive researchers might show how meanings are constituted both in relation to and within the interview environment' (Ritchie and Rigano, 2010: 755).

This concept of researchers having a 'position' has implications that reach far beyond purely theoretical understandings, because the position a researcher takes (either knowingly or unknowingly) can impact not only on the research design but also on the ethical nature of the research process itself. This is an issue that is dealt with by Khawaja and Lerche Mørck (2009: 28) in their work on research positioning and Muslim 'otherness'. According to them, in order to adopt an ethical stance to research on marginalised groups such as Muslims in Western societies and to help transcend objectifying representations, researchers need to have:

> constant awareness of and reflection on the multiple ways in which one's positioning as a researcher influences the research process. Studying the other calls for close reflections on one's own position, theoretically, personally, and politically, taking into account one's complicity in either overcoming or reproducing processes of othering and marginalisation.
>
> (Khawaja and Lerche Mørck (2009: 28)

Such concerns over position therefore connect closely with parallel concerns over the ethics of undertaking research generally (as detailed further in Chapter 21).

Position and its impact on research

A whole range of studies, not only those in education, have explored the impact that position (and awareness or non-awareness of position) has on the research process and findings. The examples provided here suggest that a lack of self-awareness about a researcher's own stance – including the kinds of normative assumptions, biases and background knowledge that researchers bring with them – can have negative impacts on the validity and veracity of the research findings. These examples provide a cautionary tale regarding non-reflexive forms of research, illustrating the need for care to be taken when designing your research project. One example comes from the field of education research, while the other is taken from health research.

Example 1: Researchers' assumptions and the ideology of 'normality'

Source: Benincasa, L. (2012) 'Teaching lessons in exclusion: Researchers' assumptions and the ideology of normality'. *International Journal of Qualitative Studies in Education*, 25:8, 1087–1106.

In this research, Luciana Benincasa examined a range of studies that attempted to investigate the attitudes of Greek pupils towards fellow-pupils who were defined as 'different'. She wanted to explore the assumptions that inform the selection and construction of survey questions in questionnaires administered to Greek pupils to measure their acceptance or rejection towards 'diversity', and also what kind of worldview respondents were exposed to through contact with the selected questions. She concluded that such surveys themselves embody assumptions that are likely to encourage attitudes and practices potentially leading to the marginalisation of children who are defined as 'different':

> "A closer examination of the questionnaire items brings to light an underlying set of presuppositions about the respondents. Those questions appear thus to address a 'mainstream respondent' who, besides being a 'Greek pupil', has also a number of additional characteristics that are part of the culturally taken-for-granted idea of what is 'normal'. In this context normality includes being Greek, Christian-Orthodox, non-Roma and 'white', 'bodily able', 'mentally able', 'without learning disabilities' and at least 'average' from a socio-economic point of view. Whenever this bundle of characteristics is evoked the underlying ideology is strengthened. In this sense the questionnaire items contribute to maintaining the status quo".
>
> (Benincasa, 2012: 1095).

One of the recommendations she makes is to introduce other methods into the research, because the questionnaires used often 'impose categories that the young respondents do not necessarily share'. She believes that research on pupils' attitudes would be improved by making use of participant observation, which aims at 'letting respondents' meanings emerge, without imposing previously defined categories on them' (Benincasa, 2012: 1098).

Example 2: Conceptions of race and health among health researchers

Source: Baer, R., Arteaga, R., Dyer, K., Eden, A., Gross, R., Helmy, H., Karnyski, M., Papadopoulos, A. and Reeser, D. (2012) 'Concepts of race and ethnicity among health researchers: Patterns and implications'. *Ethnicity and Health*, 2012, 1–15iFirst article.

Baer *et al.* (2012) used seventy-three interviews with research scientists to explore their conceptions about race and ethnicity – a significant and serious area of study, as it has been suggested that the 'scientific validity of research done using vague notions of race and ethnicity may be in question' (2012: 14). Of concern is that they identified:

> a core model of how race and ethnicity are understood. The respondents were confused about the concepts of race and ethnicity and their link to genetic differences between populations; many treated these concepts as interchangeable and genetically based. Although ethnicity was considered somewhat more socially constructed, it was often felt to cause unhealthy behavior. In addition, the situation is not improving; the younger health researchers tended to put a stronger emphasis on the genetic aspects of race than did the older health researchers.
>
> (Baer *et al.*, 2012: 14)

It was evident from these findings that health researchers' stance (in this case their implicit understanding) of the difference between race and ethnicity was shaky at best:

- 'Race and ethnicity are blurred concepts'.
- 'I know it is different from race, but I am not sure as to how'.
- 'There is a fuzzy line between race and ethnicity'.
- 'Some people try to use ethnicity rather than race, [be]cause race is a very political term'.
- 'I don't differentiate between the two [race and ethnicity] … there is a political tone at play here and there is need to be careful'.
- 'Same as race, redundant. [The] rules [are]: Black, White, Hispanic, etc.'.

What is significant about this conceptual vagueness is that most respondents felt that ethnic differences affect health. About half related the effect of ethnicity on health to genetic differences, a fifth to physical traits, and about a third related it to individual behavior:

- 'Ethnicity is part of culture and culture affects behavior and diet, which affect health'.
- 'Eating, lifestyle, religion, Christian background, use of alcohol can cause a predisposition to certain types of cancer'.

Baer *et al.* (2012: 14) concluded that better training in concepts such as race and ethnicity was necessary in formal and continuing educational training of health researchers: 'Such training should build on the actual perspectives of this population, beginning with discussions of human diversity, and then move into what race and ethnicity are and are not'.

Other types of positioning: Role play

Glesne and Peshkin (1992: 112–114) described how there are several dramaturgical roles that researchers, especially novice researchers, can assume, each bringing its own ethical dilemmas. These can be summarised briefly as:

Exploiter   The relationship between research and exploitation is a fraught and challenging one, and reflects the importance placed on debates about positionality. Glesne and Peshkin are correct to caution the researcher against falling into such a trap of manipulation: 'Do researchers, as welcomed but uninvited outsiders, enter a new community, mine words and behaviours, and then withdraw to process those words into a product that serves themselves and, perhaps, their professional colleagues?'

Intervener/reformer   This is a role that 'researchers may consciously decide to assume': a kind of action/reconstructive form of research that sees professional researchers caught in ethical dilemmas not of their own making (such as when they acquire knowledge about criminal activity). It also relates to the presence of what Glesne and Peshkin refer to as 'dangerous knowledge' (1992: 11) – knowledge gained during the research process that could have potentially damaging consequences for individuals and organisations.

Advocate   Given the amount of time and effort (both physical and emotional) spent with research participants, it is unsurprising that the role of the researcher can sometimes be transformed into that of advocate. Glesne and Peshkin provide a revealing example of a researcher (Lynne) who was tempted into advocacy in her research on university custodians:

I keep asking myself to what extent the research should improve the situation for custodians. This is magnified somewhat by my feeling that I have been a participant in the process, raising issues with custodians that many by now have come to terms with or raising expectations that some good will result. Even though my research was for the purpose of understanding and not 'fixing', how can one come so close to what is judged to be a very bad situation and walk away? I keep asking myself 'do I owe them solutions or at least some relief?' My answer is always 'no', but then I keep asking myself the same question, probably because I just don't like my answer.

(in Glesne and Peshkin, 1992: 115–16)

Friend   The relationship between the researcher and friends who are research participants can be valuable but also awkward, both emotionally and ethically. This situation does occur, but it has its own set of ethical dilemmas attached. For example, you can gain access to intimate information given to you in your researcher role, but 'should you use such data?' (Glesne and Peshkin, 1992: 116).

Positioning and alternative forms of research

These concerns over researcher positioning and its impact on methods and outcomes have led some researchers to 'take the idea of responsibility to participants further than others' (Curtis and Pettigrew, 2010: 62). Curtis and Pettigrew point to the existence of research that represents a third paradigm, one 'which extends the interpretivist criticism of positivist objective neutrality and argues that researchers should be openly and actively committed to contributing directly to educational change'. They point to the likes of Griffiths (1998) and Thompson and Gunter (2006) as good examples of such a paradigm.

Other approaches have developed as part of this third paradigm, such as what Burke (2002) calls 'reflexive collaboration' and what Flecha and Gomez (2004) refer to as 'dialogic research'.

Reflexive collaboration   In her work on access to higher education Penny Burke (2002: 40) positions the research process as part of a broader political project, believing that joint participation in the research (from both herself and those who are being researched) helps to facilitate a more ethical form of data gathering and meaning making, made easier by the fact that she researched her own students, something that helped to:

> identify important interconnections between the private (e.g. their experiences of family and mothering, the emotional and subjective) and the public (e.g. their experiences of access education) as lived out by the women and men participating in the research. Such inter-connections have crucial ramifications for understanding, reconstructing and reshaping meanings around adult educational participation. The collaborative approach enabled students to contribute actively to a research project of which they felt they had some ownership.
>
> (Burke, 2002: 40)

Dialogic research   In their paper 'Participatory paradigms: researching "with" rather than "on"', Flecha and Gomez argue that much interpretivist research still views the researcher's position as expert even when it takes into account the voices of the researched subjects, with the researcher 'considering his or her interpretations more valid to his or her position of power' (2004: 132). Their dialogic approach, based on a communicative model of human understanding and meaning-making, 'offers scientific knowledge and methodologies that incorporate people's voices, with the aim of providing elements that favour overcoming the social exclusion they face'.

According to them, the core priority of dialogic research is not the accumulation of information, but 'its use and results' (Flecha and Gomez, 2004: 132).

Other considerations

Research as quasi-therapy – as indicated above, roles during the research process can become quite fluid, altering shape dramatically depending on the research and the researcher. For example, it is quite common for the researcher to morph into the role of therapist, whether they like it or not. As Glesne and Peshkin (1992: 123) point out, 'self-reflections can produce pain where least expected, and interviewers may suddenly find themselves face to face with a crying interviewee. Tears do not necessarily mean that you have asked a bad or a good question, but they do obligate you to deal sensitively and constructively with the unresolved feelings'.

Impact on researcher – it is also sometimes the case that while research can have implications for those who are being researched, it can also have a considerable impact on those undertaking the research. This was the conclusion of Poole *et al.* (2004: 79) in their review of research on sexuality and sexual issues – particularly in the field of non-consensual sex. Here, it was evident 'that the consequences of carrying out sexuality research are typically negative (for example, the impact on personal relationships)' (Poole *et al.*, 2004: 85), with researchers in this field encountering experiences that had detrimental effects on both their professional and personal lives.

Chapter summary

This chapter explored the notion of positionality and what it means for education researchers to take a 'stance' in relation to their subject or the participants being researched. It examined the kinds of impacts that researcher position can have on the research process and included two examples (including one from outside education). The chapter then outlined a set of other roles that the researcher may encounter – those of exploiter, intervener, advocate and friend. It also looked at how the more recent focus on positionality has resulted in a third alternative paradigm of research with a more explicit political agenda. The chapter concluded by considering the quasi-therapeutic nature of research and the potential impacts that research can also have for the researcher.

Further reading

McGinity, R. (2012) 'Exploring the complexities of researcher identity in a school based ethnography'. *Reflective Practice: International and Multidisciplinary Perspectives*, 13 (6), 761–773.

- An article by Ruth McGinity (2012) presents an interesting reflexive analysis of the first year of a PhD studentship which involved working and researching in a university and a school. In the paper, McGinity presents a theory of what it means to be simultaneously in, out and between, and what this means for the development of a project that meets the requirements of the school and university simultaneously.

Purdy, L. and Jones, R. (2011) 'Changing personas and evolving identities: The contestation and renegotiation of researcher roles in fieldwork'. *Sport, Education and Society*, 2011, 1–19, iFirst article.

■   Another recommended paper is by Laura Purdy and Robyn Jones (2011), who discuss the evolution of particular personas in their research with a special focus on the role of the principal author as a female ethnographer (and the sole female) in the world of elite male rowing.

21

Ethical issues in educational research

Introduction

Sometimes in our everyday lives we have to make difficult decisions. When there is no definitive 'right' or 'wrong' answer we use our individual morals and principles to guide our choices. Carrying out research can also be fraught with ethical dilemmas. Ethical research guidelines are codes of conduct which outline a system of moral principles which researchers are expected to follow. For ethical guidance, refer to the documents provided by your institution and the educational association you are most closely aligned to; for instance, this might be the British Educational Research Association (BERA), the American Educational Research Association (AERA) or the European Educational Research Association (EERA). The ethical guidelines outlined by BERA can be downloaded from their website: www.bera. ac.uk. The BERA ethical guidelines are underpinned by principles of respect for:

- The person – treating them fairly, sensitively and with dignity. This applies to research participants and researchers as well.
- Knowledge – we should respect the information that we gain from our research participants.
- Democratic values – this means carrying out research in a way that is not authoritarian. Participants should take part in research voluntarily, and have ownership over the information that they give to researchers.
- The quality of educational research – this means conducting research to the highest standard and not sensationalising research findings.
- Academic freedom – being able to put forward new ideas and ask questions, but not abusing this privilege.

(adapted from the BERA guidelines, 2011: 4).

Therefore, an overriding concern when thinking about ethics is one of respect (BERA, 2011: 5). Respect is an important principle which you should keep at the forefront of your mind during the entire research process. Ethical guidelines are put in place to protect the researcher and the researched. We have a duty of care to the participants in our research, and we also need to make sure that we do not put ourselves in dangerous situations. Research ethics help us to remember why it is unacceptable to report our findings inaccurately, and why covert research is generally not appropriate. In addition, ethical guidelines help us to respond to difficult situations such as finding out that your research participants are involved in illegal activities. Overall, we need to remember that educational research brings ethical responsibilities to a number of stakeholders: participants, sponsors of the research, the community of educational researchers, educational professionals, policy makers and the general public (BERA, 2011: 5). This chapter discusses the most likely ethical considerations you will need to think about as you prepare to undertake a piece of education research: anonymity, confidentiality, informed consent, potential harm to participants, gaining ethical approval for your research from an ethics committee, and writing up your research.

Anonymity

Anonymity is important for participants in research – after all, they are unlikely to disclose information if it will be possible to identify them in later reports or publications. Consequently, a guarantee of anonymity will allow participants to feel confident in providing their perspectives or experiences. Generally when you carry out research you change the names of the participants. This is known as providing each participant with a pseudonym – for example, 'Mrs Smith, a Year 3 teacher' may be referred to throughout the reporting stage as 'Ms Jones, a Key Stage 2 teacher'. If you have a very small number of participants you may need to go further still in ensuring their anonymity by actively obscuring any features which may identify them. For example, if your participants are teachers from a small village school with only one male member of staff, any readers of your research who are familiar with the school may be able to guess his identity. The names of locations in your research should also be changed – for example, 'Borrow Wood Primary School in Walsall' could become 'Greenfields Primary School in the West Midlands'. By changing any distinguishing features of your research participants and their location, you should be able to ensure their anonymity.

Confidentiality

Maintaining the confidentiality of your research participants implies that you do not disclose information that was given to you during the data collection. This means that you cannot repeat any 'juicy gossip' given to you by a participant in an interview. If you are going to share a recording of an interview with your dissertation supervisor, or if someone else is transcribing your data, participants should be made aware of this. Additionally, you should remind any third parties sharing your data that it is important that they keep this information confidential. However, at the same time you should be aware that there may be limitations to the level of confidentiality you can provide participants – and you should be honest with them about this. A good example of this is police officers who undertake educational research as part of their qualifications to support them in training newly appointed officers. If police officers are made aware of illegal activities they have a duty to report them, and therefore they make this clear to potential research participants at the outset. You could find yourself in a similar situation in your own research, for instance if your teenage participants tell you about their drug-taking habits. Ethical guidelines suggest that you must not keep this information confidential.

With regard to disclosure, the BERA guidelines state: 'Researchers who judge that the effect of the agreements they have made with participants, on confidentiality and anonymity, will allow the continuation of illegal behaviour, which has come to light in the course of the research, must carefully consider making disclosure to the appropriate authorities. If the behaviour is likely to be harmful to the participants or to others, the researcher must apprise the participants or their guardians or responsible others of their intentions and reasons for disclosure' (2011: 8). At times it will be ethically impossible to maintain confidentiality. For example, an interview with a child could cause you real concern if they disclose that they may be suffering from abuse in the home, and in this instance you must make your unease known to the relevant professionals. Other incidents may also cause you more of an ethical dilemma in terms of maintaining confidentiality, as the description below indicates.

ACTIVITY

Andrew Barbour's description of observations in the classroom highlighted some challenging ethical dilemmas for him. His observations were allowed by 'gatekeepers' who were his colleagues – other further education lecturers – so from that perspective he felt loyal towards them. However, the teaching practices he observed were of poor quality, and his interviews with students reinforced this point. Additionally, when lecturers were being peer observed by colleagues there was a distinct change in their teaching approaches, suggesting that they were aware of the poor quality of their teaching in general.

> If my interpretations of data were accurate, to avoid confrontation yet identify this unprofessionalism in my research, however anonymously, could become tantamount to a betrayal of trust to my colleagues. After all, without their permissions the research would not have been able to take place. I was caught in a dilemma of being torn between disloyalty to colleagues and a moral obligation to those students who were receiving a less than ideal education. These considerations were compounded with the risk, aversion even, of losing access to this fertile research site. However, by avoiding these questions and remaining as a more passive observer I could aim to gain a clear, accurate and non-judgmental account of the cultures of the classroom and also remain within the original aims of the research.
>
> (Barbour, 2010: 167)

- How does this situation challenge the principles of anonymity and confidentiality?
- To what extent should he have remained loyal to the 'gatekeepers'?
- How would you write up findings that are potentially controversial or damaging?
- What was more important – publishing his research or the quality of the education that the students were receiving?

'Informed' consent

Homan and Bulmer (1982) describe the principle of informed consent as meaning that in all circumstances participants should be completely aware of factors that affect them, and based on this information they choose freely to take part (or not) in the research. You should also be aware that consent is an ongoing process – just because participants have signed a consent form does not mean that they have to continue with the research. Participants can change their mind about their involvement in your project at any time. Should participants decide not to continue their involvement in your research (for whatever reason), this should be respected and their decision should not have any negative consequences for them.

> **ACTIVITY**
>
> A participant gives the most brilliant interview material for your research, but then says, 'Actually, I don't want to be part of your research project anymore. Please don't use my interview'.
>
> ■ Will the participant ever know if you do use the interview transcript against their wishes (after all, they are not an avid reader of dissertation theses in the university library)?
>
> ■ What about the grade for your research project? (Your dissertation supervisor might give you a First if you use the data from that interview, and you really need to pull up your whole degree classification to a 2:1 if you are going to be accepted on a PGCE course.)

Making decisions about whether to participate in research assumes that participants understand what the research involves. It can be difficult to know whether some participants are truly able to give 'informed consent'. A variety of ways have been developed to ensure that more vulnerable participants can give consent, for example by the use of participatory research methods (Hart, 1992) in which children carry out the research themselves if they want to. The mosaic approach (Clark and Moss, 2001) is a good example of a research method that allows participants to give 'informed consent'. There are examples within education research in which participants have not been in full possession of all the facts when making a decision to take part, as this case study suggests:

> **ACTIVITY**
>
> Levinson (2010: 198–199) discusses the difficulties of informed consent, which was especially problematic because the nature of his research into the homeschooling of Gypsy children shifted as his research progressed:
>
>> To what extent is a researcher misleading participants when (s)he her/himself does not know where it is heading? Initially, my attempts to justify my study revolved around the position that research was beneficial; only with such knowledge and

understanding could one hope for changes to an educational system increasingly shaped by didacticism and intolerance of non-conformity, in which the outcome of much research seemed to be the confirmation and support of pre-established positions. I allowed this initial conviction to justify enquiry that was somewhat tangential... As suggested already, my own research began as a restricted study. The focus, at the outset of data collection in the 1990s, the initial study, investigated reasons for the difficulties encountered by Gypsy children in schools. As it became evident that understandings based on such research could only be partial, the research gradually moved towards the home environment. Meanwhile, it also became clear that to understand the experiences of children, it was necessary to explore the perspectives of older members of the communities. From my perspective, this seemed to significantly enrich the data that were being gathered. This view was not necessarily shared by participants:

> Ethan (30s): I thought your research was about our kids' education.
> Me: It is.
> Ethan: So why are you asking me now about how I feel about moving from my trailer to a house?
> Me: Well, as I've been talking to people, I've come to realise that there are all sorts of things involved that affect attitudes, and I think it's important to find out what parents are feeling if I'm going to understand where their children are coming from.
> Ethan: So, what you said the first time was just bollocks, and what you're doing now is trying to find out about lots of new things.
> Me: OK – if you want to put it like that, but it's not as if I ever set out to deceive you.
> Ethan: 'Course, if I'd known that from the start, I might never have agreed to talk to you.
> Me: Fair enough – 'course you can still tell me to get lost.
> Ethan: I can – and I might – but all this time you've been talking to Jack and Crystal (Ethan's children), and I don't know what sort of things they've been telling you.

■ How has the principle of informed consent been challenged here?

■ To what extent do you agree with Levinson about his justification for the shift in research focus?

■ Goffman (1959) argues that complete openness is impossible to achieve. If we conceal our intentions or mislead people in our everyday lives, is it OK to do this in research?

■ Discuss your thoughts with a partner.

The general consensus within education research is that it is important to be honest about your identity and the aims of your research so that participants can make an informed decision, in possession of all the facts, about whether they wish to participate. This information can be incorporated into your participant consent form.

Exemplar participant consent form:

Consent form for participants (volunteers) taking part in research

Name of researcher: Sam Shields

Title of project: Assessment reassessed: A student and lecturer collaborative enquiry into current practice.

Research Statement:
In this research project we are focusing on exploring the concept of collaborative assessment feedback, for example the use of peer assessment.

Our key questions are:

■ What good practice in assessment feedback currently exists on Education Studies programmes?

■ How do students and lecturers in different HEIs feel about the assessment feedback practices on their course?

1 I confirm that I have read and understood the research statement for the above study.

2 I confirm that I have had the opportunity to discuss my decision to participate in this research study with others.

3 I understand that my participation is voluntary and that I am free to withdraw at any time, without giving any reason.

4 I understand that the decision I take regarding my participation in this research will in no way affect or influence my academic progress.

5 I understand that any research findings related to this project will be anonymous.

6 I understand that data collected for this research will only be accessed by the research project team and any other parties with permission from the research project team.

7 I understand that following any publications the research data will be destroyed by the deletion of files and paper shredding.

I agree/do not agree (delete as appropriate) to take part in the above study.

Name of participant: _____

Signature of participant: _____   Date: _____

Potential harm to participants

The Hippocratic Oath taken by doctors requires them to 'do no harm' – and this is a good starting point for thinking about the way in which we conduct all research, not just research in medicine! A questionnaire about how children would like to improve the playground facilities at their school is unlikely to cause any distress to participants. Nevertheless, you should always be mindful of the potential for research to harm participants. For example, if you are using a narrative life history approach when asking participants to reflect on their school days, this could dredge up memories of being bullied. Providing potential participants with a research statement about your research (see the exemplar participant consent form) means that they can make an informed decision about whether they are likely to be harmed in any way by taking part in your research.

There are lots of examples of research (including education research) that have been conducted in an unethical fashion. Based on what you have read about ethical dilemmas in research, evaluate this well known case study below.

ACTIVITY

Rosenthal and Jacobson (1968) conducted an experiment in an American elementary school. They wanted to identify to what extent (if any) teachers' expectations of pupils influenced the levels of pupil achievement. The researchers told teachers that particular children in their classrooms were likely to make more academic progress than their peers based on the students' results in the 'Harvard Test of Inflected Acquisition' test. In reality, the test did not exist and the children who were identified as 'Spurters' had been randomly picked.

In small groups:

- Discuss the ethical issues that are raised by this study.
- Does the end justify the means?
- Could this research be re-designed to avoid ethical problems? How?

Gaining ethical approval

As part of the process of undertaking any research you need to get approval from your university *before* starting. Universities have ethics committees which meet to decide if you can carry out your research. In order to get approval you generally have to submit an ethics form, possibly with additional documentation such as a copy of the questionnaire you wish to use, a copy of your interview schedule or exemplar consent forms.

Ethical approval process

Complete ethics paperwork
↓
Submit paperwork
↓
Ethics committee meets
↓
Decision is made about granting ethical approval:

■   YES

■   WITH AMENDMENTS/FURTHER INFORMATION

■   NO

You are informed of the decision

The likelihood of gaining ethical approval often depends on what you are trying to find out and the research methods you wish to use. For example, if you are interested in researching the teaching and learning strategies teachers use in the classroom and you wish to carry out non-participant observation, this is unlikely to be problematic. Anonymity and confidentiality are probably the biggest ethical concerns, and you will need to reassure the ethics committee and your participants that you can guarantee this. On the other hand, if you want to interview children (vulnerable participants who may not be able to give 'informed' consent) about their experiences of being bullied (with potential for emotional distress), this may be much more difficult to gain ethical approval for. In this case you may need to think of alternative strategies or a different research focus.

EXEMPLAR ETHICS FORM

The University of Newtown requires that approval is obtained by members of staff of the University and by students of the University who wish to engage in research. Please complete this application for ethical approval if your anticipated research involves:

1   Gathering information about human beings (and organisations) through:

■   interviewing

■   surveying

■   questionnaires

■   observation of human behaviour

■   Using archived data in which individuals are identifiable.

APPLICATION FORM FOR RESEARCH ACTIVITY REQUIRING HUMAN RESEARCH ETHICS CONSIDERATION OR APPROVAL

Staff/Student Name
Sarah Miller

Programme (if relevant)
BA Educational Studies

Title of Research Project
A study into the free play choices of Year 1 children at a suburban infant school

Brief description of proposed activity and its objectives
This research will involve identifying the choices of children in Year 1 with regards to free play opportunities through non-participant observation.

- The data collection methods will involve non-participant observation of Year 1 children and;
- Teachers will be asked to take part in semi-structured interviews about their perceptions of Year 1 children's free play experiences.

Ethical issues
- Protection of participants' identities
- Informed consent from children, teachers, parents and headteacher required.

How ethical issues will be addressed
- Anonymity and confidentiality (number reference instead of name)
- Participant consent form.

To which ethical codes of conduct have you referred?
BERA (2011) Ethical Guidelines for Educational Research www.bera.ac.uk/guidelines.html

Have you considered the following?
Providing participants with full details of the objectives of the research

Providing information appropriate for those whose first language is not English

Voluntary participation with informed consent

Written description of involvement

Freedom to withdraw

Keeping appropriate records

Signed acknowledgement and understanding by participants

Consideration of relevant codes of conduct/guidelines

> ### Are there other/additional factors that could/will give rise to ethical concerns?
>
> List of accompanying documentation to support the application:
>
> 1   A copy of the research proposal.
>
> 2   The details of arrangements for participation of human subjects (including recruitment, consent and confidentiality procedures and documentation as appropriate).
>
> 3   A copy of all the documentation provided to the volunteers to ensure the clarity of information provided.
>
> 4   Copies of appropriate other ethical committee permissions (internal or external) or supporting documentation.
>
> There are four possible outcomes from reviewing the activity against the procedures in place:
>
> 1   no ethical issues.
>
> 2   minor ethical issues which have been addressed and concerns resolved.
>
> 3   major ethical issues which have been addressed and concerns resolved.
>
> 4   ethical issues that have not been resolved/addressed.
>
> (Adapted from De Montfort University Ethics paperwork, 2011)

Writing up your research

When writing up your research you may wish to include a discussion of any ethical issues you encountered as an indicator of your reflexivity. Reflexivity means that we acknowledge we are part of the social world that we are studying (Atkinson and Hammersley, 1989) and as such our identity can influence the research process. Cicourel (1964) argues the importance of explaining the set of circumstances and conditions that favourably or unfavourably influence data collection. For example, you may be concerned that you were 'exploiting' participants during the interview process, if you felt your identity could be seen as one of 'authority' and 'dominance' because you were asking the interview questions and probing for further explanation. Also, as the researcher you are in a more powerful position because you have control over writing up the findings. If you have spent time gaining the trust of your participants, what happens if your findings cast the participants in a negative light? Do you try to 'skew' your findings to avoid the participants being shown in a negative way? Issues regarding bias may also occur if your research is funded. The funding body may anticipate certain outcomes, and you may be under pressure to write up your research in a certain way to satisfy the funding body.

Chapter summary

Hopefully the ethical dilemmas that you face in your research will not be too challenging. In general, ethical concerns such as anonymity, confidentiality and informed consent should be fairly straightforward to address. Nevertheless, this chapter will have given you an insight into educational scenarios where this is not always the case, and how it can be difficult to resolve these concerns. As Ferdinand *et al.* argue, 'how researchers deal with ethical dilemmas ultimately comes down to personal choice and the responsibility that goes with this' (2007: 540). However, the BERA guidelines are an excellent reference source and it is important to remember the key principle of respect when carrying out your research.

Further reading

Mauthner, M., Birch, M., Jessop, J. and Miller, T. (eds) (2002) *Ethics in qualitative research.* London: Sage.

■   This book explores ethical issues in a theoretical and practical way. It is written from a feminist perspective and is particularly useful for understanding the concept of 'informed' consent.

22

Educational research with children and young people

Introduction

By its very nature, the majority of educational research involves children and young people. This chapter considers the kinds of strategies that are most effective for working alongside younger people. It asks questions about how one might gather data from very young children, and considers how schools, colleges and universities elicit 'data' from their students. It distinguishes between the various levels of participation – for instance, research conducted *about, on, for, with* and *by* children. Approaches involving students as researchers and co-researchers are outlined and discussed. The chapter concludes by outlining key issues for these approaches to research – most notably, issues of power in terms of differences and equity in adult–child research relations.

Constructions of childhood and young personhood

Since Phillipe Aries wrote his landmark book *Centuries of Childhood* in 1960 (translated 1962) the idea that 'childhood' is a social construction has prevailed. This notion suggests that what it means to be a child is shaped and defined by the cultural, environmental, economic, political and social contexts of a given time and place. 'Childhood' changes over time and means different things in different places. In recent years, debates about the changing nature of childhood have been dominated by moral panics – a decline in children's safety and innocence, a 'commodification' of childhood, a potential 'end of childhood', or, as Palmer (2006) famously suggested, the emergence of 'toxic childhood'.

However, a more positive reading of childhood in Western societies today would point to a growth in children's prominence, status and 'voice'. Advances in technology, mass media, education and the leisure industries provide children with far more access to products and information, and many more opportunities to express their viewpoints. Children are no longer 'seen but not heard'. Arguably, adults listen to children more and their rights, needs and interests are taken far more seriously than in the past. The United Nations Convention on the Rights of the Child was enshrined in international law in 1990 and ratified in the UK in 1991. In theory, the convention provides all young people under the age of eighteen with specific protections, entitlements and services. It also affords children rights to be informed and to participate. Consider the following activity.

ACTIVITY

Read the following extracts from two articles in the UNCRC.

Article 12:
States Parties shall assure to the child who is capable of forming his or her own views the right to express those views freely in all matters affecting the child, the views of the child being given due weight in accordance with the age and maturity of the child.

Article 13:
The child shall have the right to freedom of expression; this right shall include freedom to seek, receive and impart information and ideas of all kinds, regardless of frontiers, either orally, in writing or in print, in the form of art, or through any other media of the child's choice.

(Extracts taken from UNCRC, date accessed 2012)

Now respond to the following questions:

1   How do you think these two articles might inform an educational researcher's methods of studying school children?
2   What approaches to data collection might enable children to utilise these rights in educational research?
3   How might research approaches differ when conducted in:
   a   Pre-school?
   b   Primary school?
   c   Secondary school?
   d   Further education?
   e   Higher education?

Levels of participation

As you would expect, the majority of educational research is concerned with children and young people. This research takes various forms and has many different purposes – from a teacher's research to inform and improve her own practice, to large-scale longitudinal and international projects. Hart's highly influential 'ladder of participation' (1992) has had a considerable impact upon conceptualisations of children's participation, see Figure 22.1.

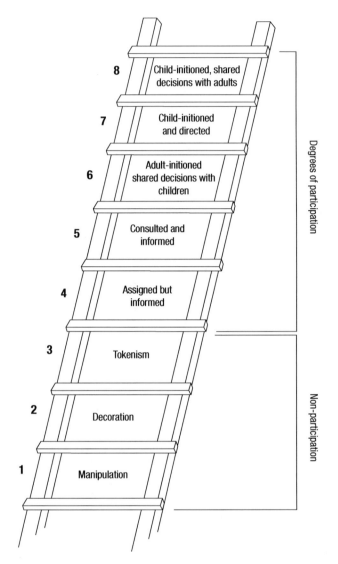

FIGURE 22.1 Hart's ladder of participation

Hart's ladder encourages educational researchers to rethink the relationship between children and their research. One potential direction of travel is shown in Figure 22.2.

Children as objects of research

(educational research is about children but does not involve them)

↓

Children as subjects in research

(children are part of the data collection process)

↓

Children as (co-)researchers

(children participate in data collection and analysis)

FIGURE 22.2 Potential direction of travel

There are various ways that children and young people might engage with educational research, including:

- *About but without* **children** – research might be concerned with the experiences of children, but not include their perspectives in data collection or analysis. For instance, a researcher might choose to interview teachers or parents rather than children because the children of interest are too young. Alternatively, depending on the topic, there might be ethical concerns regarding the children's involvement in terms of adverse effects on their social or emotional wellbeing or their academic achievement.

- *For* **children** – adult researchers might conduct research on behalf of children. The purpose of the project might be to make recommendations that will improve the conditions that children and young people live and learn within, whether or not they take part in the research itself.

- *On* **children** – educational research today frequently involves children participating as respondents/sources of data. For example, Piaget famously conducted research on children to identify different stages of development (see Voyat, 1982), and his observations have had tremendously positive impacts on learning and teaching ever since. Depending on ethical constraints and the children's age, communication and skill levels, different modes of involvement may be possible and/or desirable. Data collection can involve children in many different activities, including:
  - Keeping diaries
  - Drawing pictures
  - Making models
  - Completing surveys
  - Being interviewed
  - Taking photographs
  - Making films
  - Participating in stimulated discussion
  - Telling stories
  - Developing spider diagrams or mind maps
  - Completing worksheets
  - Being the focus of observations.

Methods are frequently combined – most influentially in Clark and Moss' 'mosiac approach' to understanding young children's perspectives on early years settings (2001).

- *With* **children** – increasingly, children and young people participate in the collection and analysis of the data – especially in research intended to evaluate and enhance existing educational provision. Working alongside more experienced researchers, children and young people become active participants in the research process (see overleaf for further details).

- **By children** – while still relatively uncommon, some educational research is conducted by children, who might take responsibility for all or particular stages of enquiry (developing aims and objectives, gathering and analysing data, presenting findings). For example, some universities offer opportunities for students to design research projects and apply for funding (see below).

Enhancing participation – Harry Shier's 'pathways to participation'

Increasing interest in the promotion of young people's participation in educational research has encouraged educationalists to reflect on strategies to enhance best practice. Perhaps the most well-known model has been developed by Harry Shier in his 'pathways to participation', see Figure 22.3, providing an excellent framework for planning and evaluating children's participation.

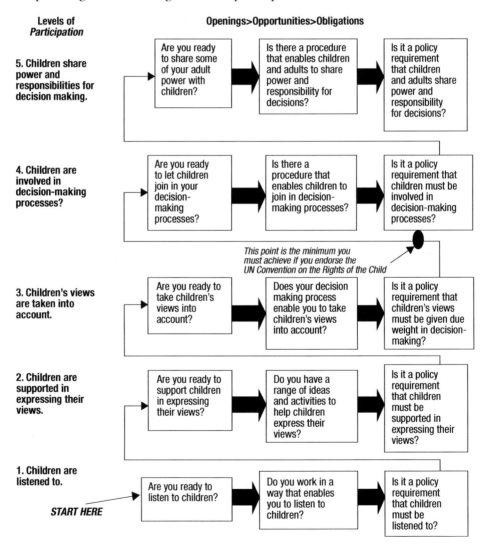

FIGURE 22.3 Pathways to participation

ACTIVITY

Michael Fielding outlines six 'patterns of partnership' between adults and young people within schools and other educational contexts:

- Students as data source – in which staff utilise information about student progress and wellbeing
- Students as active respondents – in which staff invite student dialogue and discussion to deepen learning/professional decisions
- Students as co-enquirers – in which staff take a lead role with high-profile, active student support
- Students as knowledge creators – in which students take lead roles with active staff support
- Students as joint authors – in which students and staff decide on a joint course of action together
- Intergenerational learning as lived democracy – in which there is a shared commitment to/responsibility for the common good

(Fielding, 2012: 49–50)

Complete the following table, identifying an example of research that utilises each of Fielding's six 'patterns of partnership', and a strength and limitation/difficulty for each – you should read the full article to get more detail about the studies you focus on.

	Example	Strength	Limitation/difficulty
'Data source'			
'Active respondents'			
'Co-enquirers'			
'Knowledge creators'			
'Joint authors'			
'Lived democracy'			

Students as researchers and co-researchers

Recent years have witnessed considerable interest in strategies that encourage students to take an active role in research, in particular as a means of enhancing educational provision. In the UK, Michael Fielding has been the most influential advocate for both 'students as researchers' and 'students as co-researchers' – that is, as *partners in research* with teachers or academics. Projects that involve students as 'co-researchers' generally take the form of collaborative enquiry, whereby the different experiences, skills and knowledge of young people and adults are brought together to generate new knowledge and to improve current practice. Projects are commonly instigated by academics or practitioners, and interested students are invited to join and form a research team. Conversely, 'student as researcher' projects are initiated and shaped by student interests. With the support of teachers and academics, individual (or groups of) students embark on their own research projects.

Projects involving students as researchers or co-researches often make use of participatory action research (PAR). This entails participants theorising their own lives and using collaboration and reflection to improve current circumstances (see Bland and Atweh, 2007 for a discussion of students as researchers and PAR).

The Children's Research Centre at the Open University

The OUs 'Children's Research Centre' is a great example of the promotion of students as researchers. Below is an extract from the programme's home page:

> Here at CRC, our primary objective is to empower children and young people as active researchers. We recognise that children are experts on their own lives and we value their perspectives and knowledge. The CRC promotes children's and young people's voices by training and supporting them to investigate issues they identify as important to them. We offer diverse groups of children and young people a taught programme on all aspects of the research process followed by support to design and carry out an original research study. Since our launch in 2004 we have worked with several hundred children through links with schools, youth organisations and charities nationally and internationally. An important part of our mission is to contribute to the body of knowledge on childhood and children's lived experiences. Helping children and young people to disseminate their research is integral to that goal. There are over 150 research outputs by children and young people featured on this site. (From: http://www.open.ac.uk/researchprojects/childrens-research-centre/)

Students as (co-)researcher projects are designed to empower students and to enable them to participate in the evaluation and development of their own learning environments. They are also intended to impact positively on educational practice. Reviewing the literature on 'students as researchers', Lena Bahou identifies five common aims:

1 Address issues that matter to students.

2 Create new knowledge about education for critical evaluation and action.

3 Set an agenda for students to make a difference.

4 Enable students to develop a kind of professionalism whereby student voices can be taken seriously by adults.

5 Enhance the conditions and processes of learning and teaching.

(Bahou, 2011: 7)

Advantages of children and young people as researchers

There are many advantages of employing 'students as researchers'. In this section these are grouped around three headings:

- Improving the quality of research
- Benefiting the children who participate
- Enhancing democracy, citizenship and social relations.

The quality of research can be improved in the following ways:

- **Collecting data** – student researchers share more in common with young respondents. When gathering data, they arguably are more able to relate to other young people, making interview settings less formal and putting interviewees at ease. They are more likely to be able to recognise when young respondents are exaggerating or messing about.

- **'Agents of change'** – the idea that children and young people are effective 'agents of change' (Kay, Dunne and Hutchinson, 2010) has gained increasing currency in recent years. Many educational institutions encourage their students to play an active role in the research, evaluation and development of new assessments, curriculums and resources. Young people might be more able to articulate change because they are less constrained by existing assumptions and practices.

- **Multiple voices** – 'researcher triangulation' entails increasing validity by employing a number of different researchers in research design, data collection and analysis. Validity is likely to be further increased if these researchers come from groups that are generally marginalised or excluded from such processes. Despite changes in society noted above, the voices of children and young people remain relatively unheard.

Children and young people can also benefit in the following ways:

- **Sense of ownership and involvement** – as Hart (1992) argues, young people can demonstrate great competence if they feel some sense of ownership and are involved in the design and management of the project. Participation encourages young people to feel they can make a meaningful contribution.

- **Improved academic performance** – there is compelling evidence that engagement in research impacts positively on the attainment of those who take part. As Fielding and Bragg (2004) argue, student researchers are likely to develop in confidence and motivation, become more engaged and develop academic skills.

- **Personal and social development** – students will also develop wider skills, associated with relating to other people and working effectively as a member of a team. They develop a greater understanding of their learning contexts and are likely to play a more active role in their school and their wider environment.

Benefits to wider democratic society include:

- **Democratic engagement** – active participation in the development and evaluation of knowledge and practice will foster the kinds of qualities and skills ideally suited to active citizenship and democratic engagement. If young people are able to participate and shape the settings they study within, they are far more likely to take part in the wider world in adulthood.

- **Promoting** *'intergenerational learning'* – these strategies enable people from different generations to work together. This creates opportunities for children and adults to collaborate on projects and learn from one another. For Fielding, such 'intergenerational learning' fosters a sense of collegiality and develops a shared sense of 'mutual responsibility' and 'energising adventure' (2012: 53).

ACTIVITY

Read at least two of the following four articles, which present accounts of educational research with young participants from different age groups:

Christine Pascal and Tony Bertram (2009) 'Listening to young citizens: The struggle to make real a participatory paradigm in research with young children.' *European Early Childhood Education Research Journal*, 17 (2).

Niamh O'Brien and Tina Moules (2007) 'So round the spiral again: A reflective participatory research project with children and young people.' *European Action Research*, 15 (3).

David Leat and Anna Reid (2012) 'Exploring the role of student researchers in the process of curriculum development.' *Curriculum Journal*, 23 (2).

Sue Cox and Anna Robinson-Plant (2008) 'Power, participation and decision making in the primary classroom: children as action researchers.' *Educational Action Research*, 16 (4).

Draw up a list of the different approaches to utilising students as researchers or co-researchers. According to your reading, identify the main advantages and difficulties in adopting this approach to educational research.

Eliciting student voices

Since the beginning of the twenty-first century, legislation in England has dictated that schools must consult with their students about provision. There is considerable evidence that schools, colleges and universities engage with their students in a variety of ways. Most have a 'school council' or something similar, which discusses and informs institutional policy. Some schools and universities ensure they have student representation on interview panels, boards of governors and other institutional committees. Most educational establishments survey their learners to evaluate modules, curriculums and student experience. For universities, the

National Student Survey has become a vital instrument in measuring student satisfaction in various aspects of provision. As these examples indicate, student voices are sought to evaluate existing practice as well as to inform future developments.

While enabling the student voice is valuable in and of itself, there is a big difference between providing opportunities to speak and ensuring that such contributions are meaningful and have impact. There is a danger that such activities are *tokenistic* – that critical student perspectives are ignored, or that consultation is only offered on relatively insignificant issues. Moreover, it is relatively straightforward to elicit the opinions of confident and articulate young people. It may be more difficult to do so with students who are reticent, disengaged or who have special educational needs. Effective strategies should always seek to promote dialogue with more marginalised or 'silent' students.

Evaluating educational research with children

There are many issues to consider when conducting research with child participants. Among the questions to reflect on are:

Levels of participation

- What stages of research might children be involved in?
- What are the advantages and disadvantages of children participating in or being excluded from:
    - developing research design and research questions
    - data collection
    - data analysis
    - writing up and presenting work?

Power relations

- How do you avoid exploitation of child researchers?
- Can research participation be empowering? If so, how can this be ensured/maximised?
- How far is the relationship between adult and child equal?
- How can you facilitate shared decision-making?
- How do roles differ?

Avoiding tokenism

- How can you ensure the process is meaningful and worthwhile?
- Are the children who participate listened to seriously?
- Does the research have real outcomes and impact?

Representing divergent voices

- How are child participants recruited/selected?
- Do participants share the same characteristics as the whole (student) population?
- How do you ensure that quieter and/or marginalised voices are heard?

Developing appropriate research skills

- How are 'novice' researchers supported in the fieldwork site?
- How will child participants be trained and supervised to develop the relevant skills?
- Who provides this support?

The impact of participation

- Are children safe and protected?
- Are child researchers likely to be exposed to distressing situations and/or feelings?
- How is participation likely to impact on children's wider relationships?

ACTIVITY

Using the questions above, develop a 'student as co-researcher' strategy for each of the following topics of study:

- To compare differences in boys' and girls' numeracy development.
- To evaluate the impact of new special educational needs provision in a secondary school.
- To identify effective strategies for supporting school leavers' choices.
- To investigate school gang cultures.

Chapter summary

Changing conceptions of childhood, especially as ratified in the UNCRC, promote greater involvement of children and young people. This chapter has outlined some of the different ways that children and young people might be involved in educational research, identifying a number of 'levels of participation'. The chapter has focused on notions of the student as 'researcher' and as 'co-researcher'. Evidence suggests that the participation of children and young people in educational research improves the depth and validity of the findings. It also appears to benefit the children and young people who take part, increasing engagement as well as social and academic development. The chapter concludes by offering a series of questions with which to evaluate the efficacy of a research project involving children as researchers.

Further reading

Fielding, M. and Bragg, S. (2003) *Students as researchers: Making a difference.* London: Pearson.

- Michael Fielding's work on 'students as researchers' has been especially influential. This book, written with Sara Bragg, provides an excellent introduction to this work. After this, you should look at Fielding's later work on 'patterns of partnership' as discussed earlier in this chapter.

Christensen, P. and James, A. (Editors) (2008) *Research with children: Perspectives and practices (2nd edition).* London: Routledge.

- A great introduction to different approaches to working with children, covering a wide range of methodological strategies and issues.

UNICEF *Child and youth participation resource guide* – http://www.unicef.org/adolescence/cypguide/resourceguide_basics.html

- An extensive resource bank covering material in a range of relevant areas. The sections on ethics and capacity building are particularly useful.

Glossary

Action research – a cyclical research process of reflection, research and action intended to solve practical problems.

Case study – aims to explore a specific 'case' that can help illuminate whatever research question is under investigation.

Coding – putting labels on data to categorise it into themes and patterns.

Descriptive statistics – they describe. Typically descriptive statistics may take the form of percentages or fractions.

Documentary research – a form of research that analyses documents as a primary research tool, and can encompass the study of documents such as records, government publications, diaries, photographs, and drawings.

Epistemology – a framework or theory for specifying the constitution and generation of knowledge about the social world.

Ethnography – an in-depth study of the culture(s) of a particular group of people.

Experiment – researchers manipulate specific variables within controlled conditions.

Focus group interviews – a way of collecting qualitative data from a group of people in order to explore their perceptions, opinions, beliefs or attitudes. They differ from one-to-one discussions as the researcher asks questions in an interactive group setting where participants respond by entering into group discussion with one another.

Grounded theory – analysis that generates theory from empirical data.

Interpretivism – a theoretical approach that views research as an interpretive rather than scientific act. Usually described as an opposing view to positivism in research contexts.

Memos – notes about any thoughts, ideas or questions that are emerging from the concepts in the data.

Member-checking – asking participants to check their contribution to data collection for accuracy, such as an interview transcript. Member-checking should give a participant the opportunity to add to or amend their original contribution.

Methodology – a discussion of the principles and values that underpin research which explain the decisions taken, such as the approach (e.g. positivism vs. interpretivism) and how research methods are selected.

Naturalism – studying people and activities as they ordinarily take place (often via observations).

Paradigm – a set of beliefs which have particular epistemological and ontological values.

Positionality – the notion that the 'position' or 'stance' a researcher takes (either knowingly or unknowingly) can impact on the research design and also on the ethical nature of the research process.

Positivism – an approach to research that assumes the neutrality and objectivity of a detached researcher, believed to be free from any bias related to social, political or cultural context.

Quantitative/qualitative research – quantitative research is an approach to research that places the emphasis on the analysis of numbers, popular in large scale studies, while qualitative research places emphasis on meaning, and is more popular in smaller-scale research projects.

Reflexivity – when the researcher reflects honestly about all the steps taken in the research and how she has influenced the process of the research.

Reliability – the consistency and dependability of research processes and measurements.

Research bias – research bias is the existence of subjective assumptions that negatively affect the veracity of the research findings.

Social theories – social theories are analytical frameworks or paradigms used to examine social phenomena, and are commonly used in educational research to explore how education connects to issues of power and structural inequalities such as gender, ethnicity and social class.

Subjectivity – a belief that a researcher's views are not neutral, but are mediated by their experiences of life, and these experiences are (consciously or unconsciously) influenced by class, gender, ethnicity and age as well as other factors. Researchers who accept their subjectivity in the research process will consider the impact that their own identity can have on participants when conducting research.

Triangulation – the use of a variety of research methods to enhance the validity of the findings.

Validity – literally meaning truth, validity identifies how truthfully an account represents participants' realities of social phenomena.

Variable – an attribute that describes a person, place, thing or idea. Qualitative variables take on values that are names or labels. Quantitative variables are numeric, which means they can be measured.

References

Adams, D. (2002) 'The unintended consequences of deregulation: Australian higher education in the marketplace.' In P. Trowler (ed), *Higher education policy and institutional change: Intentions and outcomes in turbulent environments*, 108–125. Buckingham: Open University Press.

Aggleton, P. (1987) *Rebels Without a Cause*. London: Falmer Press.

Ahmed, J.U. (2010) 'Documentary research method: New dimensions.' *Indus Journal of Management and Social Sciences*, 4 (1), 1–14.

Alsup, J. (2005) *Teacher identity discourses: Negotiating personal and professional spaces*. Oxon: Routledge.

Angrist, J. (2004) 'American education research changes tack.' *Oxford Review of Economic Policy*, 20 (2), 198–212.

Apted, M. (1999) *7up*. Heinemann: London.

Aries, P. (1962) *Centuries of childhood: A social history of family life*. Trans. Robert Baldwin. New York: Vintage Books.

Baer, R., Arteaga, R., Dyer, K., Eden, A., Gross, R., Helmy, H., Karnyski, M., Papadopoulos, A. and Reeser, D. (2012) 'Concepts of race and ethnicity among health researchers: Patterns and implications.' *Ethnicity and Health*, 2012, 1–15, iFirst article.

Bahou, L. (2011) 'Rethinking the challenges and possibilities of student voice and agency.' *Educate*, 2–14.

Balfe, T. and Travers, J. (2011) 'The Children's Voice: What makes students feel included.' *REACH Journal of Special Needs Education in Ireland*, 25 (1), 8–24.

Ball, S. (1981) *Beachside comprehensive: A case study of a secondary school*. Cambridge: Cambridge University Press.

——(1987) *The micropolitics of the school: Towards a theory of school organisation*. London: Methuen.

——(1994) *Education reform: A critical and post-structural approach*. Buckingham: Open University Press.

Ball, S., Davies, J., David, M. and Reay, D. (2002) "Classification' and 'judgement': Social class and the 'cognitive structures' of choice of higher education.' *British Journal of Sociology of Education*, 23 (1), 51–72.

Barbour, A. (2010) 'Exploring some ethical dilemmas and obligations of the ethnographer.' *Ethnography and Education*, 5 (2), 159–173.

Barone, C. (2006) 'Cultural capital, ambition and the explanation of inequalities in learning outcomes: A comparative analysis.' *Sociology*, 40 (6), 1039–1058.

Barraket, J. (2004) 'E-learning and access: Getting behind the hype.' In M. Osborne, J. Gallacher and B. Crossan (eds), *Researching widening access to lifelong learning: Issues and approaches to international research*, pp. 191–202. London: RoutledgeFalmer.

Bell, J. (1999) *Doing your research project: A guide for first-time researchers in education and social science.* Buckingham: Open University Press.

Benincasa, L. (2012) 'Teaching lessons in exclusion: Researchers' assumptions and the ideology of normality.' *International Journal of Qualitative Studies in Education,* 25 (8), 1087–1106.

BERA (2011) 'Ethical guidelines for educational research.' *British Educational Research Association.* Accessible at http://content.yudu.com/Library/A1t9gr/BERAEthicalGuideline/resources/index.htm?referrerUrl=http%25253A%25252F%25252Fwww.yudu.com%25252Fitem%252525 2Fdetails%25252F375952%25252FBERA-Ethical-Guidelines-2011

Besley, T. and Peters, M. (2007) *Subjectivity and truth: Foucault, education and the culture of the self.* New York: Peter Lang.

Biel, A., Eek, D., Garling, T. and Gustafson, M. (2007) *New issues and paradigms in research on social dilemmas.* New York: Springer.

Bland, D. and Atweh, B. (2007) 'Students as researchers: Engaging students' voices in PAR.' *Educational Action Research,* 15 (3), 337–349.

Booth, A., McLean, M. and Walker, M. (2009) 'Self, others and society: A case study of university integrative learning.' *Studies in Higher Education,* 34 (8), 929–939.

Booth, W.C., Colomb, G.G. and Williams, J.M. (1995) *The craft of research.* Chicago: University of Chicago Press.

Bouguen, A. and Gurgand, M. (2012) *Randomized Controlled Experiments in Education*: EENEE Analytical Report No. 11 prepared for the European Commission. European Expert Network on Economics of Education (EENEE), February, 2012. Available at: http://www.eenee.de/portal/page/portal/EENEEContent/_IMPORT_TELECENTRUM/DOCS/EENEE_AR11.pdf

Brinkmann, S. (2007) 'The good qualitative researcher.' *Qualitative Research in Psychology,* 4 (1–2), 127–144.

Brydon-Miller, M., Kral, M., Maguire, P., Noffke, S. and Sabhlok, A. (2011) 'Jazz and the banyan tree: Roots and riffs on participatory action research.' Chapter 23, pp. 387–414, in N.K. Denzin and Y.S. Lincoln (eds) (2011) *The SAGE Handbook of Qualitative Research.* Thousand Oaks, California: SAGE.

Burgess, R. (1984) *In the Field: An Introduction to Field Research.* Oxon: Routledge.

Burke, P.J. (2002) *Accessing education: Effectively widening participation.* Stoke: Trentham Books.

Bushnell, M. (2003) 'Teachers in the schoolhouse panopticon: Complicity and resistance.' *Education and Urban Society,* 35 (3), 251–272.

Callinicos, A. (2007) *Social theory: A historical introduction.* Cambridge: Polity Press.

Campbell, D. and Stanley, J. (1963) Experimental and quasi-experimental designs for research on teaching. In N. Gage (ed.) *Handbook of research on teaching.* Chicago: Rand McNally.

Carr, M. and Lee, W. (2012) *Learning stories: Constructing learner identities in early education.* London: Sage.

Carr, W. and Kemmis, S. (1986) *Becoming critical: Education, knowledge and action research.* London: RoutledgeFalmer.

Carspecken, P. (1996). *Critical ethnography in educational research: A theoretical and practical guide.* London: Routledge.

Casey, A., Dyson, B. and Campbell, A. (2009) 'Action research in physical education: Focusing beyond myself through cooperative learning.' *Educational Action Research,* 17 (3), 407–423.

Chappel, C., Rhodes, C., Solomon, N., Tennant, M. and Yates, C. (2003) *Reconstructing the lifelong learner: Pedagogy and identity in individual, organisational and social change.* Oxon: Routledge.

Charmaz, K. (2011) 'Grounded Theory Methods in Social Justice Research', Chapter 21, pp. 359–380 in N. Denzin and Y. Lincoln (eds) (2011) *Handbook of Qualitative Research.* London: Sage Publications.

Christensen, P. and James, A. (eds) (2008) *Research with children: Perspectives and practices* (2nd edition). London: Routledge.

Christensen, P.H. (2004) 'Children's participation in ethnographic research: Issues of power and representation.' *Children and Society, 18.*

Cicourel, A. (1964) *Method and Measurement in Sociology.* New York: Collier-Macmillan.

Cigman, R. (ed.) (2006) *Included or excluded? The challenge of the mainstream for some SEN children.* Oxon: Routledge.

Clark, A. and Moss, P. (2001) *Listening to young children: The Mosaic Approach.* London: National Children's Bureau.

Cline, T. and Frederickson, N. (2009) *Special educational needs: Inclusion and diversity.* Buckingham: Open University Press.

Cohen, L., Manion, L. and Morrison, K. (2007) *Research methods in education* (6th edition). London: Routledge.

Connelly, P. and Healy, J. (2004) 'Symbolic violence and the neighbourhood: The educational aspirations of 7–8 year old working-class girls.' *The British Journal of Sociology,* 55 (4), 511–529.

Connolly, P. (2007) *Quantitative data analysis in education: A critical introduction using SPSS.* London: Routledge.

Cousin, G. (2009) *Researching learning in higher education: An introduction to contemporary methods and approaches.* London: Routledge.

Cox, J. and Cox, K.B. (2008) *Your opinion please! How to build the best questionnaires in the field of education* (2nd edition). Thousand Oaks, CA: Corwin Press.

Cresswell, J.W. and Miller, D.L. (2000) 'Determining validity in qualitative inquiry.' *Theory into Practice,* 39 (3), 124–130.

Crosskey, L. and Vance, M. (2011) 'Training teachers to support pupils' listening in class: An evaluation using pupil questionnaires.' *Child Language Teaching and Therapy,* 27 (2), 165–182.

Crotty, M. (1998) *The foundations of social research: Meaning and perspective in the research process.* London: Sage.

Croxford, L. (2002) 'The Youth Cohort Survey Data, Working Paper 5.' ESRC Research Project on *Education and Youth Transitions in England, Wales and Scotland, 1984–2002.*

Curtis, W. and Pettigrew, A. (2010) *Education studies: Reflective reader.* Exeter: Learning Matters.

Danaher, P., Gururajan, R. and Hafeez-Baig, A. (2009) 'Transforming the practice of mobile learning: Promoting pedagogical innovation through educational principles and strategies that work.' In H. Ryu and D. Parsons (eds) *Innovative mobile learning: Techniques and technologies.* Hershey: IGI Global.

Davies, B. and Harré, R. (1990) 'Positioning: The discursive production of selves.' *Journal for the Theory of Social Behaviour,* 20 (1), 43–63.

——(1999) 'Positioning and personhood.' In R. Harré and L. van Langenhove (eds), *Positioning theory: Moral contexts of intentional action* (pp. 32–52). Oxford: Blackwell.

De Montfort University (2010) *Standard ethics application forms* accessible at http://www.dmu.ac.uk/research/ethics-and-governance/faculty-specific-procedures/health-and-life-sciences-ethics-procedures.asp

Denissen, J., Neumann, L. and van Zalk, M. (2010) 'How the internet is changing the implementation of traditional research methods, people's daily lives, and the way in which developmental scientists conduct research.' *International Journal of Behavioural Development,* 34 (6), 564–575

Denscombe, M. (1998) *The good research guide for small-scale social research projects.* Buckingham: Open University Press.

——(2003) *The good research guide for small-scale research projects.* Buckingham: Open University Press.

Denzin, N.K. (1994) 'The Art and Politics of Interpretation.' In N.K. Denzin and Y.S. Lincoln (eds) *Handbook of Qualitative Research.* London: Sage.

——(2011) 'The Politics of Evidence.' Chapter 39, pp. 645–657 in N.K. Denzin and Y.S. Lincoln (eds) *The Sage Handbook of Qualitative Research* (4th edition). Thousand Oaks: California.

Denzin, N.K. and Lincoln, Y.S. (eds) (2000) *The SAGE handbook of qualitative research* (2nd edition). Thousand Oaks, California: Sage.

——(2011) *The SAGE Handbook of Qualitative Research* (4th edition). Thousand Oaks, California: Sage.

Douglas, P. (2010) "Problematising' inclusion: Education and the question of autism.' *Pedagogy, Culture and Society,* 18 (2), 105–121.

Dressman, M. (2008) *Using social theory in educational research: A practical guide.* Oxon: Routledge.

Duffy, B. (1999) 'The analysis of documentary evidence.' In J. Bell *Doing your research project: A guide for first-time researchers in education and social science,* pp. 106-117. Buckingham: Open University Press.

Eder, D. and Fingerson, L. (2002) 'Interviewing children and adolescents.' In: J.F. Gubrium and J.A. Holstein (eds), *Handbook of interview research: Context and method,* pp. 181–201. Thousand Oaks, CA: Sage.

Elliott, A. (2008) *Contemporary social theory: An introduction.* London: Routledge.

Evans, L. (2012) 'Breadline Britain: 83% of teachers see evidence of hungry children in their class.' *The Guardian datablog,* Tuesday 19 June 2012.

Exley, S. (2009) 'Exploring pupil segregation between specialist and non-specialist schools.' *Oxford Review of Education,* 35 (4), 451–470.

Ferdinand, J., Pearson, G., Rowe, M. and Worthington, F. (2007) 'A different kind of ethics.' *Ethnography,* 8 (4), 519–543.

Ferguson, D.L., Hanreddy, A. and Draxton, S. (2011) 'Giving students voice as a strategy for improving teacher practice.' *London Review of Education,* 9 (1), 55–70.

Fielding, M. (2012) 'Beyond student voice: Patterns of partnership and the demands of deep democracy.' *Revista de Educación,* 359, September-December 2012, 45–65.

Fielding, M. and Bragg, S. (2003) *Students as researchers: Making a difference. Consulting pupils about teaching and learning.* Cambridge: Pearson Publishing.

Fielding, N., Lee, R. and Blank, G. (eds) (2008) *The Sage handbook of online research methods.* London: Sage.

Finch, J. (2012) *Accessibility, sustainability, excellence: How to expand access to research publications: Report of the Working Group on Expanding Access to Published Research Findings.* London: Research Information Network. Available at: http://www.researchinfonet.org/publish/finch/

Fine, M. and Weiss, L. (2000) 'Compositional studies in two parts: Critical Theorizing and Analysis on Social (In) Justice.' In N.K. Denzin and Y.S. Lincoln (eds) (2000) *The SAGE handbook of qualitative research* (2nd edition). London: Sage.

Fink, A. (2013) *How to conduct surveys: A step-by-step guide* (5th edition). Thousand Oaks, CA: Sage.

Finkel, D. and McGue, M. (1993) 'Twenty-five year follow-up of child-rearing practices: Reliability of retrospective data.' *Personality and Individual Differences,* 15, 147–154.

Finney, H.C. (1981) 'Improving the reliability of retrospective survey measures: Results of a longitudinal field survey.' *Evaluation Review,* 5, 207–229.

Flanders, N. (1970) *Analyzing teaching behavior.* New York: Addison-Wesley.

Flecha, R. and Gomez, J. (2004) 'Participatory paradigms: researching 'with' rather than 'on''. In M. Osborne, J. Gallacher and B. Crossan (eds), *Researching widening access to lifelong learning: Issues and approaches to international research,* pp. 129–149. London: RoutledgeFalmer.

Fontana, A. and Frey, J. (1994) 'Interviewing: The art of science', in N.K. Denzin and Y.S. Lincoln (eds), *The SAGE Handbook of Qualitative Research,* pp. 361–376. Thousand Oaks, CA: Sage.

Francis, B., Skelton, C. and Read, B. (2012) *The identities and practices of high achieving pupils: Negotiating achievement and peer cultures.* London: Continuum.

Freire, P. (1972) *Pedagogy and the oppressed.* London: Continuum.

Fryer, M. (2012) 'Facilitative leadership: Drawing on Jürgen Habermas' model of ideal speech to propose a less impositional way to lead.' *Organisation,* 19, 25.

Gaiser, T. and Schreiner, A. (2009) *A guide to conducting online research.* London: Sage.

Gallard, D. and Garden, A. (2011) 'The Psychology of Education.' In B. Dufour and W. Curtis (eds) *Studying education: An introduction to the key disciplines in education studies.* Maidenhead: Open University Press.

Garcia, F. (2010) 'MBA lecturers' curriculum interests in leadership.' *Management Learning,* 41 (1), 21–36.

Geertz, C. (1973) *The interpretation of cultures: Selected essays.* New York: Basic Books.

Gibbs, A. (1997) *Focus groups.* Social Research Update No. 19, Winter, University of Surrey.

Gibbs, G. (2007) *Analysing qualitative data.* London: Sage.

Giddens, A. (1987) *Social theory and modern sociology.* Cambridge: Polity Press.

Gillies, D. (2008) 'Quality and equality: the mask of discursive conflation in education policy texts.' *Journal of Education Policy*, 23 (6), 685–699.

Glaser, B. and Strauss, A. (1967) *Discovery of grounded theory: Strategies for qualitative research.* London: AldineTransaction.

Glesne, C. and Peshkin, A. (1992) *Becoming qualitative researchers: An introduction.* White Plains, New York: Longman.

Goffman, E. (1959) *The presentation of the self in everyday life.* London: Penguin Books.

Gold, R. (1958) 'Roles in sociological field observations.' *Social Forces*, 36 (3), 217–223.

Gorard, S. (2001) *Quantitative methods in educational research: The role of numbers made easy.* London: Continuum.

Gorely, T., Holroyd, R. and Kirk, D. (2003) 'Muscularity, the habitus and the social construction of gender: Towards a gender-relevant physical education.' *British Journal of Sociology of Education*, 24 (4), 429–448.

Gouthro, P. (2009) 'Neoliberalism, lifelong learning, and the homeplace: Problematizing the boundaries of 'public' and 'private' to explore women's learning experiences.' *Studies in Continuing Education*, 31 (2), 157–172.

Gray, K., Thompson, C., Sheard, J., Clerehan, R. and Hamilton, M. (2010) 'Students as web 2.0 authors: Implications for assessment design and conduct.' *Australasian Journal of Educational Technology*, 26 (1), 105–122.

Grenfell, M. and James, D. (1998) *Bourdieu and education: Acts of practical theory.* London: Routledge.

Griffiths, G. (1985) 'Doubts, dilemmas and diary-keeping: Some reflections on teacher-based research.' In R. Burgess (ed.) *Issues in Educational Research: Qualitative Methods*, pp. 197–215. London: Falmer Press.

Griffiths, M. (1998) *Educational research for social justice: Getting off the fence.* Buckingham: Open University Press.

Haahr, J.H. (2003) 'The provocation of plaiting palm leaves: Habermas, Foucault and media presentations of education in Danish television.' *Journalism*, 4 (2), 203–223.

Hackett, L., Theodosiou, L., Bond, C., Blackburn, C., Spicer, F. and Lever, R. (2010) 'Understanding the mental health needs of primary school children in an inner-city local authority.' *Pastoral Care in Education*, 28 (3), 205–218.

Hamilton, L. (2011) 'Case studies in educational research.' *British Educational Research Association* online resource. Available online at: www.bera.ac.uk/.../Case%20studies%20in%20 educational%20researc... Last accessed 22.1.2012.

Hammersley, M. (1992) *What's wrong with ethnography.* London: Routledge.

——(2012) 'Troubling theory in case study research.' *Higher Education Research and Development*, 31 (3), 393–405.

Hammersley, M. and Atkinson, P. (1989) *Ethnography: Principles in practice,* London: Routledge.

——(1995) *Ethnography: Principles in practice* (2nd edition). London: Routledge.

Hancock, R. (1997) 'Why are class teachers reluctant to become researchers.' *Journal of In-Service Education*, 23 (1), 85–99.

Hargreaves, A. and Woods, P. (eds) (1984) *Classrooms and staffrooms: The sociology of teachers and teaching.* Milton Keynes: Open University Press.

Hargreaves, D. (1967) *Social relations in the secondary school.* London: Routledge.

Harper, R. (2000) 'The social organisation of the IMF's mission work: An examination of international auditing.' In M. Strathearn (ed.), *Audit cultures: Anthropological studies in accountability, ethics and the academy,* 21–53. London, Oxon: Routledge.

Harrington, A. (2005) 'Introduction: What is social theory?' In A. Harrington (ed.) *Modern social theory: An introduction.* Oxford: Oxford University Press.

Hart, C. (1998) *Doing a literature review: Releasing the social science research imagination.* London: Sage.

Hart, R. (1992) *Children's Participation: From tokenism to citizenship.* Florence: UNICEF Innocenti Research Centre.

Hesse-Biber, S. and Griffin, A. (2012) 'Internet-mediated technologies and mixed methods research: Problems and prospects.' *Journal of Mixed Methods Research*, 7 (1), 43–61.

Hine, C. (ed.) (2005) *Virtual methods: Issues in social research on the internet.* Oxford: Berg.

Hobson, A.J., Malderez, A., Tracey, L., Homer, M., Mitchell, N., Biddulph, M., Giannakaki, M.S., Rose, A., Pell, R.G., Roper, T., Chambers, G.N. and Tomlinson, P.D. (2007) *Newly Qualified Teachers' Experiences of their First Year of Teaching: Findings from Phase III of the Becoming a Teacher Project*. Nottingham: University of Nottingham, research report DCSF-RR008.

Hodkinson, A. and Vickerman, P. (2009) *Key issues in special educational needs and inclusion*. London: Sage.

Hodkinson, P. and Hodkinson H. (2001) 'The strengths and limitations of case study research.' Paper presented to the *Learning and Skills Development Agency conference, Making an impact on policy and practice*, Cambridge, 5–7 December 2001, downloaded from http://education.exeter.ac.uk/tlc/docs/publications/LE_PH_PUB_05.12.01.rtf. 26.01.2013

Homan, R. (1991) *The ethics of social research*. Harlow: Longman.

Homan, R. and Bulmer, M. (1982) 'On the merits of covert methods: a dialogue.' In M. Bulmer (ed) *Social Research Ethics*. London: Macmillan Press.

Hope, A. (2009) 'CCTV, school surveillance and social control.' *British Educational Research Journal*, 35 (6), 891–907.

Huisman, J. (2010) *International perspectives on the governance of higher education: Alternative frameworks for co-ordination*. London: Routledge.

Hutchinson, D. and Styles, B. (2010) *A guide to running randomised controlled trials for educational researchers*. Slough: National Foundation for Educational Research.

Jæger, M.M. (2011) 'Does cultural capital really affect academic achievement? New evidence from combined sibling and panel data.' *Sociology of Education*, 84 (4), 281–298.

James, A., Jenks, C. and Prout, A. (2001) *Theorizing childhood*. Cambridge: Polity Press.

Jeffrey, B. and Troman, G. (2004) 'Time for ethnography.' *British Educational Research Journal*, 30 (4), August, 2004.

Jennings, J. and DiPrete, T. (2010) 'Teacher effects on social and behavioral skills in early elementary school.' *Sociology of Education*, 83 (2), 135–159.

Jesson, D. (2004) *Educational outcomes and value added by specialist schools – 2003*. London: Specialist Schools Trust.

Kamberelis, G. and Dimitriadis, G. (2013) *Focus groups: From structured interviews to collective conversations*. Oxon: Routledge.

Kanes, C. (2012) *Elaborating professionalism: Studies in practice and theory (innovation and change in professional education)*. New York: Springer.

Kay, J., Dunne, E. and Hutchinson, J. (2010) 'Rethinking the values of higher education – students as change agents?' *The Quality Assurance Agency for Higher Education*. Gloucester: QAA.

Kearney, M., Schuck, S., Burden, K. and Aubusson, P. (2012) 'Viewing mobile learning from a pedagogical perspective.' *Research in Learning Technology*, 20.

Kelly, L., Burton, S. and Regan, L. (1994) 'Researching women's lives or studying women's oppression?: Reflections on what constitutes feminist research.' In M. Maynard and J. Purvis (eds) *Researching Women's Lives from a Feminist Perspective*. London: Taylor and Francis.

Kerr, D., Cleaver, E., Ireland, E. and Blenkinsop, S. (2003) *Citizenship Education Longitudinal Study First Cross-Sectional Survey 2001–2002*, Research Report RR416. DfES NFER.

Khawaja, I. and Lerche Mørck, L. (2009) 'Researcher positioning: Muslim "otherness" and beyond.' *Qualitative Research in Psychology*, 6: 1–2, 28–45.

King, P. and Howard, J. (2010) 'Understanding children's free play at home, in school and at the After School Club: A preliminary investigation into play types, social grouping and perceived control.' *The Psychology of Education Review*, 34 (1), 32–41.

Kitzinger, J. (1994) 'Focus groups: method or madness?' In M. Boulton (ed.). *Challenge and innovation: Methodological advances in social research on HIV/AIDS*, pp. 159–175. London: Taylor and Francis.

——(1995) 'Introducing focus groups.' *British Medical Journal*, 311, 299–302.

Klopfer, E., Squire, K. and Jenkins, H. (2002) 'Environmental detectives: PDAs as a window into a virtual simulated world.' In Proceedings of IEEE international workshop on wireless and mobile technologies in education. *IEEE Computer Society*, Vaxjo, Sweden, 95–98.

Koole, M.L. (2009) 'A model for framing mobile learning.' In M. Ally (ed.) *Empowering learners and educators with mobile learning*. Athabasca: Athabasca University Press.

Kozinets, R. (2010) *Netnography: Doing ethnographic research online.* London: Sage Publishing.

Krathwohl, D. and Smith, N. (2005) *How to prepare a dissertation proposal: Suggestions for students in education and the social and behavioral sciences.* Syracuse, NY: Syracuse University Press.

Lather, P. (1986) 'Issues of validity in open ideological research: Between a rock and a soft place.' *Interchange,* 17 (4), 63–84.

——(1993) 'Fertile obsession: Validity after poststructuralism.' *The Sociological Quarterly,* 34 (2), 637–673.

Laugharne, J. and Baird, A. (2009) 'National conversations in the UK: Using a language-based approach to interpret three key education policy documents (2001–2007) from England, Scotland and Wales.' *Cambridge Journal of Education,* 39 (2), 223–240.

Leathwood, C. and O'Connell, P. (2003) "It's a struggle': The construction of the 'new student' in higher education.' *Journal of Education Policy,* 18 (6), 597–615.

Levey, H. (2009) '"Which One Is Yours?": Children and Ethnography.' *Qualitative Sociology,* 32 (3).

Levinson, M.P. (2010) 'Accountability to research participants: Unresolved dilemmas and unravelling ethics.' *Ethnography and Education,* 5 (2), 193–207.

Lewin, K. (1946) 'Action research and minority problems.' *Journal of Social Issues,* 2 (4), 34–46.

Lewis, K. and Brzyska, B. (2012) *NFER Teacher Voice Omnibus April 2012 Survey: Volunteering in schools.* Slough: NFER.

Liamputtong, P. (2011) *Focus group methodology: Principles and practice.* London: Sage.

Liasidou, A. (2011) 'Unequal power relations and inclusive education policy making: a discursive analytic approach.' *Educational Policy,* 25 (6), 887–907.

Lincoln, Y.S. and Guba, E.G. (1985) *Naturalistic Inquiry,* Beverly Hills, CA: Sage.

lisahunter, Rossi, T., Tinning, R., Flanagan, E. and Macdonald, D. (2011) 'Professional learning places and spaces: The staffroom as a site of beginning teacher induction and transition.' *Asia-Pacific Journal of Teacher Education,* 39 (1), 33–46.

Litosseliti, L. (2003) *Using focus groups in research.* London: Continuum.

Livingstone, D.W. (2006) 'Informal learning: Conceptual distinctions and preliminary findings.' In Z. Bekerman, N.C. Burbules and D. Silberman Keller (eds) *Learning in places: The informal education reader,* pp. 203–228. New York: Peter Lang.

Lovat, T., Holbrook, A. and Bourke, S. (2008) 'Ways of knowing in doctoral examination: How well is the doctoral regime?' *Educational Research Review,* 3, 66–76.

Mac an Ghaill, M. (1994) *The making of men: Masculinities, sexualities and schooling.* Maidenhead: Open University Press.

Macfarlane, K. (2008) 'Playing the game: Examining parental engagement in schooling in post-millennial Queensland.' *Journal of Education Policy,* 23 (6), 701–713.

Malik, S. and Courtney, K. (2011) 'Higher education and women's empowerment in Pakistan.' *Gender and Education,* 23 (1), 29–45.

Mark, R. (2004) 'The case study approach to research in adult literacy, numeracy and ESOL.' In M. Osborne, J. Gallacher and B. Crossan (eds), *Researching widening access to lifelong learning: Issues and approaches to international research,* pp. 207–230. London: RoutledgeFalmer.

Masterman, E. and Shuyska, J. (2011) 'Digitally mastered? Technology and transition in the experience of taught postgraduate students.' *Learning, Media and Technology,* 37 (4), 335–354.

Maunder, R., Harrop, A. and Tattersall, A.J. (2010) 'Pupil and staff perceptions of bullying in secondary schools: Comparing behavioural definitions and their perceived seriousness.' *Educational Research,* 52 (3), 263–282.

Mauthner, M., Birch, M., Jessop, J. and Miller, T. (eds) (2002) *Ethics in qualitative research.* London: Sage.

Mayer, R. (2005) 'The failure of educational research to impact educational practice: Six obstacles to educational reform.' In G.D. Phye, D. Robinson, and J. Levin (eds), *Empirical methods for evaluating educational interventions.* San Diego: Elsevier Academic Press.

Maynard, M. and Purvis, J. (eds) (1994) *Researching women's lives from a feminist perspective.* London: Taylor and Francis.

McCulloch, G. (2000) *Historical research in educational settings (Doing qualitative research in educational settings).* Buckingham: Open University Press.

——(2004) *Documentary research: In education, history and the social sciences.* London: Routledge.

McGinity, R. (2012) 'Exploring the complexities of researcher identity in a school based ethnography.' *Reflective Practice: International and Multidisciplinary Perspectives,* 13 (6), 761–773.

McGinty, S. (2011) *First year Humanities and Social Science students' experiences of engaging with written feedback in a post-1992 university.* Unpublished PhD thesis.

McGuigan, M., McNally, S. and Wyness, G. (2012) *Student awareness of costs and benefits of educational decisions: Effects of an information campaign.* London: Centre for the Economics of Education.

McNiff, J. (1988) *Action research: Principles and practice.* London: Routledge.

Meighan, R. and Siraj-Blatchford, I. (1997) *A sociology of educating* (3rd edition). London: Continuum.

Mercieca, D. (2013) 'Engaging with students on reflective writing: Reclaiming writing.' In M. Murphy (ed.), *Social theory and education research: Understanding Foucault, Habermas, Bourdieu and Derrida,* pp. 200–211. London: Routledge.

Merriam, S.B. (1998) *Qualitative research and case study applications in education.* San Francisco: Jossey-Bass.

Miedel, W. and Reynolds, A. (1999) 'Parent involvement in early intervention for disadvantaged children: Does it matter?' *Journal of School Psychology,* 37 (4), 379–402.

Miles, M. and Huberman, M. (1994) *An Expanded Sourcebook: Qualitative Data Analysis* (2nd edition). London: Sage.

Milgram, S. (1974) *Obedience to authority: An experimental view.* Hammersmith: Harpercollins.

Mirza, H. (1992) *Young, female and black.* London: Routledge.

Moore, A. (2012) *Teaching and learning: Pedagogy, curriculum and culture.* Oxon: Routledge.

Morgan, A. (2005) 'Governmentality versus choice in contemporary special education.' *Critical Social Policy,* 25 (3), 325–348.

Morgan, D. (1997) *Focus groups as qualitative research.* London: Sage.

Munns, G. and Woodward, H. (2006) 'Student engagement and student self-assessment: The REAL framework'. *Assessment in Education,* 13 (2), 193–213.

Murphy, M. (2009) 'Bureaucracy and its limits: Accountability and rationality in higher education.' *British Journal of Sociology of Education,* 30 (6), 683–695.

——(ed.) (2013a) *Social theory and education research* (four-volume set). London: Sage.

——(ed.) (2013b) *Social theory and education research: Understanding Foucault, Habermas, Bourdieu and Derrida.* London: Routledge.

Murphy, M. and Bamber, J. (2012) 'Introduction: From Fromm to Lacan: Habermas and education in conversation.' *Studies in Philosophy and Education,* 31, 103–107.

Murphy, M. and Fleming, T. (eds) (2010) *Habermas, critical theory and education.* New York: Routledge.

Murphy, M., Morgan-Klein, B., Osborne, M. and Gallacher, J. (2002) *Widening participation in higher education: Report to the Scottish Executive.* Stirling: Centre for Research in Lifelong Learning.

Murphy, M. and Skillen, P. (2013) 'The politics of school regulation: Using Habermas to research educational accountability.' In M. Murphy (ed.), *Social theory and education research: Understanding Foucault, Habermas, Bourdieu and Derrida,* pp. 84–97. London: Routledge.

Myklebust, J.O. (2007) 'Diverging paths in upper secondary education: Competence attainment among students with special educational needs.' *International Journal of Inclusive Education,* 11 (2), 215–231.

Nelson, S., de la Colina, M. and Boone, M. (2008) 'Lifeworld or systemsworld: What guides novice principals?' *Journal of Educational Administration,* 46 (6), 690–701.

Nestel, D., Ivkovic, A., Hill, R.A., Warrens, A.N., Paraskevas, P.A., McDonnel, J.A., Mudarikwa, R.S. and Browne, C. (2012) 'Benefits and challenges of focus groups in the evaluation of a new Graduate Entry Medical Programme.' *Assessment and Evaluation in Higher Education,* 37 (1), 1–17.

Newby, P. (2010) *Research methods for education.* Harlow: Pearson.

O Dochartaigh, N. (2012) *Internet research skills* (3rd edition). London: Sage.

Oakley, A. (1981) *Becoming a mother.* Oxford: Martin Robertson.

——(2005) *The Ann Oakley Reader.* Bristol: The Policy Press.

Olesen, V. (1994) 'Early millenial feminist qualitative research: Challenges and contours.' In N. Denzin and Y. Lincoln (eds) (1994) *Handbook of qualitative research.* London: Sage.

Ozga, J., Dahler-Larson, P., Segerholm, C. and Simola, H. (2012) *Fabricating quality in education: Data and governance in Europe*. Oxon: Routledge.

Pachler, N., Cook, J. and Bachmair, B. (2010) 'Appropriation of mobile cultural resources for learning.' *International Journal of Mobile and Blended Learning* 2 (1), 1–21.

Palmer, S. (2006) *Toxic childhood: How the modern world is damaging our children and what we can do about it*. London: Orion Books.

Pantell, R.H. and Lewis, C.C. (1987) 'Measuring the impact of medical care on children.' *Journal of Chronic Diseases*, 40 (1), 99–108.

Papasolomontos, C. and Christie, T. (1998) 'Using national surveys: A review of secondary analyses with special reference to education.' *Educational Research*, 40 (3), 295–310.

Papatheodorou, T., Luff, P. and Gill, J. (2011) *Child observation for learning and research*. Harlow: Pearson Education.

Parsons, D., Ryu, H. and Cranshaw, M. (2007) 'A design requirements framework for mobile learning environments.' *Journal of Computers*, 2 (4), 1–8.

Patrick, J. (1973) *A Glasgow gang observed*. London: Eyre Methuen.

PISA (2012) http://www.oecd.org/pisa/[accessed [December 2012].

Podmore, V. and Luff, P. (2012) *Observation: Origins and approaches in early childhood*. Maidenhead: Open University Press.

Pollard, A. (1985) 'Opportunities and difficulties of a teacher-ethnographer: A personal account.' In R. Burgess (ed.) *Field methods in the study of education*, pp. 217–233. London: Falmer Press.

Poole, H., Giles, D.C. and Moore, K. (2004) 'Researching sexuality and sexual issues: implications for the researcher?' *Sexual and Relationship Therapy*, 19 (1), 79–86.

Popkewitz, T. (2012) *Paradigms and ideology in education research: The social functions of the intellectual* (volume 30, Routledge library editions: Education). New York: Routledge.

Postholm, M.B. (2009) 'Research and development work: Developing teachers as researchers or just teachers.' *Educational Action Research*, 17 (4), 551–565.

Postman, N. and Weingartner, C. (1971) *Teaching as a subversive activity*. Harmondsworth: Penguin Books.

Pring, R. (2004) *Philosophy of education research* (2nd edition). London: Continuum.

Punch, K. (2005) *Introduction to social research: Quantitative and qualitative approaches*. London: Sage.

——(2006) *Developing Effective Research Proposals* (2nd edition). London: Sage.

Purdy, L. and Jones, R. (2011) 'Changing personas and evolving identities: The contestation and renegotiation of researcher roles in fieldwork.' *Sport, Education and Society*, 1–19, iFirst article.

Pykett, J. (2007) 'Making citizens governable? The Crick Report as governmental technology.' *Journal of Education Policy*, 22 (3), 301–319.

Quality Assurance Agency for Higher Education (2009) *Access to HE data trends survey – final report: March 2009*.

Ranson, S., Martin, J and Vincent, C. (2004) 'Storming parents, schools and communicative inaction.' *British Journal of Sociology of Education*, 25 (3), 259–274.

Read, B. (2011) 'Britney, Beyoncé, and me – primary school girls' role models and constructions of the 'popular' girl.' *Gender and Education*, 23 (1), 1–13.

Reason, P. and Bradbury, H. (eds) (2006) *Handbook of action research: Participative inquiry and practice*. London: Sage.

Reay, D. (2007) 'Unruly Places': Inner-city comprehensives, middle-class imaginaries and working-class children.' *Urban Studies*, 44 (7), 1191–1201.

Ridley, D. (2012) *The literature review: A step-by-step guide for students* (2nd edition). London: Sage Study Skills Series.

Ritchie, S.M. and Rigano, D.L. (2001) 'Researcher-participant positioning in classroom research.' *International Journal of Qualitative Studies in Education*, 14 (6), 741–756.

River City Project (2013) *The River City project: A multi-user virtual environment for learning scientific inquiry and 21st century skills*. http://muve.gse.harvard.edu/rivercityproject/ [date accessed: 29/01/2013].

Robson, C. (2002) *Real world research* (2nd edition). Oxford: Blackwell Publishing.

Rosenthal, R. and Jacobson, L. (1968) *Pygmalion in the classroom: Teacher expectation and the pupils' intellectual development*. New York: Holt, Rinehart and Winston.

Rubin, R.J. and Rubin, I.S. (2005) *Qualitative interviewing: The art of hearing data* (2nd edition). London: Sage.

Sanders, L. (2008) 'Power in operation: a case study focussing on how subject-based knowledge is constrained by the methods of assessment in GCE A Level Dance.' *Research in Dance Education,* 9 (3), 221–240.

Scott-Bauman, A. (2003) 'Teacher education for Muslim women: Intercultural relationships, method and philosophy.' *Ethnicities,* 3 (2), 243–261.

Sharp, J. (2012) *Success with your education research project* (2nd edition) (Study Skills in Education Series). Exeter: Learning Matters.

Shepard, J. (2012) 'Schools aren't fit for pupils to learn in, warn four in ten headteachers.' *The Observer,* Sunday, 20 May 2012.

Shier, H. (2001) 'Pathways to participation: Openings, opportunities and obligations: A new model for enhancing children's participation in decision-making, in line with article 12.1 of the United Nations Convention on the Rights of the Child.' *Children and Society,* 15 (2), 107–117.

Silverman, D. (2001) *Interpreting qualitative data methods for analysing talk, text and interaction* (2nd edition). London: Sage.

Skeggs, B. (1997) *Formations of class and gender: Becoming respectable*. London: Sage.

Smith, R. (2007) 'Work, identity and the quasi-market: The FE experience'. *Journal of Educational Administration and History,* 39 (1), 33–47.

Solberg, L. (2012) 'Regulating human subjects research in the information age: Data mining on social networking sites.' *Northern Kentucky Law Review,* 39 (2), 327–358.

Somekh, B. (2006) *Action research: A methodology for changes and development*. Maidenhead: Open University Press.

Sparks, A. (2008) 'Embodiment, academics, and the audit culture: A story seeking consideration.' *Qualitative Research,* 7 (4), 521–550.

Starr, L.J. (2012) 'The use of autoethnography in educational research: Locating who we are in what we do.' *Canadian Journal for New Scholars in Education,* 3 (1).

Stenhouse, L. (1975) *An introduction to curriculum research and development*. London: Heinemann Educational.

Strauss, A. (1987) *Qualitative analysis for social scientists*. New York: Cambridge University Press.

Strauss, A.L. and Corbin, J.M. (1998) *Basics of qualitative research: Techniques and procedures for developing grounded theory* (2nd edition). London: Sage.

Swann, J. (2011) *Learning, teaching and education research in the 21st century: An evolutionary analysis of the role of teachers*. London: Continuum.

Swann, J. and Ecclestone, K. (1999) 'Improving lecturers' assessment practice in higher education: A problem-based approach.' *Educational Action Research,* 7 (1), 63–87.

Tesch, R. (1990) *Qualitative research*. New York: Falmer.

Thomas, J. (1993) *Doing Critical Ethnography (Qualitative Research Methods)*. London: Sage.

Thompson, P. and Gunter, H. (2006) 'From 'consulting pupils' to 'pupils as researchers': A situated case study.' *British Education Research Journal,* 32 (6), 839–856.

Tomlinson, S. (2005) *Education in a post-welfare society* (2nd edition). Buckingham: Open University Press.

Torrance, H. and Pryor, J. (2001) 'Developing formative assessment in the classroom: Using action research to explore and modify theory.' *British Educational Research Journal,* 27 (5), 615–631.

Traxler, J. (2009) 'Learning in a mobile age.' *International Journal of Mobile and Blended Learning.* 1 (1), 1–12.

UNCRC (1989) http://www.unicef.org.uk/UNICEFs-Work/Our-mission/UN-Convention/ [accessed 12th November 2012].

——(2012) *United Nations Convention on the Rights of the Child*. Accessed at http://www2.ohchr.org/english/law/crc.htm

UNICEF *Child and youth participation resource guide* – http://www.unicef.org/adolescence/cypguide/resourceguide_basics.html

Vander Schee, C. (2008) 'The politics of health as a school-sponsored ethic: Foucault, neoliberalism, and the unhealthy employee.' *Educational Policy,* 22 (6), 854–874.

Vavoula, G. and Sharples, M. (2009) 'Meeting the challenges in evaluating mobile learning: a 3-level evaluation framework.' *International Journal of Mobile and Blended Learning,* 1 (2), 54–75.

Voyat, G. (1982) *Piaget systematized.* Hillsdale: Lawrence Erlbaum Associates.

Walliman, N. and Buckler, S. (2008) *Your research project in education (Sage Study Skills Series).* London: Sage.

Watson, D. (2011) '"Urban, but not too urban": Unpacking teachers' desires to teach urban students.' *Journal of Teacher Education,* 62 (1), 23–34.

Weems, L. (2003) 'Representations of substitute teachers and the paradoxes of professionalism.' *Journal of Teacher Education,* 54 (3), 254–265.

Wellington, J. (2000) *Educational research: Contemporary issues and practical approaches.* London: Continuum.

Willer, D. and Walker, H. (2012) *Building Experiments: Testing Social Theory.* Stanford: Stanford University Press.

Willis, P. (1978) *Learning to labour: How working class kids get working class jobs.* Farnham: Ashgate.

Wilson, R. Gosling, S. and Graham, L. (2012) 'A review of Facebook research in the social sciences.' *Perspectives on Psychological Science,* 7 (3), 203–220.

Wilson, V. (1997) 'Focus groups: A useful qualitative method for educational research?' *British Educational Research Journal,* 23 (2), 209–224.

Winter, C. (2006) 'Doing justice to geography in the secondary school: Deconstruction, invention and the national curriculum.' *British Journal of Educational Studies,* 54 (2), 212–229.

Wolcott, H. (1990) *Writing up qualitative research.* London: Sage.

Woods, P. (1986) *Inside schools: Ethnography in educational research.* London: Routledge.

Youdell, D. (2006) 'Subjectivaction and performative politics – Butler thinking Althusser and Foucault: Intelligibility, agency and the raced-nationed-religioned subjects of education.' *British Journal of Sociology of Education,* 27 (4), 511–528.

Young, S. and Perez, J. (2012) '"We-research': Adopting a wiki to support the processes of collaborative research among a team of international researchers.' *International Journal of Music Education,* 30 (1), 3–17.

Zimdars, A., Sullivan, A. and Heath, A. (2009) 'Elite higher education admissions in the Arts and Sciences: Is cultural capital the key?' *Sociology,* 43 (4), 648–666.

Index

Page numbers in **bold** indicate information contained in a table. *Italic* page numbers indicate a figure.